FRENCH AND FRANCOPHONE STUDIES

Adapting Nineteenth-Century France

FRENCH AND FRANCOPHONE STUDIES

Adapting Nineteenth-Century France

Literature in Film, Theatre, Television, Radio and Print

KATE GRIFFITHS and ANDREW WATTS

UNIVERSITY OF WALES PRESS

Reprinted (paperback) 2015

www.uwp.co.uk

British Library Cataloguing-in-Publication Data
A catalogue record for this book is available from the British Library.

ISBN 978-1-7831-6308-3
eISBN 978-0-7083-2595-7

Typeset by Mark Heslington Ltd, Scarborough, North Yorkshire
Printed by CPI Antony Rowe, Chippenham, Wiltshire

Contents

Contents

Series Editors' Preface

This series showcases the work of new and established scholars working within the fields of French and francophone studies. It publishes introductory texts aimed at a student readership, as well as research-orientated monographs at the cutting edge of their discipline area. The series aims to highlight shifting patterns of research in French and francophone studies, to re-evaluate traditional representations of French and francophone identities and to encourage the exchange of ideas and perspectives across a wide range of discipline areas. The emphasis throughout the series will be on the ways in which French and francophone communities across the world are evolving into the twenty-first century.

Hanna Diamond and Claire Gorrara

Acknowledgements

I would first like to thank Swansea University for the research leave that made the first stage of this monograph possible. A variety of colleagues have helped this project in its various stages. I am very grateful for their time, patience and insight. Particular thanks are owed to Sarah Lewis for her forbearance, to Roger Bickerton and Nigel Deacon for their help locating Zola adaptations in radio, to Diana Griffiths for her generosity with radio scripts and insight into radio in practical terms, to Bradley Stephens and Elaine Canning for reading the various versions of my chapters, to Tim Unwin for sharing his knowledge of flying machines, to Clair Rowden for her musical advice and to Rob Stone for his help with all things media related. Finally, I am grateful to be able to record again in print my thanks to Margaret and John Griffiths and to Richard Sheppard for their backup at all times. The biggest thanks of all, though, go to Genevieve Sheppard whose drawings grace every draft of this book and made me smile every time I picked it up.

Kate Griffiths

This monograph owes much to the University of Birmingham, and to the combination of research leave and teaching relief that enabled me to begin work on the project during the 2010–11 session. I would like to record my special thanks to those friends and colleagues who have supported this book in a variety of ways. I am particularly indebted to my co-author, Kate Griffiths, who encouraged me to develop my interest in adaptation, and who has been an invaluable source of advice at every stage. Michelle Cheyne, Ceri Crossley, Tim Unwin and Dennis Wood have all read and commented on my chapters, and I am very grateful for their time, generosity and scholarly insight. I am equally delighted to be able to express my thanks to Posy Simmonds for making the visit to Birmingham that inspired my work on Flaubert, and for responding patiently to my questions about *Gemma Bovery*. As ever, I extend my warmest thanks to John and Janet Watts, for never failing to ask when this book would be finished, and to Claire Watts, for her patience and support in helping me towards that goal.

Andrew Watts

Introduction

KATE GRIFFITHS

The French nineteenth century and its cultural products have long fascinated those who adapt. Adaptation, as a cultural phenomenon, is key to the artistic life of this era, characterised as it is by cross-media/genre dialogues as novels, plays, operas and paintings nourish each other adaptively. Zola's *Nana* (1880) offers a powerful case in point. The novel mocks, in adapted form, the operettas of Offenbach (*La Belle Hélène* is recalled in Nana's abysmal *La Blonde Vénus*). It is comparably indebted to the painting of its heroine done by Edouard Manet in the winter of 1876, based on Nana's brief appearance in Zola's previous novel *L'Assommoir*, a painting it ekphrastically reproduces in its narrative.[1] Having nourished itself on other works of art, it is perhaps then appropriate that Zola's novel was subsequently adapted into a host of other forms. With Zola's consent it was adapted into theatre at the hands of William Busnach to mediocre reviews.[2] Without Zola's consent, the novel's heroine and the superimposed identity of the actress playing her on stage (Léontine Massin) were subsequently worked and reworked in a plethora of parodies and pastiches across artistic forms and artefacts.[3] The novel triggered further art forms. Alfred de Sirven's 1880 *La Fille de Nana* depicted Nana's offspring rising to respectability in a novelistic rebuttal of both Zola's novel and the author's theories of heredity. Moreover, widely translated in translations which themselves deploy adaptive strategies in their composition at times, the novel found its way into a variety of languages. An 1880 version for a North American publishing house, Peterson and Brooks, underlines how often contemporary translations show nothing of this novel with its pretensions precisely to show everything. Thirteen lines describing the sensual, sexual potency of

Nana's body and its ability to bring men to their knees are rendered in the following three curt lines: 'A murmur ran through the house. Every glass was riveted on Venus. Nana had conquered the public. Bordenave was correct. She had only to show herself as he had said.'[4] Bordenave may show Nana, but this translation, driven by the commercial, legal and cultural imperatives of its own context, does not. It does, however, gesture towards the adaptive afterlives of the nineteenth-century text, a text translated, transformed and transplanted in the seemingly endless exchanges of its era.

Such adaptive urges in relation to nineteenth-century France are, though, far from the preserve of the century itself. Each of the case study novelists featured in this book, Zola, Balzac, Flaubert, Hugo, Maupassant and Verne, was not only adapted and re-adapted in his lifetime, but continues to be reinvented across time, media and nation to the present day. In 2012, the screenwriter of *Larkrise to Candleford*, Bill Gallagher, transposed Zola's *Au Bonheur des dames* into a BBC television series, swapping Paris for Newcastle, the site of the first British department store (Bainbridge's – now John Lewis).[5] Adrian Penketh's adaptation of Balzac's *La Peau de chagrin* aired as the Friday play on Radio 4 on 21 January 2011, the adaptor drawing out the resonances between the financial system of the novel and the monetary issues of his own contemporary era.[6] In 2011 Adam Thorpe offered what he believes is the twentieth English translation of *Madame Bovary* (Vintage), the previous translation of which had appeared just one year earlier.[7] Having celebrated its twenty-fifth anniversary in 2010, the ever-popular stage musical of *Les Misérables* was adapted into a film in 2013 under the direction of the Oscar winner Tom Hooper, a piece in which Hugh Jackman and Russell Crowe starred. In March 2012 the adaptation by Declan Donnellan and Nick Ormerod of Maupassant's *Bel-Ami*, starring teen heart-throb Robert Pattinson, was released in the UK and the USA.[8] In February 2012 the complete works of Jules Verne, compacted into eighty comic minutes by performers David Furlong and Alex Kanefsky, could be viewed at the Lion and Unicorn Theatre, London. Whatever the media, nation or era, nineteenth-century France has always, it seems, made adaptive sense.

That contemporary media forms continue to adapt across the literary canon is clear. Critical debate as to the motivations for this adaptive interest is ongoing. Robert Giddings, Keith Selby and Chris Wensley suggest that our thirst for adaptations of nineteenth-century works is driven by a complex nostalgia. This era is, Giddings, Selby and Wensley suggest, still recognisable to us, it is 'a major warehouse of historical commodities and evidence, and a period still almost within living memory in which culture we feel we have strong roots'.[9] We do not access this past in any true form for adaptations are inevitably something of a 'fake antique'. Such works can nevertheless serve as something of an antidote, allowing us to travel away from the stresses of our contemporary era, taking us, not back to the past, but to the no-place and no-time of adaptations as they recreate a past which is always simultaneously driven by the production values and social issues of the present. For Giddings et al., the thirst for images of the past and for classic texts in the form of adaptations 'are all symptomatic of the condition of the national psyche which is shedding layers of modernity and reverting to its own past tones under the stress of contemporary economic, political and social crisis'.[10] The temporal strategies of adaptations which either modernise the source text, bringing it into our present, or go in quest of its heritage, taking us to a mythical past, appear clear cut. Yet, as Andreas Huyssen points out, the 'temporal status of any act of memory is always the present'.[11] Even those heritage adaptations that seek to take us to a mythical past are marked by their contemporary era. Both the 1972 BBC television production of Jane Austen's *Emma*, starring Doran Godwin, and its ITV counterpart from 2007, starring Kate Beckinsale, are heritage pieces that seek to reproduce Austen's era. Yet both testify to the production values and trends of their own times, the Godwin piece being marked in the mind of the modern audience as a 1970s piece by its colours, music and sets. Adaptations, moreover, whatever their approach, inevitably cater for and comment upon their era. It is not for nothing that George Cukor's 1933 *Little Women*, for example, emphasising as it does family togetherness and happiness in a time of, in Alcott's words, 'the departed days of plenty', was written as a screenplay during the Great Depression.[12] Literary adaptations have always offered the means to escape the present, even while simultaneously commenting upon it.

Attempts to assess why nineteenth-century France has proved so attractive to those who adapt must vary according to media and era. In the print fiction and musical theatre of the nineteenth century in France, adaptation often made overwhelming commercial sense. David Coward makes clear the era's growing thirst for ever-greater cultural production. Rising literacy meant that by 1900 83 per cent of French men and women could read and write in some form. Vast changes took place to the nation's social structure and the cost of books plummeted (in 1838 Charpentier started selling books for 3 francs and in 1855 Michel Lévy reduced this to just 1 franc). These factors, in association with the growing popularity of the *cabinets de lecture* until 1855 and the serialisation of novels in *feuilleton* form from 1836, meant that an ever-thirstier mass market for written fiction grew. Book production rose in an attempt to meet this thirst. Between 1812 and 1814 four to five thousand titles were published annually, a figure which rose to seven or eight thousand over the next thirty years, and stabilised at twelve or thirteen thousand between 1855 and 1914.[13] The new species of publisher, whose rise Christine Haynes charts in her survey of nineteenth-century French publishing, both commissioned and established the circulation of works as artistic commodities, adapting them, when necessary, to meet current tastes and trends.[14] Hetzel, as shall be seen in chapter six, not only modified the texts of Jules Verne to meet public taste, he also purchased manuscripts from other writers for Verne to adapt and rewrite, so as to ensure he could meet the growing public demand for the works of this author. In a century where literary property was seemingly constantly under debate, the laws governing it being assessed and reassessed by successive regimes as they debated the rights of the author and a nation to a specific work once published, publishers took advantage of this lack of fixity to adapt in different ways and forms. Jealous of Hetzel's success with Verne and his *Voyages extraordinaires*, his competitors sought to adapt both his publishing format and his key author. Daniel Compère writes:

> une véritable concurrence se met en place dans les années 1880, en particulier . . . les éditeurs Georges Decaux et Maurice Dreyfous tentent de détrôner la maison Hetzel dans le domaine du livre d'étrennes: face à sa 'Bibliothèque d'éducation et de récréation', Dreyfous crée la 'Bibliothèque d'aventures et de voyages', collection à laquelle Hetzel riposte en créant la série 'Les romans d'aventures'. Mais, comme le dit Jean-Pierre Ardoin Saint-Armand, 'pour faire du Hetzel, il leur faut des auteurs qui fassent du Jules Verne'.[15]

Enter a series of writers à la Verne, producing works which adapt, to varying degrees, the style, form and titles of Verne's novels. Jules Gros penned a work entitled *Les Secrets de la mer*, Louis Boussenard created *Le Tour du monde d'un gamin de Paris.* Both appeared in *Le Journal des voyages.* Literary adaptation, whatever its form, is a defining feature of nineteenth-century French literary production.

Adaptation was, as a phenomenon, perhaps even more embedded in the operatic productions of the era. While some librettists created works from scratch, particularly those such as Eugène Scribe who were also celebrated playwrights in their own right, and others might take a legend or a myth and extemporise on the theme, the majority of librettists worked from an existing literary source.[16] Often they made their selections in a commercial sense, basing them on the work's public success in novel or play form, a success they hoped to replicate in opera. Louise Bertin's *La Esmeralda* (1836) is a case in point. Victor Hugo provided the libretto to this grand opera that appeared just five years after his own novel's publication. The adaptive selections of librettists also served a very practical purpose in terms of the form of the work. If librettists could rely on a large part of the audience having previous knowledge of the story, they could skate over detailed plots which would otherwise take up too much time on the opera stage, contenting themselves with abbreviated character psychology and motivation. Flaubert's Emma Bovary goes to watch Donizetti's *Lucie de Lammermoor* in a Rouen theatre. Emma adapts the plight of Donizetti's heroine to her own, allowing this tale of a woman torn between the man she loves and the man she must marry to reawaken her own passions and lead her to take a lover.[17] Donizetti's opera was itself a loose adaptation of Walter Scott's successful historical novel *The Bride of Lammermoor.* While the opera was initially written in Italian for an 1835 debut, it was recreated in French in 1839 in a version that toured extensively in France. The libretto, the creation of Alphonse Royer and Gustave Vaëz, has itself to be considered an adaptation as Donizetti altered and removed scenes and characters. Adaptation, in its multiple forms, drives nineteenth-century French opera.

Adaptation, moreover, has driven cinema from its nascent moments. The link between silent cinema and nineteenth-century literature is well established. Each of the case study authors in this book are worked and reworked in silent film as the following noteworthy examples illustrate. Georges Méliès's 1902 *Le Voyage dans la lune* used Verne as a means to indulge the director's interest in trick photography. In 1918, André Antoine, a leading naturalist theatre director turned film director, used Hugo's *Les Travailleurs de la mer* as a vehicle for the director's documentary instincts and location filming. In 1902, the year of the author's death, Ferdinand Zecca's *Les Victimes de l'alcoolisme* offered viewers a five-minute adaptation of Zola's *L'Assommoir* in five tableaux. The film would be adapted a further three times in France before the outbreak of the First World War. While perhaps less beloved by silent film than his predecessor Balzac, whose prevalence in this art form is underlined by chapter two, Flaubert had still been adapted at least five times before Jean Renoir's 1933 adaptation of *Madame Bovary*. The reasons silent cinema turned to literature and to the novel in particular are legion. Successful novels generated audiences. They also provided a degree of cultural legitimacy for the nascent medium as it tried to define itself. The Lumière brothers may have seen film as a new form of science, but for those working in the magic lantern tradition, it offered the possibility of cheap, mass, sensational entertainment. While much has been said about silent film's adaptation of literature, less has been said on its relationship with theatre. Early film not only borrowed from the nineteenth-century theatre in its acting and stage conventions, but early critics tended to assume that cinema was simply 'a new form of theatre'. Silent cinema would, though, as Rick Altman points out, gradually efface its relationship with theatre, developing its own more naturalistic acting styles and moving away from its sources. Altman writes:

> Take any list of silent films apparently derived from novels, submit it to a few hours research in a serious library and you will have little trouble discovering that a very high proportion of the novels were turned into extremely popular stage shows in the years preceding the film. Yet, systematically, it is the novel that gets the attention, the novel that is mentioned in the end, the novel that draws the screen credit. For by the turn of the century novels were clearly a drawing card, cinema's tenuous connection with culture.[18]

D. W. Griffith's *The Drunkard's Reformation* (1909), offers a striking example of the phenomenon Altman evaluates. Griffith's film, a version of Zola's *L'Assommoir*, stems not from the novel, but from the British/North American theatrical version of Gastineau and Busnach's French theatrical adaptation of Zola's successful work.[19] Silent cinema's adaptive debt to theatre, as much as to literature, forms part of its very lifeblood.

Literature too provided ready-made material. The narrative structure of much realist fiction with its clear chronological progression, emphasis on visual description and character exposition, arguably does much to create an accessible first draft of a script for a screenwriter. Critics have often been tempted to explain the link between silent cinema and, in particular, realist literature, by deeming specific realist writers to be 'pre-cinematic'. Pointing to the confluence between the realists' desire to depict reality in intricate detail and the ability of the film camera to meet that aim, such critics situate early cinema as heir to the realist tradition. Sergei Eisenstein, writing of his admiration of Zola's naturalist novels, considers them to be 'in the methodological sense the greatest school for a filmmaker (his pages read like complete cue sheets)'.[20] Eisenstein claimed to have reread a Zola novel before each of his key films, drawing inspiration from their content and cinematic style. While there are intriguing crossovers between realist fiction and silent cinema as the plethora of realist writers adapted in the early years of film shows, to deem such writers pre-cinematic affords a teleology to artistic relations which is misleading. Art forms cross and recross, influencing and re-influencing each other rather than developing the one into the other. In any case, as Tolstoy pointed out in 1908, there are stark differences between realist writing and nascent film:

> You will see that this little clicking contraption with the revolving handle will make a revolution in our life – in the life of writers. It is a direct attack on the old methods of literary art. We shall have to adapt ourselves to the shadowy screen and to the cold machine. A new form of writing will be necessary . . . But I rather like it. The swift change of scene, this blending of emotion and experience – it is much better than the heavy, long-drawn-out kind of writing to which we are accustomed. It is closer to life. In life, too, changes and transitions flash by before our eyes, and emotions of the soul are like a hurricane. The cinema has divined the mystery of motion. And that is greatness.[21]

Radio, as a cultural institution, has, if anything, an even greater commitment to adaptation as an art form. In its early years, the medium turned to theatre in an attempt to define its cultural practice. Stephen Barnard writes: 'On both sides of the Atlantic, radio's institutions initially embraced drama as a demonstration of cultural commitment.'[22] As late as 1926 long BBC plays were prefaced with four or five minutes of conventional stage overture and music was always played between acts. Comparably, the Lux Radio Theatre which was produced in Hollywood by the J. Walter Thompson advertising agency had its dramas introduced by the mediating presence of Cecil B. De Mille, who introduced each production as if it were live from a theatre.[23] British radio was driven not only by the need for cultural authenticity, but also by a wider mission. The BBC under Lord Reith was early devoted to the belief that radio should be used to educate the mass audience.[24] Part of this education was to be a literary one and what were known as the Microphone Serials began in 1938 with the broadcast of twelve episodes adapted from *The Count of Monte Cristo* by Dumas. Val Gielgud writes: 'It was the first of the classical adaptations which were to settle down as regular features of the English Sunday evening at home; which were to include works by Galsworthy, Dickens, Scott, Hardy and Arnold Bennett.'[25] In its mission to define itself in cultural terms and to educate and entertain the public, radio, from its earliest days, turned both to drama and to literature in its adaptive undertakings.

The adaptive undertakings of television, in its early years, in many respects echo those of radio and its cultural mission. Writing on the birth of French television and its associated structures, Jean-Marie Dizol underlines why the new medium was so attracted to canonical literature and its adaptations in a passage which in many respects echoes the pedagogical aims of the BBC under Reith. According to Dizol:

> Enfin et surtout, il faut se rappeler que l'ambiance dans laquelle se crée la télévision française participe encore peu ou prou de l'esprit de reconstruction du pays né des années de résistance et de la libération: avec une évidente naïveté, beaucoup de ses premiers artisans pensaient inventer un outil de connaissance destiné à un peuple de citoyens. Cet environnement de la jeune télévision prédisposait donc les réalisateurs à s'y transformer en pédagogues, soucieux de la culture populaire: un Jean Prat expliquera que, malheureusement, bien des œuvres littéraires ne seraient jamais lues par la majorité des citoyens et qu'il se faisait donc une obligation personnelle de révéler notre patrimoine littéraire par le biais d'adaptations. De là à pratiquer une politique systématique de mise à l'écran des grands classiques, il n'y avait qu'un pas.[26]

Moreover, while in Britain writers such as Harold Pinter were keen to write directly for television, the attitudes of authors to the new medium in France were less open and consequently the systematic adaptation of the literary classics became something of a necessity. Such acts of adaptation offered artistic credibility and often, if one chose wisely, comparatively cheap material. Early French television, like early British radio, found artistic credibility, convenient subject matter and grist for its pedagogical mission in the art of literary adaptation.

Our attempt to underline the varying, if at times overlapping, impulses to adapt which characterise each media is deliberate. Critical writing on adaptation tends to privilege theatre and cinema. While interfictional adaptation is a growing field of study, writing on adaptation for television – a process usually elided, albeit erroneously, with its larger screen counterpart – is comparatively scarce. Writing on adaptation for radio is practically non-existent. Working against the prevalent approach which seems to imply that one adaptive strategy fits all media, *Adapting Nineteenth-Century France* seeks to focus on the way in which different media adapt differently, their very different aesthetic frameworks and practical requirements authoring adaptations almost as much as the writer penning them and the various creative identities translating them into different creative forms. That these media specific aesthetics and requirements bring some adaptive losses is inevitable. Thus, as chapter one makes clear, radio, a non-visual medium, strips Zola of the colour and detailed panoramas for which he is so renowned. Early film, as chapter two underlines, silences the linguistic exuberance that is the massive Balzacian text. But with such adaptive losses come other adaptive gains. Radio, an intimate, domestic medium, brings the listener closer to the, at times forgotten, intimacy of Zola's novels as they dissect the lives and motivations of their characters in extreme close-up. Comparably, if early film silences Balzac, it also brings to light the unexpected prevalence and importance of silence as a theme in the seemingly ceaseless words of this writer. We do not seek to evaluate all of our case study authors across all of the media on which this volume focuses. Such a task would be Herculean. Rather, our chapters evaluate the texts of a specific author in relation to a specific medium or art form with which they enjoy a telling affinity. Hence this book assesses Zola in relation to radio adaptation, Balzac on silent film, Flaubert recreated in contemporary fiction, Maupassant as seen on television, Hugo as incarnated in musical theatre and Verne as translated into sound cinema. It does so, first, to attempt to identify the specific adaptive strategies of the media in question and, second, to suggest how, in their affinities with specific media, such adaptations help us better to read the theories, form and content of the authors in question.

Our case study authors have been chosen not only for their affinities with a specific medium, they have also been selected for the resonance of their authorial approach with contemporary debates on adaptation. If fidelity approaches have dominated adaptation studies since their inception, situating adaptations as necessarily inferior copies of a superior textual original, key critical voices have made clear, and continue to make clear, the need for a more intertextual approach to the discipline. Brian McFarlane writes that adaptations are best read with an acknowledgement of the inherent intertextuality of all texts.[27] Deborah Cartmell, writing on her co-edited volume with Imelda Whelehan concurs:

> Perhaps the search for an 'original' or for a single author is no longer relevant in a postmodern world where a belief in a single meaning is seen to be a fruitless quest. Instead of worrying about whether a film is 'faithful' to the original literary text (founded in a logocentric belief that there is a single meaning), we read adaptations for their generation of a plurality of meanings. Thus the intertextuality of the adaptation is our primary concern.[28]

While *Adapting Nineteenth-Century France* is informed by the persuasive voices of such critics of adaptation and by a series of the theorists who perhaps inspired them (notably, Lacan, Kristeva, Bakhtin, de Certeau and Derrida), this book also seeks to showcase the anticipation of elements of intertextual theory in the work of our case study nineteenth-century French novelists. Adaptations, whatever their form and media, of Zola, Balzac, Hugo, Flaubert, Maupassant and Verne, cannot irrevocably be written off as inferior copies of a superior textual original, for these authors, in very different ways, self-consciously borrow from a host of different sources, dramatising their own acts of adaptation and playfully pointing to their multiple points of origin. Such authors find their own literary originality, paradoxically, by showcasing their own borrowing from elsewhere. Furthermore, the adaptations selected of them for this book frequently engage with their source author's debate on literary originality. Far from being facile, exploitative copies, these adaptations, in their form and content, reflect on their own adaptive act in highly creative ways. They contemplate their derivation from a clearly canonical source, borrowing with a reflexivity comparable to their canonical forebear. While such a claim cannot be made for all adaptations of the authors in question, this book hopes, nevertheless, to throw into relief the profoundly intertextual debate on the nature of authorship itself at play between these key nineteenth-century French writers and some of the best of the adaptations made of them.

Structured around some of the key themes of the adaptive process, sound, image, time, spectacle, space and the question of whether any individual can ultimately sign an adaptation as his/her own, each of the chapters takes on a specific theme. Sound is the central focus of chapter one: 'Labyrinths of Voices: Emile Zola, *Germinal* and Radio'. While voices commenting on the work of Emile Zola and its adaptation into film and theatre are numerous, they fall silent in relation to the novelist's adaptation for radio. The national range and extent of adaptations of Zola for radio is such that this critical silence is not driven by a paucity of output in this medium. Rather, it is part of a more general critical silence on literary adaptation in radio, a silence only in part beginning to be broken. In any case, Zola, the novelist of vast spaces and intricate detail who claimed to translate the visual techniques of the Impressionists into fiction, does not, at first glance, seem suited to the blind, black medium of radio and its dependence on sound alone. This chapter, however, uses two BBC adaptations (from 1982 and 2007 respectively) to make the case for the natural affinity between Zola and radio. These adaptations underscore the particular importance of voice in Zola's *Germinal* and also explore, as Zola's own novel does, the nature and origin of their own creative voice. As both of the BBC adaptations italicise the myriad intertextual threads from which they weave their own existence, pointing to the whispers of earlier texts, authors and moments in their creative voice, so they echo Zola's reading of authorship as the cumulative retelling of an age-old story in a new context.

As chapter one focuses on Zola and sound or Zola in sound, chapter two, 'Diamond Thieves and Gold Diggers: Balzac, Silent Cinema and the Spoils of Adaptation', moves to contemplate the silence of Balzac in early cinema. While critics have not remained silent on the many early reworkings of Balzac in this medium, such reworkings have not always garnered the critical acclaim they merit. Using two case studies, Jean Epstein's *L'Auberge rouge* (1923) and Rex

Ingram's *Eugénie Grandet, The Conquering Power* (1921), this chapter shows that, far from being technically underdeveloped artefacts that abbreviate and undo a great artist, these two films tap into key Balzacian themes. Often viewed in negative terms of theft, exploitation and plundering, these adaptations engage with the presence of such themes in Balzac's work itself. As Balzac, à la de Certeau, poached the textual property of his contemporaries and literary ancestors, so Epstein and Ingram, in adaptations precisely about theft and appropriation, reflect on their own theft and appropriation of Balzac to creative and ultimately harmonious ends. In poaching Balzac, ultimately they remain true to Balzac.

Chapter three, 'Fragmented Fictions: Time, Textual Memory and the (Re)Writing of *Madame Bovary*', considers the complexity of adaptive time in relation to inter-fictional adaptations of Flaubert's *Madame Bovary*. Some twenty-four literary homages to *Madame Bovary* have appeared in the last thirty years. This chapter, though, focuses in particular on Posy Simmonds's *Gemma Bovery* (1999) and Philippe Doumenc's *Contre-enquête sur la mort d'Emma Bovary* (2007) since both works, in keeping with their Flaubertian predecessor, throw into relief the importance of time and temporality in the adaptive process. These texts by Simmonds and Doumenc share their source novel's fascination with how works rewrite earlier texts, adapting them to fit a new era in temporal rewritings which are always, in a sense, at least double, pointing simultaneously to the time of a past work and to the era of the culture for which the rewritings are intended. Both Simmonds and Doumenc enact, this chapter argues, Kristeva's theory of texts as mosaics, fashioning the matter of past works with more recent social, cultural and artistic discourses to create an artefact at once past and present. In building their textual pictures in part from the matter of works gone by, both writers trigger a consideration of time in the text of Flaubert. If the temporal matter of works gone by destabilised Flaubert's heroine, such matter is grist for her fictional master's mill, offering him key creative materials from which to fashion his imagery.

Continuing chapter three's consideration of the expanse of matter from which Flaubert and his adaptors fashion their literary originality, chapter four, '*Les Misérables*, Theatre and the Anxiety of Excess', concentrates too on the question of excess. It takes as its case studies the West End and Broadway musical *Les Misérables* (1985–) by Alain Boubil and Claude-Michel Schönberg and José

Pliya's 2001 play *Le Complexe de Thénardier*. Critics all too often focus on what is lost as a work, whatever its length, is translated into a different medium. This chapter, however, explores the way Hugo's novel and key adaptations crafted from it revolve around notions of excess, be it in relation to extremes of violence or the fate of the chronically poor. Walter Benjamin in his 1936 essay 'The work of art in the age of mechanical reproduction' suggested that every original work of art has an aura of authority and authenticity that is manipulated and, in cases, stripped away by reproduction. In their attempts to accommodate the vastness of *Les Misérables* within their own medium, Boubil and Schönberg and Pliya strip the novel of its digressions and tendency towards narrative excess. Yet, in paring down their canonical source, they echo and reproduce the adaptive aura of Hugo himself who did likewise in his novel in relation to key literary and cultural intertexts. *Les Misérables,* a novel innately suited to the theatre, makes music one of its key themes, anticipating in part its metamorphoses in musical theatre. If Hugo, Boubil and Schönberg and Pliya all testify to a certain anxiety in relation to the theme of excess, all resolve it as they strip down and refine the work of their predecessors in their adaptive undertakings.

While Hugo's text is expansive, space in the short stories of Maupassant is usually a far more claustrophobic, restrictive concept. Chapter five, '*Chez Maupassant*: The (In)Visible Space of Television Adaptation', thus looks at how the short story writer is innately suited to the more claustrophobic visual aesthetic and structural rythms of television as a medium. Despite their prevalence and popularity, television adaptations of Maupassant have largely remained invisible in critical spheres. Focusing on the first two series of France 2's hugely popular *Chez Maupassant,* an anthology of adaptations by different renowned directors, this chapter seeks to make visible the critical value and artistic space of this anthology. The medium throws into relief the key claustrophobia of the writer's work and his innate and intriguing seriality. Moreover, the self-reflexivity of the series in question as its adaptations negotiate the space and place of their own identities alongside that of Maupassant, translates the self-reflexivity of the nineteenth-century writer himself. Maupassant, in his narrative, self-consciously reworks earlier sources in offerings in which he, like the directors of *Chez Maupassant,* effaces himself in narratives that make him very present. *Chez Maupassant* simultaneously translates the artistic identities of both Maupassant and his twenty-first-century adaptations.

This question of who ultimately signs an adaptation as his/her own is taken up, in spectral terms, by the book's final chapter, '*Le Tour du monde en quatre-vingts jours*: Verne, Todd, Coraci and the Spectropoetics of Adaptation'. Adaptations are arguably the most haunted of all art forms, spectrally incarnating Jacques Derrida's reading of the haunted nature of any canonical work's recreation at the hands of its would-be artistic heirs. Though the two case studies of this chapter, a 1956 adaptation of *Le Tour du monde* produced by Michael Todd and its far less commercially successful counterpart directed by Frank Coraci in 2004, do take great liberties with Verne's source novel, their artistic value lies in their willingness to contemplate and engage with the ghosts at the heart of adaptation. Both contemplate the ghostly presence of Verne's novel and Verne the broader cultural icon. Alongside the Vernian ghost, they dramatise the spectral traces of the authorial influence of their directors, producers and stars. They revel in the spectral intertextual dialogue that binds them to Verne.

The ghost of nineteenth-century France looms large in the output of those with a love of adaptation. A century and space in which adaptation was a dominant art form, its creative products have been worked and reworked seemingly constantly across time, space and media. The collective importance of the case study authors of this book and the selected adaptations made of them is threefold. First, they enact the very different adaptive strategies of specific media and make clear the formal affinities that at times link certain authors with certain art forms. Secondly, they underline the intricate intertextual dialogues at play in the best of the adaptations of these canonical sources. They also, though, make clear the intriguing analyses on authorship and the originality to be gleaned in the reworking of other texts that lie at the heart of these canonical sources themselves. They underline, in short, that in adaptation, true artistry may be found.

Notes

1 For a discussion of the ways in which the opening night of Nana's *La Blonde Vénus* comments on Offenbach's *La Belle Hélène*, see Roger Clark, *Zola: 'Nana'* (London: Grant and Cutler, 2004), pp. 49–50. For an exploration of the 'artistico-literary *chassé-croisé*' at play between Manet's *Nana* and that of Zola, see ibid., p. 41.

2 See Lawson A. Carter, *Zola and the Theater* (New Haven, CT: Yale University Press; Paris: Presses Universitaires de France, 1963), pp. 118–22.

3 Catherine Dousteyssier-Khoze, *Zola et la littérature naturaliste en parodies* (Paris: Eurédit, 2004), p. 130.

4 Emile Zola, *Nana* (Philadelphia: T. B. Peterson and Brothers, 1880), p. 51. Translation available on *http://archive.org/stream/nanasequeltolass00zola#page/50/mode/2up*, accessed 21 March 2012.

5 For further details see Martin Wainwright, 'Newcastle, not Paris, may set TV scene for Zola classic', *www.guardian.co.uk/media/2008/apr/05/television.bbc*, accessed 21 November 2011.

6 For further details, see Adrian Penketh, 'Adapting Balzac for the Friday play', *www.bbc.co.uk/blogs/radi04/2011/01/adapting_balzac_for_the_friday_play.html*, accessed 10 March 2012.

7 Writing on his own translation, see Adam Thorpe, '*Madame Bovary:* the Everest of translation', *www.guardian.co.uk/books/2011/oct/21/translating-madame-bovary-adam-thorpe*, accessed 10 March 2012.

8 See Philip French, '*Bel-Ami* – review', *www.guardian.co.uk/film/2012/mar/11/bel-ami-review-donnellan-ormerod*, accessed 22 March 2012.

9 Robert Giddings, Keith Selby and Chris Wensley, *Screening the Novel: The Theory and Practice of Literary Dramatization* (London: Palgrave, 1990), p. 31.

10 Ibid. p. 38.

11 Andreas Huyssen, *Twilight Memories: Marking Time in a Culture of Amnesia* (New York: Routledge, 1995), p. 3.

12 For further details, see Pat Kirkham and Sarah Warren, 'Four *Little Women*', in D. Cartmell and I. Whelehan (eds), *Adaptations: From Text to Screen, Screen to Text* (London: Routledge, 1999), pp. 81–97 (p. 83).

13 David Coward, 'Popular fiction in the nineteenth century', in T. Unwin, *The Cambridge Companion to the French Novel: From 1800 to the Present* (Cambridge: Cambridge University Press, 1997), pp. 73–92 (pp. 73–4).

14 Christine Haynes, *Lost Illusions: The Politics of Publishing in Nineteenth-Century France* (Cambridge: Harvard University Press, 2010).

15 Daniel Compère, 'Dans le sillage de Jules Verne', *Le Rocambole*, 30 (2005), 11–16 (12).

16 For further details on Scribe, see his biography by theatre historian Jean-Claude Yon, *Eugène Scribe: la liberté et la fortune* (Paris: Broché, 2000).

17 Gustave Flaubert, *Madame Bovary*, ed. Claudine Gothot-Mersch (Paris: Garnier, 1971), p. 227.

18 Rick Altman, 'Dickens, Griffith, and film theory today', in R. Abel (ed.), *Silent Film* (London: Athlone, 1996), p. 148.

19 For further details, see Diane Smith and Robert Singer, 'A drunkard's representation: the appropriation of naturalism in D. W. Griffith's Biograph Films', *Griffithiana*, 65 (1999), 96–125.

20 S. M. Eisenstein, 'Literature and cinema: reply to a questionnaire' in S. M. Eistenstein, *Selected Works*, vol. 1: *Writings, 1922–1934*, ed. and trans. R. Taylor (London: British Film Institute, 1988), pp. 95–9 (p. 95).

21 Tolstoy cited in Cartmell and Whelehan (eds), *Adaptations: From Text to Screen, Screen to Text*, p. 5.
22 Stephen Barnard, *Studying Radio* (London: Arnold, 2000), p. 113.
23 Ibid., p. 114.
24 For further details, see Andrew Crisell, *Understanding Radio* (London: Routledge, 1994), p. 19.
25 Val Gielgud, *British Radio Drama: 1922–1956* (London: Harrap, 1957), p. 70.
26 Jean-Marie Dizol, 'Maupassant de l'écrit à l'écran' in Y. Reboul (ed.), *Maupassant multiple* (Toulouse: Presses Universitaires du Mirail, 1995), pp. 87–105 (p. 94).
27 Brian McFarlane, *Novel to Film: An Introduction to the Theory of Adaptation* (Oxford: Clarendon Press, 1996), p. 10.
28 Cartmell and Whelehan, *Adaptations: From Text to Screen, Screen to Text*, p. 28.

Chapter One
Labyrinths of Voices: Emile Zola, *Germinal* and Radio

KATE GRIFFITHS

The critical silence surrounding the adaptation of Emile Zola to radio is deafening.[1] It does not stem from a paucity of adaptations of the author in radio.[2] Rather, this silence is the result of two factors. First, the discipline of adaptation studies has tended to ignore radio as an adaptive medium.[3] Secondly, Zola, an author who famously privileges the visual in his attempt to make us 'see' reality, does not appear suited to a purely aural medium that is, in the words of Andrew Crisell, 'blind'.[4] However, using two BBC radio adaptations of *Germinal* written by David Hopkins and Diana Griffiths and aired in 1982 and 2007 respectively, this chapter seeks to underline that radio is not a blind medium. Rather, in its ability to delve into the consciousness of its characters and to construct itself in the skulls of its audience, it offers an 'inner vision' essential to the success of the Zolian text. Vision is, in any case, a highly problematic sense in *Germinal*, a sense that falters and gains support precisely from the power of the word, of the voice. The powerful association between Zola's novel and its adaptation at the hands of Hopkins and then Griffiths stems precisely from their concentration on things vocal. At the level of plot, each work assesses the power of voice. However, more intriguingly, at a metatextual level, each author considers the voices within his/her own creative voice, the whispering traces of myth, contemporary history, art and literature from which his/her text is adapted. The texts of Zola, Hopkins and Griffiths are polyphonic works that encourage readers to trace their multiple vocal tracks, to engage with their labyrinthine borrowings from the voices of others.

The voice of Zola's *Germinal* still resonates in contemporary culture. In economic terms it is one of the most successful of the author's output in book form. Adapted into silent film by Alberto Capellani as early as 1913, the novel has been worked and reworked across time, media and nation. The novel formed the subject matter for Claude Berri's 1993 blockbuster starring Gérard Depardieu, the most expensive film of its era.[5] A multi-part television mini-series aired on the BBC in 1970, and, residually popular on French television with single *téléfilms* and multi-part adaptations being broadcast and re-broadcast repeatedly, a multi-part mini-series aired in 2009 on Direct 8. The two radio adaptations explored in this chapter, however, require more introduction than the novel since their voices are perhaps unknown to the reader and, if so, likely to remain so given the lack of a publicly accessible BBC radio archive.[6] Once aired, unless recorded, the voices of the adaptations of Hopkins and Griffiths disappeared. Such though is the nature of radio, for it depends on sounds and voices. In the words of W. Ong:

> Sound exists only when it is going out of existence. It is not simply perishable but essentially evanescent, and it is sensed as evanescent. When I pronounce the word 'permanence' by the time I get to the '-nence' the 'perma-' is gone and has to be gone.[7]

Mladen Dolar concurs: '[Voice] makes the utterance possible, but it disappears in it, it goes up in smoke in the meaning being pronounced.'[8] The perishable nature of voice leads to what Gregory Whitehead identifies as the central paradox of radio, the medium that is 'ubiquitous' in its popularity and open access, but ever 'fading without a trace'.[9] David Hopkins was, in many respects, a highly suitable candidate to dramatise Zola's novel for the spoken word. Like Zola his artistic interests were broad (he worked as a filmmaker, writer, cinema programmer and dramatist as well as becoming a documentary director at BBC Bristol). His university studies in zoology and drama, moreover, might arguably be seen as the perfect preparation for the animalistic thrills of *Germinal*, a text he dramatised as a five-part serial for the BBC in 1982, working from Leonard Tancock's translation.[10] If Hopkins's interest in Zola was fleeting and his interest in radio at times secondary to other media, the dramatist of the second case study, Diana Griffiths, not only focuses largely on radio, but her interest in Zola's voice is serial. Her three-part adaptation of *Germinal* that aired in 2007 on Radio 4 had been preceded by a version, in 2004, of *L'Assommoir* and was followed in 2009 by a version of *Thérèse Raquin.*[11]

Neither adaptation triggered critical comment in the sphere of Zola studies. Such critical silence has much to do with the medium of radio's message: voice/sound. Though Zola is an artist in and of words, he is repeatedly associated with vision, with an overarching desire to see and make us see everything in his twenty-novel *Rougon-Macquart* series. It is no coincidence that, in the totalising ambitions of the writer figure in Zola's *Nouveaux Contes à Ninon,* speech comes a poor third after sight: 'tout voir, tout savoir, tout dire. Je voudrais coucher l'humanité sur une page blanche, tous les êtres, toutes les choses; une œuvre qui serait l'arche immense.'[12] The breadth of the novelist's panoramas in *Germinal* is clear as Zola hints at the limitlessness of the landscape and its 'champs sans fin'.[13] His approach to such panoramas is in many respects painterly. As Monet painted the same space in different lights, seasons and times, so Zola offers the reader comparable visions of the mine in day, night, spring and winter. His visions are washed in blackness in fluid descriptions 'de cette apparition fantastique, noyée de nuit et de fumée' (p. 1134). They make clear the 'touches' and 'taches' of his textual painting: 'Très loin, de petites taches blanches indiquaient des villes' (p. 1192). Colour too proves important. Like the Impressionists, Zola plays with the colours intrinsically attributed to objects. Bonnemort spits not blood but black coal on the earth. The earth, instead of being comparably black, is as red as the blood it has drunk from him in its three attempts to kill him (p. 1135). Colour is also one of many means of highlighting the chasm between the workers and the bourgeois. While the miners live in a palette confined to just three colours (the black of the ubiquitous coal dust, the white of their anaemic bodies and the red of the blood they offer to the gluttonous mine), Cécile's entry into the action in a nasturtium colour dress opens a bourgeois world far more varied in tone and hue (p. 1308). Driven by vision at the level of plot and by a desire at the level of form to explore the capacity of words to 'see', the affiliation of *Germinal* with things visual is clear.

Radio, as has already been suggested, by stark contrast, is traditionally considered to be a blind, black medium. Val Gielgud, for so many years the guiding force of BBC radio drama concurs. He suggests that radio's blindness is in fact double. Not only does the dramatist see 'himself deprived of visual effect, of costume-colour, of scenic atmosphere', but 'he is also robbed of all audience reaction'.[14] BBC radio drama has made something of a leitmotiv of this blindness. The first play written for radio, *A Comedy of Danger* (1924) by Richard Hughes, is set in the darkness at the bottom of a coal mine and opens with the words 'The lights have gone out'.[15] The BBC sought to maximise this sense of darkness, advising the audience to listen to the radio play in the dark for fear that the public's surroundings would distract them. Hopkins's *Germinal* takes up this leitmotiv of blindness, reflecting on the medium of its own existence. Hopkins's Jeanlin reflects on the darkness of the mine in which he and Etienne hide: 'It's odd that you can hear better down here especially when it's really dark. Things sound so much more.' Radio does black out aspects of Zola's text. Neither Hopkins nor Griffiths allow us to see the full cast of Zola's novel for the darkness of radio imposes specific constraints on dramatists. Large cast dramas, of which *Germinal* is a prime example, are impossible. If a character falls silent at any time they disappear in radio. Moreover, neither Hopkins nor Griffiths can show us the spaces of Zola's panoramas. Place, the theme so important to Zola with his belief in the formative nature of environment, can only ever be minimal in radio, refracted through the words of characters or conveyed in descriptions from a narrator. The former possibility can be clumsy and the latter is regarded with artistic suspicion by the radio profession. Gielgud writes: 'If it is to be effective and justifiable, narrative requires extreme discrimination in use and particular care in its writing. Used merely as a device to save the writer trouble it is – often literally – unspeakable.'[16]

To dismiss radio solely as a blind medium, though, is in many respects to misunderstand it as the adaptation of Griffiths in particular demonstrates. Though their radio adaptations cannot 'show' the breadth and detail of Zola's panoramas, they offer a different type of vision, a type highly suited to Zola's fictional project: inner vision. Radio's vision (and, indeed, that of literature, Zola's medium,) is interior in two key respects. First, radio infiltrates the heads of its listeners, inhabiting the recesses of their minds, recesses in which its action is staged. As Frances Gray puts it, 'the stage of radio is the darkness and silence of the listener's skull'.[17] Gray continues:

> As soon as we hear a word in a radio play, we are close to the experience it signifies; in fact the sound is literally inside us. To submit to

> this invasion, to allow another's picture of the universe to enter and undermine our own, is to become vulnerable in a way we do not when we watch a film or a play, where the alien world is demonstrably outside.[18]

However, radio's inner vision is not restricted to the mind of its listener. Radio blacks out the outside world and its scenery and consequently is, in the ensuing darkness, particularly adept at the 'dramatisation of consciousness'.[19] It is a medium that can enter, without unnerving the listener, the unexplored recesses of its characters' minds. 'Remember', said writer Tyrone Guthrie of his heroine at the start of a radio play in the 1920s, 'you are overhearing her thoughts'.[20] Such inner vision is a key characteristic of Zola's literary mission in the *Rougon-Macquart* series in general. The novelist dissects the lives and minds of characters as they battle beneath the controlling weight of their era, environment and heredity. Writing in advance of the *Rougon-Macquart* in a statement which nevertheless anticipates the penetrating scalpel of his narrative, he claims of *Thérèse Raquin*: 'J'ai simplement fait sur deux corps vivants le travail analytique que les chirurgiens font sur des cadavres.'[21] *Germinal* exemplifies this inner vision in its opening pages as Zola contrasts and moves between the endlessness of the 'immense horizon plat' and the stifling confines of the protagonist's mind as he walks in that landscape, a mind made smaller by its fixation on a single repeated thought: 'Une seule idée occupait sa tête vide d'ouvrier sans travail et sans gîte, l'espoir que le froid serait moins vif après le lever du jour' (p. 1133). Moreover, critics have taken the mine with its unknown recesses and seams as a metaphor for the human psyche. It is the space where unspoken desires grow, where Etienne and Catherine give in to the love they have forbidden themselves, where Etienne surrenders to his urges to kill. For Henri Mitterand the mine is the 'place where instinctive impulses – hunger, sex, murder – which daylight normally censures or controls, break loose freely . . . This is the place where man reverts to beast'.[22] Zola's narrative offers its reader a privileged vision of the mind, inner impulses and hidden desires of specific characters. Radio, a medium suited to the interiority of Zola's narrative vision, can do likewise.

Griffiths's adaptation plays precisely on the inner vision so central to Zola's text and to the medium in which she works. While she cannot describe the external landscape in the breadth her source novel does, she allows the listener access to the landscape of her characters' minds. She does in places have her narrator pronounce externally on the hidden thoughts of her characters, thoughts they have not yet fully formulated for themselves: 'Although he hardly realises it yet, Etienne is excited to feel his popularity growing daily, to find himself the centre of attention and to feel the whole world revolving around him.' Yet, more often than not she simply allows the listener into her characters' heads, permitting him/her to hear the thoughts that go unvoiced. As Maheu arranges accommodation and finance for his new work mate, Etienne's brain objects vociferously in words which do not leave the confines of his skull: 'I'd rather drop dead of hunger than go back down that hell hole.' Moreover, in a series of letters to Pluchart, letters for our ears only, Etienne analyses events in a light he will not share with his comrades. Griffiths intersperses these letters with personal reflections that Etienne does not share with Pluchart, blurring the invisible boundary between what the protagonist puts down on paper and what he does not.[23] Such acts of radio voyeurism, if such visual vocabulary can pertain, find a metaphor in Griffiths's gleeful use of the eavesdropping scene in Zola, a scene in which Cécile and Paul watch the miners' delegation through a keyhole, observing from afar and commenting from outside (p. 1316). Like Cécile and Paul we eavesdrop on a world which is not our own, but unlike them we are not held at the same distance, barred by a door through which we can only peer. Griffiths plays with sound and its distance to take us into the room, to let us hear events, exploiting the innate intimacy of the medium of radio.

The panoramic vision of the external world so often associated with Zola, the vision radio cannot reproduce, is, in any case, *Germinal* makes clear, a highly problematic sense. Zola repeatedly highlights the incapacities of sight. Etienne struggles to comprehend the minescape in the opening pages of the novel. It dissolves in form and sense before his eyes in a tableau replete with verbs of hazy perception. The fluid imagery used both underlines how the landscape eludes him and anticipates the deluge at the novel's close. The landscape is, in his eyes, '[une] apparition fantastique, noyée de nuit et de fumée' (p. 1134). Before his gaze, 'la vaste salle . . . se noyait, peuplée de grandes ombres flottantes' (pp. 1151–2). Words, in this case those of the seasoned miners, are needed to make sense of this world for Etienne. The protagonist's eyes prove no more able to master space, place and detail below ground as he walks through the mine, 'un dédale d'escaliers et de couloirs obscurs' (p. 1157). 'La voix de Catherine', a voice detached from the body he cannot see in the inky subterranean blackness, guides and situates him, building in his mind a vision of the space he cannot make out (p. 1163). The gaze of the narrative itself might also be seen to fail for, in describing the scenery, it repeatedly points to the space which exceeds its fictional vision, moving beyond the pages of its own text: 'Puis, les champs se déroulaient, des champs sans fin de blé et de betteraves' (p. 1192). Space and its contents dissolve beneath the gaze of this novel: 'La nuit venait par grandes fumées, noyant les lointains perdus de la plaine. Sur cette mer immense de terres rougeâtres, le ciel bas semblait se fondre en noire poussière' (p. 1235). The novel's close appears to offer a return to clarity and light, a return to visual mastery and a clear sense of space. Etienne, in daylight, dominates the landscape that has allowed him to follow in the footsteps of his mentor, the labour leader Pluchart, in Paris. However, vision is problematic to the last in this novel. What Etienne sees, in a parody of the systematic panoramic structure to which Zola so frequently has recourse in his novels, is debris: matter decomposing, presence becoming more of an absence, something becoming nearly nothing. Zola writes, in a passage at once geographically fixed and absent, '*A droite,* il apercevait Montsou qui dévalait et se perdait. *En face,* il avait les décombres du Voreux' (p. 1591).[24] In any case, what Etienne sees is obfuscated by the words on which he concentrates as he practises speeches he hopes to give in Paris. His words block the landscape he has already metaphorically left behind, transporting him to his new life in the capital. Zola's novel might be seen to be more blind than the medium of radio.

However, words and voices, in Zola's *Germinal,* might initially seem as frail as vision itself. Words, Zola underlines in the novel, are essentially evanescent, and often ultimately silent. Etienne's rousing speech in the clandestine strike meeting appears reinforced as it is echoed by the mass of workers, thus ratifying Etienne. But the worker's chants fill the sky only to dissipate into nothingness: 'L'ouragan de ces trois mille voix emplit le ciel et s'éteignit dans la clarté pure de la lune' (p. 1386). Words dissipate. Bonnemort and Etienne converse in the opening pages of the text but 'une rafale leur coupa la parole' (p. 1135), 'leurs voix se perdaient, des bourrasques emportaient les mots dans un hurlement mélancolique'

(p. 1136). Words are lost the moment they leave the speaker's mouth. Etienne's words are not only lost to the marauding miners as they march on various pits but, in a highly Lacanian manner, they appear alien to him the moment that he hears them. His inner voice of reason questions his words urging revolt.[25] Words, at the level of plot in *Germinal* fade and apparently leave little trace. They are also often essentially silent. For a novel of so many words, silence proves key. The miners are silent and silenced in the initial stages of the text. Bonnemort, the aged miner, has the few words he does utter cut off by coughing fits caused by the mine (p. 1138). La Maheude can only stammer in the presence of the rich Hennebeau family as she asks for charity (p. 1213). Maheu sits in the presence of his immediate boss and cannot speak: 'Il voulut protester, ne put prononcer que des mots sans suite . . . et se rétira, en bégayant' (p. 1290). So silent are the miners that the elements, the night and the wind, speak for them. We hear 'un cri de famine que roulait le vent de mars' (p. 1137), 'la seule plainte des rafales' (p. 1142). Much is made of Maheu's accession to speech midway through the novel and La Maheude's spoken prophecies of social revolution at the text's close. Irving Howe contends that '*Germinal* releases one of the central myths of the modern era: the story of how the dumb acquire speech'.[26] Maheu apparently confirms this when he temporarily finds his voice when leading the deputation to negotiate with the mine bosses:

> Maintenant, il était lancé, les mots venaient tout seuls. Par moments, il s'écoutait avec surprise, comme si un étranger avait parlé en lui. C'étaient des choses amassées au fond de sa poitrine, des choses qu'il ne savait même pas là, et qui sortaient, dans un gonflement de son cœur. (p. 1320)

However, the novel's close silences Maheu definitively with a bullet. La Maheude appeals to him as he lies dead on the floor: 'Parle donc' (p. 1510). She receives no reply. Her prophetic speech in the final pages of the book, a speech with the potential to be taken as a beacon of hope in Zola's novel is ultimately even more silent. Not only are her words borrowed from the rhetoric of Etienne, rhetoric that has already been derided as empty and a failure, they are not even given to us from her mouth. The text metaphorically speaks for her, paraphrases her, silences her:

> On n'aurait pas même besoin de s'en mêler, la boutique sauterait seule, les soldats tireraient sur les patrons, comme ils avaient tiré

> sur les ouvriers. Et, dans sa résignation séculaire, dans cette hérédité de discipline qui la courbait de nouveau, un travail s'était ainsi fait, la certitude que l'injustice ne pouvait durer davantage. (p. 1586)

The words with which the reader is left at the novel's denouement belong to Etienne.[27] Etienne's words, though numerous, are ultimately silent. With their message of social hope and change, his words repeat the phrases that have failed in the course of the novel. Bonnemort repeatedly underlines the ultimate silence of Etienne's words of revolution which circulate in a cyclical manner in generation after generation: 'Dis ce que tu voudras, et ce sera comme si tu n'avais rien dit' (p. 1318). The silence of the words of the novel's close, words that take up these incantatory phrases once more, is deafening.

Griffiths's piece echoes, at the level of plot, much of this silence. As an adaptation it testifies to a certain wariness in relation to the power of the word. When the miners present their demands to the bourgeois managers, 'saying that the workers are going to make sure things change', the response is damning: 'they always say that'. The circles and cycles of history and the revolutionary cries of their ancestors, far from amplifying the voice of the miners, dispossess and silence it still further. Griffiths keeps Zola's image of words dissipating despite the passion with which they are spoken. The miners shout their determination that their world will change: 'the tempest of their voices rose and filled the heavens and then gradually dissolved in the clear, cold, bright moonlight'. And, in keeping with this image, Etienne's words, in this adaptation, achieve nothing bar allowing him to move beyond this world. La Maheude does echo them in the closing scene of the play:

> Next time it'll be the real thing . . . Next time we'll be a peaceful army . . . and the day will come when we'll find ourselves shoulder to shoulder, millions of workers . . . able to seize power and become masters.

But this act of endorsement is undercut in two respects. La Maheude rubbished such words only a few scenes earlier: 'I had my head in the clouds, imagining a life where everyone lived in friendship and equality – but now I know it could never happen. Never!' Moreover, her dreams of worker solidarity and power are undercut by the brutal interruption of her conversation with Etienne by a fellow worker ordering her, uncaring of her identity, into the prison of the mine: 'Hey, woman. The cage is waiting for you.' And Etienne's words in the Griffiths adaptation are, perhaps, ultimately to be as mistrusted as those of La Maheude. Griffiths, early in the adaptation, gives space to Zola's chaffinch contest – the event at the Montsou fair where the winning bird is the one who sings the same tune the most times in an hour (p. 1266). Such repetitive tunes find something of an amusing echo in Etienne's words of social revolution, words he repeats as seemingly endlessly as the chaffinches. Significantly, when Etienne makes an impassioned speech in the forest pushing for the strike to continue, in Griffiths's adaptation his words are immediately preceded by bird song. Such song, getting louder and louder, similarly precedes the visionary words of hope pronounced at the adaptation's close. In both instances the song might be read as an indication of the harmony and beauty to come from these revolutionary words. Or, in light of the chaffinches and their endless tune repeated by rote, such birdsong may silence the adaptation's final words of possibility, rejecting them as a platitude recycled endlessly, to little effect.

Words, though, in radio and in *Germinal*, retain a clear power even as they fade and dissipate. They are the source of power of Rasseneur ('il laissa couler son éloquence facile, d'une douceur apaisante d'eau tiède' p. 1520), Pluchart ('il avait une éloquence qui tenait du prône, une façon religieuse de laisser tomber la fin des phrases, dont le ronflement monotone finissait par convaincre' p. 1347) and Etienne ('Tous le disaient, il n'était pas grand, mais il se faisait écouter' p. 1379). Thanks to their words, each of these men, in their own ways, achieves both eminence and a living. Etienne's words may be lost to the other that is the mass of miners, turned against him in mocking parody when the strike fails, but by dint of repeating them he still manages to use them to advance socially and professionally in post-novelistic time. He leaves for Paris repeating the words that have failed the miners in Montsou, words that secure his future. Words too hold the key to Zola's success for, however problematic they are in the novel, the words of the novel bring him both financial success and a degree of cultural acclaim. And, as Zola speaks silence in *Germinal*, so, in Griffiths's adaptation of it, silence speaks. Radio can do silence like no other form. Silence is, as McWhinnie suggests, a natural ingredient in 'the creation of the radio illusion' as the medium 'comes out of silence, vibrates in the void and in the mind, and returns to silence'.[28] Griffiths makes eloquent use of the absence of words, using silence as a scene transition in places. She chooses to follow Catherine's death with 'dead ambience', a total silence which both underlines the silence of the state which has embraced the character, Etienne's shock and the definitive break this scene represents in Etienne's life: he subsequently cuts all ties with Montsou and leaves. Similarly Griffiths uses silence to depict the horror of Maigrat's castration, a horror made somehow all the more poignant by her refusal to name it:

> Etienne: No, he's dead, let him be.
> Narrator: Etienne realises with growing horror what these women are about to do.
> . . .
> Etienne: Oh, no, no, no.
> Women: Yes! Yes! Yes!
> Etienne: God.

Griffiths's words, even in their silence, like Zola, achieve a vocal power.

That both of the radio adaptations in question silence aspects of Zola's voice is clear. Constrained by their time slots (Griffiths's piece is made up of three parts, Hopkins's of five), both have to alter elements of Zola's text. Hopkins cuts Etienne's love affair with La Mouquette, making his love for Catherine purer, he makes Alzire the hunchback child a far feistier child than her softly spoken Zolian counterpart and endows M. Grégoire, one of the shareholders in the mine, with a calculating canniness alien to Zola's character. Griffiths does away with Rasseneur and merges the mine's owners largely into one. Neither animalises characters in the way Zola does, though both seek equivalents. Animal comparisons find their way into the prose Griffiths gives her narrator – he suggests that Jeanlin is 'slowly reverting to his animal origins'. Hopkins parallels the habits of Bonnemort and his horse as both function to exactly the same timetable. Neither dramatist personifies the inanimate as Zola does and in neither play does the mine 'speak' as it does in Zola's novel. Both, however, use sound to underline the omnipresence of the mine. Hopkins opens each episode with the roll of a coal truck in a mine, a roll made elemental by its association with thunder, and the gulps of the pump which keep the mine water at bay, gulps which sound like a throat gasping for air. The significance of these alterations is minor and, indeed, the usefulness of listing them limited. What is more significant is the way in which both dramatists privilege one aspect of Zola's voice as a whole. Zola is a polyphonic writer. His novels seek to depict the everyday world, offering an accurate vision of a sociological reality, but they are also the products of a poet, literary works steeped in symbolism and imagination. Both adaptations introduce a narrator absent in Zola's novel that is refracted to a large extent through the consciousnesses and voices of his characters.[29] While the personality of these narrators in both texts is very different, one a social realist, one more of a poet, neither narrator ultimately expresses both of these Zolian voices.

As Zola aimed for a panoramic vision of the external world in novels that offered incisive sociological commentary by dissecting the personalities and thoughts of characters, the command of Hopkins's narrator over time, character and action is pronounced. He not only has a full grasp of what has been, but also continually gestures to what will be, mastering past, present and future. As Etienne enters the action, Hopkins's narrator states: 'It'll be over a year before he leaves, but in that time there'll be more upheaval than his present companion [Bonnemort] has seen in a lifetime.' Catherine whispers her desire to herself for 'peace, peace', and the narrator responds 'But that's not to be, not for a long time'. Moreover, Hopkins's narrator extends his vision panoramically to cover the world: 'If the contrast between the Grégoires and the Maheus seems to be too strong for your liking, too exaggerated, let me tell you that it's true and repeated one hundred times over in northern France, perhaps the whole world.' The narrator's total vision extends also to complete mastery over his characters as he peers invasively, in a detached fashion, inside their skulls and actions. He not only ratifies for the reader what they say in places ('it's true, the things he says', 'and he's right', 'and she's right'), he fills in the gaps in their speech. He offers the listener a technical explanation for the oasis of warmth and growth above the abandoned mine which has a fire still burning in it, a technical explanation Paul Négrel does not give, even though asked, within the play itself. The narrator voices the gratitude for the brioche that Alzire does not utter: 'And the poor, starving brat goes gratefully out, respectfully holding the pieces of brioche.' He speaks Etienne's silent horror in his first day at the mine: 'It's cramped and awkward. Cold and wet. He's tired and miserable. And he hasn't even started his day's work yet.' Indeed, Hopkins uses his scene length to allow us to share the initiatory experience of his character. A series of short sharp different scenes open the play, but they are followed by a long set of interlinked scenes focusing on Etienne's first day in the mine which echo the protagonist's belief that it seems 'to go on forever'. The language of Hopkins is, as the quotation in relation to Etienne's horror suggests, precise, prosaic and absolute. In relation to the Grégoires, Hopkins's narrator claims: 'They have four servants to minister to their needs. They are very rich. They believe in charity.' Using his words far more sparingly and simply than his source text, Hopkins seeks to give us a total vision of his characters and their world. The totality of his vision finds physical expression in the repeated use by Hopkins's narrator of two adjectives linked by 'and', adjectives that balance and in a sense seal the description. The narrator seemingly enters into a conversation with the listener, addressing him/her directly. Speaking of the Hennebeaus, he says: 'We have not met either of them, so I will tell you.' He adds later: 'I don't suppose it will surprise you to be told that not everyone in the village thinks of Etienne as a liberator.' But the conversation is one in which the audience is silenced and which, the narrator makes clear, brooks no response. Describing to the listener the chaffinch contest and explaining its direction by the nail-makers he states: 'Why? Why is the sky blue and rain wet? It just is.' The voice of Hopkins's dramatisation is that of Zola the would-be sociologist seeking to analyse, dissect and pronounce on his characters' lives in their entirety.

If Hopkins's dramatisation gives voice to the sociological aspect of Zola, that of Griffiths is far closer to Zola the poet. The baldness and symmetry of Hopkins's language, with its absence of ostentation and imagery, contrasts starkly with the artistry of Griffiths. Her narrator claims: 'There's no sign of dawn yet, to relight the dead sky; only the distant furnaces bloody the shadows.' This narrative voice offers much more scenic utterances which attempt to give the listener a sense of space, sight, colour and metaphor: 'the sun's last dark rays dye the road and the plain red. The people seem bathed in blood like butchers in a slaughter house.' Such statements underline Zola's belief in the importance of milieu, in his idea that environment shapes personalities. They reflect too his tendency to use the surrounding scenery as a mirror for and of events. Griffiths's poetry seemingly clashes with the obscenity her dramatisation includes ('piss off', 'you skyving bastard') yet this seeming contradiction is perfectly in keeping with Zola, the novelist committed to using current slang and contemporary words in his at times highly poetic, beautiful writing.

While both adaptations might be criticised for silencing one of Zola's voices, be it the sociological or the poetic, Zola, as Alain Pagès points out, silenced himself in a tellingly comparable way while his text was being written. Before *Germinal* was complete, Zola agreed its publication in *feuilleton* form. It subsequently appeared in *Gil Blas* (November 1884–February 1885) and *La Vie populaire* (April–July 1885). While such publications allowed Zola the time and means to complete and edit his textual voice, they also silence that voice in two key respects. First, the spatial constraints of the *feuilleton* form and its very different audiences require aspects of Zola's novel to be silenced, a fact Zola recognised when he authorised the *Gil Blas* to cut what they believed their readers would not accept.[30] Secondly, regardless of the words these publications print, their ideological identities filter and privilege one of Zola's voices. Pagès explains:

> Le premier feuilleton . . . , placé dans un espace journalistique hétérogène [*Gil Blas*], est un événement littéraire qui redouble l'actualité du moment (la grève d'Anzin de février–avril 1884, notamment): il propose un contrat de lecture idéologique. Le deuxième feuilleton, situé dans un espace homogène [*La Vie populaire*], est un produit de consommation littéraire dont l'impact est banalisé: il offre un contrat de lecture essentiellement narratif.[31]

The very different Zolas these publications voice, the social commentator and the artistic narrative producer, both have a basis in Zola's text. However, the publications prove unable to allow both voices to be spoken simultaneously. Aspects of the voices in Zola's *Germinal* are silenced even while they are being written.

The adapted voices drawn from Zola's text, however, need to be paralleled with the adapted voices in Zola's text itself. Words, texts and voices are, at the level of plot, adapted and reiterated seemingly constantly. The miners echo and adapt, albeit minimally, the words of Etienne, their new leader, just as they echoed and will echo again those of their previous figurehead Rasseneur (p. 1521). Yet the source of their adaptations, Etienne's voice, is itself an adapted one. He reads voraciously if, at times, uncomprehendingly and weaves his phrases from a twisted mass of threads drawn from the printed words of others. He speaks, inspired by 'cette lecture mal comprise' (p. 1524). From his reading he fashions his calls for social revolution: 'Sur les moyens d'exécution, il se montrait plus vague, mêlant ses lectures, ne craignant pas, devant des ignorants, de se lancer dans des explications où il se perdait lui-même' (p. 1279). Etienne adapts repeatedly, endlessly and ultimately badly, 'en phrases dont la confusion gardait un peu de toutes les théories traversées et successivement abandonnées' (p. 1340). Jeanlin is, Manfred Schmeling suggests, one of Etienne's doubles: 'Jeanlin est l'autre moi, le moi obscur du héros.'[32] Both seek refuge in the same space in the mine, both kill and use the mine as a haven for those acts of murder and indeed Etienne thinks explicitly of Jeanlin once he has killed Chaval (p. 1572). Jeanlin's prolific thefts resonate with Etienne's life. While Jeanlin steals food and tangible objects, Etienne pilfers words, concepts and other peoples' voices.

Zola's own voice might be seen to be as borrowed, as adapted as that of his protagonist. The seams of Zola's borrowing and adaptation in *Germinal* are rich. He borrows, in the first instance, from himself, from the icons and iconography of the earlier novels of his corpus. *Germinal*, Becker asserts, adapts and extends the themes of *L'Assommoir*, a novel to which it serves as a companion volume.[33] *Germinal* might also be seen as the adaptive precursor to Zola's *Travail*, the post-*Rougon-Macquart* novel which sees some of the collectivist, utopian theories Etienne voices enacted. Jean Bourgeois highlights some of the similarities that tie *Germinal* to its precursor, *Thérèse Raquin*.[34] Both have inescapable love triangles (Thérèse, Camille, Laurent/Catherine, Etienne, Chaval). Camille's watery death in *Thérèse Raquin* is echoed by that of Chaval in *Germinal*. In both works the bloated, disfigured established male partner comes back to haunt the lover who seeks to usurp him. In *Thérèse Raquin* this return is metaphorical, taking place only in the terrified imaginings of the lovers, in *Germinal* it is literal as Chaval's body poisons the water of the cave in which Etienne and Catherine shelter (p. 1576). *Germinal* not only repeats Zola's earlier works, it might also be seen to repeat itself, structured as it is around returns and replays. Catherine leads Etienne through the mine, guiding him through its perils safely in the opening pages. He will lead her in the same way, albeit unsuccessfully, in the novel's closing pages in a passage whose reflections are in fact double. The passage simultaneously echoes that of Chaval, Etienne's rival and yet another of his doubles, leading Catherine safely out of the mine. Zola's text resonates with the echoing voices of his earlier novels as well as those of its own pages.

The whispered voices of myth also resound in the pages of *Germinal*. Catherine serves as an Echo to Etienne's Narcissus. Not only does she frequently prove incapable of authentic speech, echoing the voices and ideas of the men in her life, but Etienne, whose narcissicism is underlined by Rasseneur (p. 1340), uses her as an acoustic mirror, to use Kaja Silverman's term.[35] He searches for her in the crowd of the outdoor meeting of the striking miners, hoping to find in her eyes, in a supremely Lacanian manner, the ratification of his words and speech (p. 1384). Etienne's attempted rescue of Catherine in the mine is reminiscent of Theseus's attempt to take Persephone from the underworld. Persephone is the child who causes her mother so much grief when she is abducted, just as La Maheude is devastated by the financial loss of Catherine when Chaval forces her to live with him (p. 1331). As her mythical predecessor is the consort of Hades when he governed the underworld, so Catherine is the sexual partner of Chaval as he is promoted to oversee the blackleg Belgians brought down to run the mine. The myth of Orpheus and Eurydice, a myth precisely about another subterranean rescue and the power of the voice, resonates in *Germinal*. Orpheus, renowned for the power of his singing, just as Etienne becomes renowned for the power of his speech, can tame wild beasts and change the course of rivers with his song. Etienne, like his mythical forebear, for a limited time, enjoys the ability to tame the marauding mass of miners, a mass Zola depicts precisely in bestial, fluid terms. He diverts them from their murderous course: 'Mais un nouveau flot arrivait du coron, et Levaque qui marchait en tête ... criait "A mort, les Borains! pas d'étrangers chez nous! à mort! à mort!" Tous se ruaient, il fallut qu'Etienne les arrêtât' (p. 1501). Orpheus was famously one of the few heroes to visit the underworld and return. Even in Hades his singing and lyre music apparently did not lose their power. Etienne, like Orpheus, exits the mine unscathed, leaving behind his Eurydice, Catherine, having looked at a future with her for the first time (p. 1580). His voice speaks on unaltered, reciting, like an incantation, the words of social revolution which won him power over the miners, the words which secure him a future with Pluchart in Paris. As Eurydice dies twice in the myth, Catherine might be seen to die twice in the mine. While her first stay in the underworld in the accident with Chaval is temporary, her second, like that of her mythical forebear, is definitive.

Zola's adaptation of various mythical voices in *Germinal* is labyrinthine. It finds an analogy in the novel's relationship with the myth of the Minotaur. While the word labyrinth is never used in the novel, the image of the elaborate maze-like construction clearly hovers over the text. Zola describes the mass of corridors and seams in the mine: 'Ce convoi sous la terre, au milieu des épaisses ténèbres, n'en finissait plus, le long des galeries qui bifurquaient, tournaient, se déroulaient' (p. 1298). Etienne loses himself in the passages of the maze which miners have walked 'depuis des éternités' (p. 1212) according to La Maheude. Zola writes: 'Ils allaient toujours, elle [Catherine] silencieuse à présent, lui [Etienne] ne reconnaissant pas les carrefours ni les rues du matin, s'imaginant qu'elle le perdait de plus en plus sous la terre' (p. 1180). Not only is the subterranean landscape labyrinth-like, but so too is the surface landscape which, in its endless uniformity, deprives the viewer of fixed reference points: 'A droite et à gauche du chemin, se déroulaient les mêmes terrains vagues clos de palissades moussues, les mêmes corps de fabriques' (p. 1210).[36] Etienne, like Theseus, sets himself the task of conquering the Minotaur that feeds itself gluttonously from the human flesh of miners. His links with Theseus are pronounced. The mythical figure was a hero who fought enemies identified with an archaic system and was hailed by Athenians as a great reformer. Etienne pits himself against the beast of capitalism and offers in place of this economic, social system a vision of a brave, new world. However, the image of the labyrinth is relevant on an entirely different level in the novel – it embodies the way in which Zola borrows from myth. Zola's adaptation of myths is so profuse that a list of his potential sources exceeds the possibilities of this chapter. But what matters is not what Zola borrows from myth but, rather, the way in which he borrows from myth. The author, like Etienne with his political tracts, partially adopts, adapts and discards mythical sources, moving easily between them. He encourages the reader to recognise and follow the threads of these well-known myths. Zola seeks to lose his reader in a labyrinth of mythical intertexts for which ultimately there is no endpoint. Myth, as Julie Sanders, writes is a metaphor for the adaptive process.[37] And Zola's labyrinth of mythical voices in a sense anticipates her ideas for the novelist characterises the act of authorship precisely as an adaptation, as the retelling of an age-old story in a new voice.

Both Griffiths and Hopkins echo in their adaptations fragments of the mythical voices from which Zola weaves his narrative. At the level of plot, whispers of various myths can be heard. In the Griffiths adaptation, Négrel greets Etienne like a defeated Theseus as he goes back down the pit after the strike: 'The company must have good points after all, if the great giant-killer from Montsou is returning to ask for bread.' Chaval taunts Etienne in the Hopkins dramatisation after his stay in the cave, hiding from the police: 'So you've come back to the land of the living have you?' His words gesture to the presence of the Theseus myth in Zola's *Germinal* as does the welcome the horses get in the Griffiths adaptation in the underworld that is the mine. We witness the descent of 'the latest prisoner, who would never be sent back alive' from the maze-like corridors. Both dramatisations echo Zola's mythical borrowings at the level of dialogue, be it that of the characters or of the narrator. But the Hopkins piece takes things further, leading us, Theseus-like, through the maze of Zola's fiction by spinning a narrative thread so strong we cannot lose either it or the path this adaptation would have us take. This thread is woven by Hopkins's highly reflective scene transitions. The adaptation opens with a scene perforated by Bonnemort's coughs. While such coughs gesture to the very real physical degradation his profession has wrought on him, they also serve as a scene transition, leading into Catherine's coughs in the opening moments of the next scene and those of Alzire subsequently. These coughs establish the blood link between these family members in their degeneration and lead us seamlessly through the opening scenes. Hopkins's scene transitions are nearly always mirror-like in their symmetries. Etienne, penniless, sums up the horrors of his first day at the work he cannot abandon. Hopkins cuts, in a telling contrast, to the following dialogue in the wealthy Grégoire household which echoes, albeit grotesquely, the vocabulary of work and necessity:

> Mme Grégoire: Will you be working today?
> Cécile: I must. I must get it finished.
> M. Grégoire: What's that?
> Cécile: My psalter.

Similarly, Hopkins cuts from the habitual evening sex scene between the Maheus to move to Catherine's initiatory sex scene with Chaval, underlining that there is but one trajectory for girls in this mining village. The adaptation's opening scene commences with Bonnemort spitting out the remnants of the mine, the coal dust that has seeped into his being. It is followed by a scene that focuses inversely on ingestion as the mine swallows cage after cage of men, gluttonously. Dual reflections are common in this dramatisation. Hopkins moves from a scene with Paul Négrel, the Hennebeaus' lodger, to one with Etienne, the Maheus' lodger. Triple reflections, moreover, also occur. Denuelin offers Négrel a coffee before a scene in which Chaval argues with Catherine over his coffee not being hot enough. The adaptation then transitions into a scene at the Maheu house in which there is no coffee: 'Water's been strained through that twist of grains for three days.' The narrative thread of the Hopkins dramatisation is so strong that it does not permit us to get lost. It leads us, like Theseus, through Zola's fiction.

The voices from which Zola fashions that fiction are not just mythical, they are also literary. While critics have identified a variety of potential literary intertexts for *Germinal,* Ida Marie Frandon's tracing of a trio of now comparatively unknown writers – Guyot, Talmeyr and Malot – is particularly intriguing.[38] While the influence of Talmeyr is minor, perhaps limited to the comparable solitude and stance of the entrances of Etienne and Talmeyr's Jean Jaquemin in *Le Grisou,* in Guyot's *La Science économique* one finds much of the basis for Zola's economic descriptions, particularly those relating to overproduction/over-consumption. The impact of Malot's *Sans Famille* is stronger. From it, Zola gets the flooding of the mine, the counting of Davy lamps as a means to try to assess those left behind in an accident and perhaps his inspiration to use the ignorance of a novice to explain to the reader the workings and subterranean landscape of a mine. Rémi, Malot's hero, serves, like Etienne, as a 'fil conducteur' leading the reader through the maze of his fiction. However, Malot's novel itself borrows from an earlier work which Zola himself consulted extensively: the technical writing of mine engineer Louis-Laurent Simonin in *La Vie souterraine.* While Zola clearly owes much of the mechanical detail of his fiction to Simonin, *La Vie souterraine* proves as shifting and retreating a point of origin as the myths already described, for Simonin depicts the ontological reality he knew so well precisely through the retreating, adaptive coils of myth. Simonin writes of the mine: 'le bruit métallique du marteau et des laminoirs résonne de tous côtés; les fictions de l'antiquité ont pris un corps: on dirait le pays des Cyclopes'.[39] Of the miner emptying his coal he claims : 'Puis il redescend à vide pour recommencer, nouveau Sisyphe, et ainsi de suite entre matin et soir.'[40] Of the pit head itself, he concludes: 'A la bouche du puits brûle . . . le charbon sans cesse allumé. C'est comme le feu des Vestales, qui jamais ne devait s'éteindre.'[41] Zola's literary source texts prove as elusive and as shifting as those from which Etienne adapts his own voice.

If the voices of contemporary literature surface in Zola's novel, those of twentieth-century New Wave film whisper in Griffiths's *Germinal* and, to a lesser extent, that of Hopkins. Griffiths fissures the speech of characters and narrator alike, gluing together fragments of both in what becomes something of a dialogic mosaic. Etienne appears in the murk of the opening scene:

> Narrator: And he recognises
> Etienne: A pit head! It's a pithead! And the fires
> Narrator: Are burning in cast-iron braziers part-way up a heap.

Such speech mosaics appear comparatively frequently in Griffiths's piece. While they are rarer in Hopkins's adaptation, they do occur. Souvarine, for example, counts the steps on the ladder of the mine, seeking the correct rung from which to attack the mine lining:

> Souvarine: One, two
> Narrator: Three.

These speech mosaics are highly reminiscent of the vogue in New Wave French cinema for mixing intra- and extra-diegetic speech, a trend demonstrated by François Truffaut's *Jules et Jim* (1962). Truffaut's narrator starts sentences that his characters subsequently finish, and the director at times even superimposes fragments of sentences on the screen itself. He does so in order to throw into relief the mechanics of film itself, denaturalising it to an extent. The effect of the speech mosaics in Griffiths's dramatisation is somewhat different. They testify, in the first instance, to the power of the narrator and his ability to explain and complete the characters' thoughts. However, such mosaics are also inescapably resonant in a work of adaptation that by its very nature melds elements from an earlier voice with those of the new dramatist. The effect of these mosaics is not one of fragmentation – they do not disrupt the narrative flow but, rather, they testify precisely to a sense of flow, gesturing, like Zola's novel, to the highly original art which can be created from the voices of others.

Zola's adaptation of voices in *Germinal* extends too, famously, to the sphere of reality. A variety of critics have underlined the historical and contemporary events that found their way into Zola's pages. Zakarian describes Zola's fictional strike as a 'mosaic of Anzin, 1884, Aubin and Ricamarie, 1869, with an occasional reference to Fourchambault, 1870'.[42] When taken to task for the outlandishness of his novel's ending, Zola himself pointed to his work as an adaptation of reality: 'Ce n'est que l'adaptation d'un fait célèbre dans l'histoire des mines: la catastrophe du puits de Marles dans le Pas-de-Calais.'[43] Zola adapted not just events but people. In the quest to identify models for *Germinal*'s labour leaders, critics have suggested Basly (whom Zola met), Assi and Rondet as possible models for Rasseneur, Etienne and potentially Souvarine.[44] If Zola adapts these men, he does so partially and in a mobile form. Zakarian writes:

> It is only exceptionally that Zola finds all the material for a dramatic incident or technical fact in one reading. More often than not he synthesises several accounts . . . found in three or four different sources, or he compresses several facts into one fictional incident.[45]

The same is true of Zola's character studies. Elements of the description Zola made of Basly feed into Rasseneur and Etienne, men who echo and replace each other in the novel.[46] Moreover, Zola gave voice to the stereotype of the labour leader voiced by Leroy-Beaulieu: 'Leur parole est toujours facile, au besoin elle est élégante: produits curieux d'une époque où l'ambition pénètre et soulève toutes les classes, où une instruction toute de surface aiguise et polit les esprits.'[47] The voices of Zola's contemporary history whisper in the pages of *Germinal*.

As Zola adapted the voices of his contemporary era, so the adaptations of Hopkins and Griffiths reflect on recent British industrial history in the shape of the 1984 Miners' Strike. The iconography of this strike is etched onto the British cultural consciousness precisely as a result of the unparalled exposure it received and Arthur Scargill's 'well-established skill in front of a television camera'.[48] Much is made in *Germinal* of the circles and cycles of history as centuries pass but events ultimately remain the same. The resonance of Zola's novel with the 1984 strike is clear. It is not for nothing that Scargill claimed it was his favourite fictional work in an interview with *The Guardian*.[49] While improvements had taken place in relation to mining conditions, Adeney and Lloyd, in an unknowing echo of Zola's description of the Maheu seam, claim that, in the 1980s, 'it was still possible to find a few pits where men had to work at heights of less than three feet and often in water and intense heat too'.[50] As Zola's novel underlines that Etienne is just the latest in the line of would-be social reformers dreaming of a brave new world, so the veteran Labour politician Lord Shinwell, on his hundredth birthday in 1984 claimed: 'There is always an Arthur Scargill. In my day he was called Arthur Cook.'[51] Hopkins's adaptation, a piece that precedes the strike but not the rise of Scargill, has a mine owner discuss Etienne in the following terms: 'Every now and then they crop up. People who speak out against authority, against accepted order and he's one so I've heard.' Scargill, gifted with the same oratorical power Etienne cultivates, was according to Adeney and Lloyd, 'the most compelling activist-orator of his generation.'[52] Moreover, the words of Wilsher, Macintyre and Jones on Scargill could also apply to Etienne: 'Scargill was intent to make it especially clear that he regarded the year-long stoppage as merely an episode in the great working-class struggle against capitalism.'[53] John Lloyd concurs: 'the real strike had a politically revolutionary dimension intertwined with and indissoluble from its quite real industrial objectives'.[54] Both Hopkins and Griffiths set their adaptations in the coalfields of Yorkshire, areas so central to Scargill's strike. This act of relocation triggers a series of associations in the mind of the British listener, allowing the voices of contemporary and earlier British industrial disputes to whisper through the words of these two Zola adaptations.

Hopkins and Griffiths, however, do not just vocalise both Zola and a range of his sources in their adaptations; like Zola, they reflect precisely on the adapted nature of their own authorship, on the originality they wrest from their ultimately borrowed words. Creators of artefacts in a medium that depends, like Zola's novel, entirely on the word, Hopkins and Griffiths echo and perhaps amplify Zola's exploration of the ephemerality of words. In Hopkins's piece a series of characters belittle the power of the word. Bonnemort, for Hopkins a clear-sighted truth-teller, belittles Etienne's impassioned belief that words can change the world: 'Oh I've been hearing that sort of talk all my life. And that's all it is, talk. Things go on just the same as they did before.' Souvarine concurs that 'You don't change things by talking', as does La Maheude: 'Oh, they're just words, pretty words, yes, but words.' Even Catherine, in a departure from the meekness of Zola's heroine, questions the power of his speech: 'All I know is that you talk and talk and talk and nothing changes . . . People were talking like you a thousand years ago.' Hopkins's adaptation distrusts Etienne's words so much that in a series of scenes it cuts them in their entirety. When Etienne seeks to respond to those who will not believe his words, on at least two occasions the adaptation fades out those words, implying in its silence that the audience will have heard them all before. Etienne's words continue to circulate unaltered to the close of the adaptation. Hopkins, in a move that appears to distrust the ostensibly hopeful ending Zola's *Germinal* offers, places the words of Zola's denouement entirely in the mouth of its protagonist. Thus, he posits them as Etienne's dreams for the future, visions in words that we cannot fully believe, having heard them fail repeatedly in the course of the adaptation.

Both adaptations engage in a consideration of their own adaptive act. The Hopkins adaptation, itself a replication in altered form of Zola's novel, takes up the theme of replication in vocal terms. The reflective structure of this adaptation has already been discussed, but acts of vocal reflection and repetition pervade the piece as a whole. The narrator claims: 'In another bedroom, in another place, another couple are sleeping.' Of Jeanlin and Alzire he reflects: 'Life will never be a problem for him. Life will always be a problem for her.' Introducing episode 3, the narrator plays again on the repetitions and returns of his own words: 'Everything is quiet except for the relentless wind and everywhere is bleak and white except for the bare branches of the trees.' A comparable effect is achieved at the start of episode 4:

> Village 240 is still deep in its freezing winter. The inhabitants are still cold and very hungry . . . Today they are going to march on the mines that are still working. One way or another they will close them. One way or another they will bring the mine owners to their knees. One way or another they are determined to end the starvation and the misery.

Such vocal repetitions may indicate that the narrator's words, in another moment of *style indirect libre,* become those of the miners, of Etienne as he seeks out rhetorical repetition for impact, or they may, via the double stasis of the meaning and repetition of the word 'still', underline the unchanging nature of the miners' situation even while they speak for change. However, they also become poignant as an act of vocal repetition in an essentially replicatory vocal act: that of radio adaptation.

Both adaptations, despite their very different artistic personalities, might also be seen to reflect on the limitations of the adaptive process, to voice what they cannot do. In both pieces the words of characters are at times faded out or cut at the end of specific scenes. In some cases such acts of fading or cutting contribute to the narrative comment on the value of the words in question. Hopkins, for example, cuts bourgeois platitudinous words on an associate's loss of his mine: 'He brought everything on himself. That's true of everything in life. Remember that my dear . . .' Both Hopkins and Griffiths at times cut Etienne's words, reflecting in those cuts on the endless sameness of his speech. However, such cuts become doubly significant in the context of an adaptation of Zola. Impressionist artists such as Manet, artists Zola defended so vigorously in his art criticism, cropped the images at the edge of their canvases in order to situate their work as a slice of life, a mere indication of the vast reality which exceeded the confines of their painting. Manet, for example, in his now canonical *Un bar aux Folies-Bergère* (1882) has the feet of an unseen trapeze artist hover in the top corner of his canvas, feet thrown into relief by the vibrant green of the shoes. Similarly in his Zola-inspired canvas, *Nana* (1877), Manet slices in half the formally dressed gentleman who watches the prostitute in her state of undress. Such acts of narrative cropping find an equivalent in Zola's own descriptions which themselves indicate what seeps beyond their pages: the wealth of reality that eludes them. In cropping character dialogue in mid-flow, both Griffiths and Hopkins, artists in a purely verbal medium, both find something of an equivalent to the visual cropping of the Impressionists and indicate in a sense the aspects of Zola that necessarily escape them. They also give voice to an essentially visual intertext: nineteenth-century French Impressionist painting.

The case for studying Zola and radio is a compelling one. The blind darkness of radio parallels the inky blackness of Zola's *Germinal*, a novel in which the author delves into the consciousness and hidden seams of his characters' minds in a way so suited to the intimacy of radio. Radio's focus on the question of voice and silence, moreover, echoes Zola's exploration of these themes in *Germinal*. While Zola is more readily associated with the trope of vision, in

Germinal vision falters and words step in to buttress it. Such words may themselves prove ephemeral, fading into the night sky in the novel having changed little and fading into the blackness of the listener's mind in radio. However, words are far from powerless. Within the text, they gift Etienne his future, allowing him to leave Montsou. Via the text, words sustain and create Zola the novelist. Beyond the text, words ensure that this novelist continues to resonate in the series of adaptations created from *Germinal.* The adaptations of Diana Griffiths and David Hopkins not only echo the detail of Zola's text, they also engage, in a highly intriguing manner, with the novelist's conception of artistry as the latest retelling of an age-old story in a new voice. As Zola's artistry is woven from the whispering voices of myths, fictional works and reality, the voices of the plays by Hopkins and Griffiths adapt Zola, his sources and elements of their own contemporary history, culture and art. Like Zola they find artistry in a labyrinthine series of voices.

Notes

1 For explorations of Zola and cinema, see, *inter alia,* Paul Warren, *Zola et le cinéma* (Sainte-Foy: Presses de l'Université Laval, 1995); Anna Gural-Migdal and Robert Singer (eds), *Zola and Film: Essays in the Art of Adaptation* (Jefferson: McFarland, 2005) and Kate Griffiths, *Emile Zola and the Artistry of Adaptation* (Oxford: Legenda, 2009). Analyses of the fate of Zola's texts in the medium of theatre may be found in works such as Janice Best, *Expérimentation et adaptation: essai sur la méthode naturaliste d'Emile Zola* (Paris: José Corti, 1986) and Lawson A. Carter, *Zola and the Theater* (New Haven, CT: Yale University Press; Paris: Presses Universitaires de France, 1963). Comparatively little has been written on the adaptation of Zola's texts for television, but the following articles offer initial analyses of the phenomenon: Russell Cousins, 'Adapting Zola for TV: the example of Jacques Rouffio's *L'Argent*', *Excavatio,* 12 (1999), 153–61; Gaël Bellalou, '*Nadia Coupeau, dite Nana*: a modern adaptation of Zola's eponymous work', *Bulletin of the Emile Zola Society,* 30 (2004), 16–22, and Kate Griffiths, 'Mythical returns: televising *Thérèse Raquin*', *Nineteenth-Century French Studies,* 39 (2011), 285–95.

2 The Inathèque Paris houses eighteen of the radio pieces drawn from Zola's short stories, novels and *drames lyriques* sinbe 1947 and the BBC recently broadcast three Zola adaptations in the space of six years: *L'Assommoir* (2004), *Germinal* (2007) and *Thérèse Raquin* (2009).

3 Though writing on adaptation for radio is scarce, there are key exceptions. See, for example, Amanda Wrigley, *Greece on Air: Engagements with Ancient Greek Culture on BBC Radio, 1920s–1960s* (Oxford: Oxford

University Press, forthcoming 2013). Stephen Barnard, writing on radio as a generally overlooked area of study, underlines that the studies on the medium which do exist do not favour literature: 'Academic approaches to radio have drawn on many disciplines – cultural studies, linguistic analysis, political and economic history, sociology, psychology, business studies and marketing, *even* literary criticism.' My italics. Stephen Barnard, *Studying Radio* (London: Arnold, 2000), p. 3. Ian Rodger writes: 'Because its aesthetic exploitation has varied considerably from country to country, the interest of serious literary and drama critics has been deflected and seems to have encouraged the belief that radio can only be regarded as a sociological phenomenon.' Ian Rodger, *Radio Drama* (London: MacMillan, 1982), p. 1.

4 Crisell writes: 'What strikes everyone, broadcasters and listeners alike, as significant about radio is that it is a *blind* medium . . . Radio's codes are purely auditory, consisting of speech, music, sounds and silence.' Crisell, *Understanding Radio* (London: Routledge, 1994), pp. 3–5.

5 For further details, see Alison Murray, 'Film as national icon: Claude Berri's *Germinal*', *The French Review*, 76 (2003), 906–16.

6 The sphere of radio studies is in many ways one of absence and contrasts starkly with the sheer bulk of material available on Zola's print artefacts. Early BBC programmes were often live and went unrecorded. Subsequent programmes were not always archived and to date there is no publicly searchable or accessible catalogue of radio in Britain. David Wade writes: 'Most radio plays are broadcast once; some twice; a few, a very few, three times or more and after that, if not destroyed, the recordings end up in the limbo of the Tape Library.' David Wade, 'British Radio Drama since 1960', in John Drakakis (ed.), *British Radio Drama* (Cambridge: Cambridge University Press, 1981), pp. 218–44, p. 224. I am very grateful to the Radio Collector's Group for making a loan copy of both adaptations available to me and to Roger Bickerton for his help in ascertaining the extent of Zola's adaptation for this media in the UK. A catalogue of French radio adaptations is publicly searchable and accessible at *www.ina.fr*.

7 W. Ong, *Orality and Literacy* (London: Methuen, 1982), p. 32.

8 Mladen Dolar, *A Voice and Nothing More* (Cambridge, MA: MIT Press, 2006), p. 15.

9 Whitehead cited in Barnard, *Studying Radio*, p. 1.

10 For further details, see the obituary for David Hopkins that appeared in *The Guardian: www.guardian.co.uk/news/2004/jun/16/guardianobituaries.film*, accessed 19 November 2010.

11 While French radio adaptations of *Germinal* exist and are of interest, no chapter on the adaptation of literature for radio can really be written without reference to the BBC and the privileged status such adaptations have held within the corporation from its outset. Shakespeare's *Julius Caesar* was the first piece of literature to be broadcast in 1922 (see Rodger, *Radio Drama*, p. 3). As early as April 1925 the first novel, Charles Kingsley's *Westward Ho!*, was adapted for radio (see John Drakakis, 'Introduction' in Drakakis, *British Radio Drama*, p. 3).

Rodger explains the popularity of adaptation thus: 'It was . . . recognised at an early date that radio could be used to tell a story overtly. In the absence of a large number of scripts specifically written for radio, it was soon the practice in British radio to present adaptations of classic novels' (*Radio Drama*, p. 150). However, the BBC's commitment to adaptations exceeds mere expediency – in its quest to become a national, indeed international, theatre of the air, the corporation has long been arguably the most prolific source of adaptations of both British and international texts.

12 Emile Zola, *Nouveaux Contes à Ninon* in *Œuvres complètes*, ed. Henri Mitterand, 15 vols (Paris: Cercle du Livre Précieux, 1966–9), ix, p. 351.

13 Emile Zola, *Germinal*, in *Les Rougon-Macquart: histoire naturelle et sociale d'une famille sous le Second Empire*, ed. Henri Mitterand, 5 vols (Paris: Gallimard, Bibliothèque de la Pléiade, 1960–7), iii, p. 1192. All subsequent references to the novel will be to this edition and will be made parenthetically in the text.

14 Val Gielgud, *British Radio Drama: 1922–1956* (London: Harrap, 1957), p. 86.

15 Hughes claimed: 'There had never been before anything which people had had to take in by their ears only – anything dramatic, I mean – so it occurred to me that obviously the best thing was to choose a theme which would happen entirely in the dark.' Hughes cited in Drakakis, 'Introduction', in Drakakis, *British Radio Drama*, p. 20.

16 Gielgud, *British Radio Drama*, p. 23.

17 Gray cited in Drakakis, *British Radio Drama*, p. 142.

18 F. Gray, 'The nature of radio drama', in P. Lewis (ed.), *Radio Drama* (London: Longman, 1981), p. 51.

19 Ronald Hayman cited in Crisell, *Understanding Radio*, p. 156.

20 Guthrie cited in Frances Gray, 'Giles Cooper: the medium as moralist', in Drakakis, *British Radio Drama*, p. 141.

21 Emile Zola, *Thérèse Raquin* in *Œuvres complètes*, ed. Henri Mitterand, i, p. 520.

22 Henri Mitterand, 'Ideology and myth: *Germinal* and the fantasies of revolt', in David Baguley (ed.), *Critical Essays on Emile Zola* (Boston: G. K. Hall, 1986), pp. 124–30 (p. 126).

23 ETIENNE: (WRITING) My Dear Friend Pluchart, I am so pleased to hear that recruitment is going well for the International back at Lille. 'Workers of the World Unite' indeed! Here, at Montsou, conditions are poor and likely to get worse.
FX: BRING UP SOUNDS OF MINE – CHIPPING, ETC. MEN CALLING TO ONE ANOTHER, OFF MIC
I myself am getting stronger daily, as I become more used to the work. I seem to have acquired the skills of the job very quickly –
MAHEU: Good lad. Excellent. You've got that loading done in record time. Now do some timbering for us: props are there – tools – you've seen how Chaval and Zacharie do it –
ETIENNE: Then one of our four hewers left to go and work with another team –

MAHEU: You have proved to be such a good worker, and you learn so fast that I'd be very pleased if you would be Levaque's replacement.
ETIENNE: And so I have been given a promotion and am quite accepted as a real miner now.
BEAT
FADE MINE
NARRATOR: Time is passing so quickly: Spring has come and gone – April, May, June is here already –
FX: BRING UP OUTDOORS, BIRDSONG ETC.
NARRATOR: And the wheat is high and ripples in the breeze. The lovers have vacated the slag-heaps and migrated to the fields to lie together, basking in the warmth of the evening sun. Life is on the move, sprouting out of the same earth that weighs them down with fatigue and suffering when they toil beneath it . . .
ETIENNE: (WRITING) Often, after work, when the weather is fine, I take a walk (STARTS TO TAIL OFF) But . . .
(SIGHS)
NARRATOR: But several times he has come across Chaval and Catherine – almost tripped over them. They have become an accepted couple now, and after lying together in the wheatfield, Chaval walks her back to her parents' door where he kisses her goodnight –
ETIENNE: In front of the whole village! The whole – (SIGHS)
(RESUMES LETTER) An interesting man who also lives here at the pub is a Russian. He works for the company as a mechanic. He's actually the son of a noble family, who studied medicine at university, then became a Socialist-Anarchist. He was forced to flee the country after an attempt on the life of the Tsar. That's how he has ended up here . . .

24 My italics.

25 'Mais, pendant qu'il les jetait sur Montsou, d'une voix enrouée, il entendait une autre voix en lui, une voix de raison qui s'étonnait, qui demandait pourquoi tout cela' (p. 1441).

26 I. Howe, 'Zola: the poetry of naturalism', in D. Baguley (ed.), *Critical Essays on Emile Zola* (Boston: G. K. Hall, 1986), pp. 111–24 (p. 114).

27 According to Robert Lethbridge, 'La fin du roman reprend en écho le grand discours d'Etienne'. Robert Lethbridge, 'Etienne Lantier "romancier": genèse et mise en abyme', *Cahiers naturalistes*, 59 (1985), 43–54.

28 McWhinnie cited in Rodger, *Radio Drama*, p. 111.

29 It would be wrong to suggest that Hopkins's narrator entirely replaces Zola's use of characters as a means to convey the action for the voice of Hopkins's narrator, in a manner reminiscent of *style indirect libre*, takes on in certain places the words and vocabulary of the characters, while still speaking in his own voice. The narrator states, slipping into Chaval's mocking attitude to his lover Catherine: 'what's that she asks. The chaffinch contest. She doesn't know about the highlight of the Montsou fair? Where's she been?' Similarly the narrator, when discussing Catherine's approach to men, arguably slips into her words and consciousness: 'The men will treat her hard, because life is hard.' The

same phenomenon, albeit in a more pronounced manner as a result of its pointed use of 'you', occurs in episode three. The male narrator states, 'once you belong to them, men change. That's the way of things. And never again bother their heads about your happiness.' When describing the meeting of the bourgeois as they plot cruelly to prolong the strike and the suffering of their men in order to crush all resistance, the narrator's words slip into the characters' own perception of themselves, although it is clearly one with which he does not agree. Such a slippage is indicated by the repetition of the word 'refined': 'This [the meeting] is in the refined, genteel atmosphere of La Piolaine and is between these two refined gentlemen M. Grégoire and Paul Négrel, two men who also have the interests of their men at heart.'

30 Moreover, Zola made clear his awareness of the silencing nature of *feuilleton* publication when he implored Céard not to read the novel in that form: 'Vous avez tort de lire ça [*Germinal*] dans le *Gil Blas,* car le feuilleton déforme tout.' Zola cited in Richard H. Zakarian, *Zola's 'Germinal': A Critical Study of its Primary Sources* (Geneva: Droz, 1972), p. 37.

31 Alain Pagès, 'La lysogenèse du texte romanesque', *Cahiers naturalistes,* 59 (1985), 127–34 (129).

32 Manfred Schmeling, 'Labyinthus subterraneus: *Germinal*', *Cahiers naturalistes,* 84 (2010), 255–88 (271).

33 '*Germinal* est donc le complément de *L'Assommoir,* les deux faces de l'ouvrier'. Colette Becker, *Emile Zola: 'Germinal'* (Paris: Presses Universitaires de France, 1984), p. 9.

34 Jean Bourgeois, 'De *Thérèse Raquin* à *Germinal*: une structure obsédante d'Emile Zola', *Cahiers naturalistes,* 74 (2000), 43–59.

35 Kaja Silverman, *The Acoustic Mirror* (Bloomington: Indiana University Press, 1988).

36 On this point, Roger Ripoll claims, 'Dans l'univers de *Germinal,* il n'existe aucun point de repère: labyrinthe souterrain ou plaine infinie, les décors en apparence opposés fonctionnent comme un même piège. Cette expérience d'un espace où l'on ne peut s'orienter est associée à celle d'un temps défini par la monotonie et la dégradation continue, qu'il est impossible de maîtriser.' Roger Ripoll, 'L'avenir dans *Germinal*: destruction et renaissance', *Cahiers naturalistes,* 50 (1976), 115–33 (122).

37 'Mythical literature depends upon, incites even, perpetual acts of reinterpretation in new contexts, a process that embodies the very idea of appropriation.' Julie Sanders, *Adaptation and Appropriation* (London and New York: Routledge, 2006), p. 63.

38 Ida Marie Frandon, *Autour de 'Germinal': la mine et les mineurs* (Geneva: Droz, 1955).

39 Louis-Laurent Simonin cited in ibid., p. 21.

40 Simonin cited in ibid., p. 24.

41 Simonin cited in ibid., p. 27.

42 Zakarian, *Zola's 'Germinal',* p. 186.

43 Zola cited in Elliott M. Grant, *Zola's 'Germinal': A Critical and Historical Study* (Leicester: Leicester University Press, 1970), p. 120.

44 For an overview of work on the potential identities behind Zola's characters, see Henri Marel, 'Etienne Lantier et les chefs syndicalistes', *Cahiers naturalistes*, 50 (1976), 26–39.
45 Zakarian, *Zola's 'Germinal'*, p. 51.
46 Ibid., p. 152.
47 Leroy-Beaulieu cited in ibid., pp. 153–4.
48 Peter Wilsher, Donald Macintyre and Michael Jones, *Strike: Thatcher, Scargill and the Miners* (London: André Deutsch, 1985), p. 196.
49 See David Baguley, '*Germinal*: the gathering storm', in B. Nelson (ed.), *The Cambridge Companion to Emile Zola* (Cambridge: Cambridge University Press, 2007), pp. 137–51 (p. 149).
50 Martin Adeney and John Lloyd, *The Miners' Strike 1984–5: Loss Without Limit* (London: Routledge, 1987), p. 10.
51 Shinwell cited in Wilsher et al., *Strike*, p. 2.
52 Adeney and Lloyd, *The Miners' Strike*, p. 1.
53 Wilsher et al., *Strike*, p. 257.
54 John Lloyd cited in ibid., p. 266.

Chapter Two
Diamond Thieves and Gold Diggers: Balzac, Silent Cinema and the Spoils of Adaptation

ANDREW WATTS

As Jacques Rivette's *Ne Touchez pas la hache* reaffirmed in 2007, cinematographers continue to profit from the textual riches of *La Comédie humaine*. However, while present-day filmmakers remain fascinated by Balzac, no period in the history of cinema has shown greater enthusiasm for his work than the silent era. Between 1906 and the onset of sound film in 1927, at least eighty-two silent adaptations of Balzac were either produced or planned.[1] These European and American films include adaptations of *La Peau de chagrin*, *Le Colonel Chabert*, *La Duchesse de Langeais* and *Le Père Goriot*. Silent filmmakers also reinterpreted many of Balzac's plays, early works and tales from his Rabelaisian series of *Contes drolatiques*. Scholarly interest in this extensive corpus of films is by no means new. Richard Abel has considered silent adaptations of Balzac in relation to early developments in camera technique.[2] Adopting a broader historical perspective, Anne-Marie Baron has explored the ways in which silent film throws into relief Balzac's use of close-up, flashback and *mise en scène*.[3] Nevertheless, some critics have looked disdainfully on silent cinema as an industry that ransacked earlier works of literature purely for commercial gain, and on early filmmakers themselves as thieves, plagiarists and profiteers who devalued the artistic currency of the authors they adapted. In the period before sound film, silent versions of Balzac were condemned in precisely these terms. When the Italian filmmaker Jacques de Baroncelli adapted *Le Père Goriot* in 1921, he provoked anger in France for basing his adaptation around the story of the eponymous father and reducing the characters of Vautrin and Rastignac to peripheral figures. Writing in *Cinémagazine*, the reviewer René Jeanne complained that 'Baroncelli a volontairement dépouillé son sujet de tout ce qu'il comportait encore d'extérieur et s'est surtout complu à présenter dans tous leurs détails la figure centrale de Goriot et sa passion paternelle'.[4]

The derisive rhetoric that characterises early critical responses to silent adaptations of Balzac nevertheless fails to consider the recurrence of plundering as an unavoidable reality of textual creation, or the central importance of theft as a theme in *La Comédie humaine.* Focusing on Jean Epstein's *L'Auberge rouge* (1923) and Rex Ingram's adaptation of *Eugénie Grandet, The Conquering Power* (1921), the present chapter seeks to move beyond such negative appraisals by exploring the acts of literal and figurative theft around which these films and their source texts revolve. More specifically, this discussion will mobilise *The Conquering Power* and *L'Auberge rouge* to shed new light on Balzac's representation of theft, and on the subtleties of the novelist's own position regarding artistic property. Stealing, financial plundering and the circulation of purloined goods abound in *L'Auberge rouge* and *Eugénie Grandet.* However, while these texts ultimately judge the act of theft negatively, they also reveal that Balzac himself rarely followed the moral path laid out in his plots. Despite campaigning for rights of intellectual property throughout his career, Balzac can be seen to have fuelled his own creativity by plundering other texts and artistic traditions. Indeed, his creative practices, like those of Epstein and Ingram, invite comparison with the theories of Michel de Certeau. Just as de Certeau sees any act of readership as one of poaching, as we use the textual property of others to nourish our imagination and intellect, Balzac, an avid reader, sustained his own fiction by poaching material from the literary landscape and sending it back into fictional circulation. By engaging, furthermore, with many of the sources Balzac adapts, *The Conquering Power* and *L'Auberge rouge* redeploy on the screen the novelist's conceptualisation of authorship. As Epstein and Ingram reflect on their own acts of theft and appropriation, so they, too, reveal themselves as participants in what Linda Hutcheon has termed 'Western culture's long and happy history of borrowing and stealing or, more accurately, sharing stories'.[5]

A brief review of the plots of *L'Auberge rouge* and *Eugénie Grandet* demonstrates the extent to which both narratives express anxiety over ownership and the legitimacy – or illegitimacy – of possession. Written in 1831, the short story *L'Auberge rouge* recounts the tale of a robbery committed in the depths of the Alsatian countryside. Two young army surgeons, Prosper Magnan and Frédéric Taillefer, stop to rest for the night at a roadside inn. With the establishment already full, the pair offer to share their room with a wealthy merchant, who unwisely makes known that he is carrying a hundred thousand francs in gold and diamonds. After wrestling with the temptation to steal this precious cargo, Magnan awakes the next morning to find Taillefer gone and their roommate's throat cut. Unable to account for the murder or the missing purse, Magnan goes before the firing squad while Taillefer, upon hearing the crime related at a Parisian dinner party years afterwards, suffers a nervous attack and later dies in apparent confirmation of his guilt. While *L'Auberge rouge* reflects on theft as a criminal act, *Eugénie Grandet* focuses on the legalised pillaging that followed the 1789 Revolution. In Balzac's 1833 novel the fictional winegrower Félix Grandet lays the foundations of his immense fortune by speculating on property confiscated from the Church. A man of energy and ambition, Grandet increases his wealth through a series of shrewd investments, ensuring that his money remains in constant circulation. Despite his business acumen, however, Grandet is also a miser whose avarice manifests itself in an all-consuming passion for gold. Every year he marks his daughter Eugénie's birthday by giving her a gold coin to add to her dowry. A crisis envelops this provincial household when Grandet's nephew Charles arrives unexpectedly from Paris. Eugénie soon develops a sentimental attachment to her cousin, and gives the penniless young dandy her collection of coins so that he might relaunch his career in the Indies. By the time Grandet discovers this act of love that he interprets as theft of his own property, he has already hastened Charles's departure, robbing Eugénie, in turn, of her chance of a loving marriage and eventual motherhood.

At the textual level, *L'Auberge rouge* and *Eugénie Grandet* reveal Balzac's own exploitation of an array of literary sources. In the 'Avant-propos' to *La Comédie humaine*, the novelist avoids describing himself as a thief, preferring instead to compare his creative praxis to that of a gem setter who searched for artistic jewels that could be polished and reset in his own fiction. His ambition, he explained, was not to better the achievements of his predecessors, but to enrich 'cette littérature qui, de siècle en siècle, incruste d'immortels diamants la couronne poétique'.[6] As Balzac shaped *La Comédie humaine*, he appropriated themes and techniques from writers he admired, among them Rabelais, Sterne and Walter Scott, and from genres as diverse as epic poetry and theatrical melodrama. *L'Auberge rouge* and *Eugénie Grandet* illustrate the enthusiasm with which he reinvested this artistic currency in his own realist enterprise. In both texts he adapts stories from the Bible, as well as exploiting conventions popularised by the Gothic novels of Ann Radcliffe and Charles Maturin. *L'Auberge rouge*, furthermore, reworks not only the suspense and sudden incident that was characteristic of nineteenth-century melodrama, but adapts one of the best-known plays of the period, *L'Auberge des Adrets*, which introduced audiences to the thief and murderer Robert Macaire. As *L'Auberge rouge* and *Eugénie Grandet* place stealing and financial plundering at the heart of their thematic concerns, so they expose Balzac's delight in appropriating these sources and reinventing the textual property of others.

In deciding to bring *L'Auberge rouge* to the screen in 1923, Epstein was less ambitious for monetary rewards than to develop his own cinematic artistry. At the outset, the Polish-born filmmaker was drawn to the wide-ranging appeal of Balzac's story. As Marcel Lapierre explained in reference to Epstein's choice of text, 'le sujet intéressait n'importe quel public', and so corresponded to the director's vision of cinema as an art form that should be shared with the largest possible audience.[7] Epstein identified *L'Auberge rouge*, moreover, as a work that could be used to showcase the technical possibilities of his medium. Making only minor changes to Balzac's plot, he focused instead on appropriating key episodes from the text and translating them into visual effects capable of provoking a mixture of admiration and bewilderment in spectators. The opening sequence of the film, in which he uses a smooth, circular tracking shot to introduce each of the fictional dinner guests, exemplifies this adaptive method. As the camera moves around the table, a series of inter-titles names the participants in the drama before surveying the scene from above. 'L'effet à l'écran', summarised one critic, 'est des plus curieux'.[8] In what was his first attempt at adapting a literary text, Epstein viewed *L'Auberge rouge* as an opportunity not merely to make money, but to introduce spectators to new filmmaking techniques.

While Epstein sought to profit creatively from *L'Auberge rouge*, the impetus behind Rex Ingram's adaptation of *Eugénie Grandet* was more obviously commercial. The script for *The Conquering Power* was the work of the experienced screenwriter June Mathis. In 1921, Mathis had helped to catapult Ingram into an elite group of Hollywood directors when the two worked together on *The Four Horsemen of the Apocalypse*, the first silent film to gross more than a million dollars at the North American box office. *The Conquering Power* aimed to recreate the commercial success of this earlier production by reuniting its co-stars, Rudolph Valentino and Alice Terry. Moreover, the film updated the historical context of Balzac's novel in an attempt to render the story more accessible to a twentieth-century American audience. 'Commercialism tells us that you, Great Public,' read the opening titles of the film, 'do not like the costume play. Life is life, so we make our story of today.' Mathis's desire for financial profit did not, however, invalidate the artistic ambitions that underpinned the film. For Ingram, *The Conquering Power* represented an opportunity to break with the epic drama and spectacle for which *The Four Horsemen* had made him well known. As Liam O'Leary observes, *Eugénie Grandet* appealed to Ingram as a 'small-scale story of intimate passions' that enabled him to experiment with subtle lighting effects and sparse interior sets consonant with the dark, stultifying atmosphere of the Grandet household.[9] Upon the film's release in July 1921, critics praised the director for the range and quality of his cinematography. According to one review in *The New York Times*: 'Mr. Ingram tones his scenes so that they are soft, and yet distinct. There is no difficulty in watching faces, the slightest changes of expression are immediately visible, and there are contrasts in the different scenes, but never hard outlines and conflicting elements.'[10] Two years before Epstein identified Balzac as a suitable platform on which to test his credentials as a filmmaker, Ingram used *Eugénie Grandet* to extend both his own artistic range and that of the medium itself.

It would be difficult to discuss the various acts of theft at work in these texts and their subsequent adaptations, however, without first considering why *La Comédie humaine* enjoyed such popularity among silent filmmakers. If Epstein and Ingram used Balzac to demonstrate their creative talents and the artistic potential of their medium, it is clear, too, that both directors viewed *La Comédie humaine* as a bankable commodity that would attract audiences.

Other filmmakers during the silent era were quick to identify what they saw as the proto-cinematic quality of Balzac's writing. When Max de Rieux adapted *La Cousine Bette* in 1928, he described Balzac's work as tailor-made for the screen. De Rieux claimed that with its variety of narrative situations and intensely visual sensibility, *La Comédie humaine* appealed to filmmakers as 'un long scénario plein de richesses'.[11] However, there is more to the fascination that Balzac exerted on silent cinema than the nascent industry's desire for monetary revenue, artistic inspiration, or even cultural respectability. *The Conquering Power* and *L'Auberge rouge* expose deeper aesthetic connections between Balzac and silent film that reveal his work as having been particularly well suited to the new medium and the challenges it presented.

One of the most compelling reasons for which silent film provides a natural home for Balzac's work is the way in which early cinema reflects his ambition to document society. When the Lumière brothers invented the cinematograph in 1895, their own aim had been to use the new technology to chronicle contemporary life. 'Auguste and Louis', writes Brian Robb, 'had come to film through the documentary medium of photography [and] saw film as a way to reproduce reality.'[12] Their films were *actualités* that showed everyday events such as a steam train arriving at a station and Auguste Lumière enjoying breakfast with his family. The Lumières's approach to filmmaking resonates with Balzac's earlier description of himself as the 'secretary' of French society, a dispassionate observer who recorded the minutiae of nineteenth-century life for the benefit of future generations. The 1833 preface to *Eugénie Grandet* reflects the socio-historical ambitions that Balzac claimed were integral to his literary enterprise, as he presents his story as nothing more than 'le récit pur et simple de ce qui se voit tous les jours en province' (iii, p. 1026). The extent to which Balzac drew on the narrative material provided by everyday reality is a long-standing source of critical debate. As early as 1858, for example, his sister Laure Surville claimed that *L'Auberge rouge* sprang from a true story. 'Le sujet de *l'Auberge rouge*', she wrote, 'lui fut donné par un ancien chirurgien des armées, ami de l'homme qui fut condamné injustement. Mon frère n'ajouta que le dénoûment [*sic*].'[13] While Balzac presented himself as a historian rather than a novelist, he did not restrict himself to producing a photographic copy of the world around him. In contrast to the Lumières, whose films strove for objectivity, Balzac used fiction to articulate his own perspective on nineteenth-century France. According to Albert Béguin, 'sa vue devient vision, le décor du monde s'approfondit de perspectives fantastiques au moment où il écrit'.[14] Balzac's vision of French society stems from his pessimism that the Revolution has severely damaged the institutions of religion and the family. The great aristocratic estates having been broken up, France has become locked in an evolutionary race for survival in which individuals pursue wealth and social position by whatever means they can. Thus, Prosper Magnan is prepared to resort to theft in order to satisfy his dreams of owning land, while Charles Grandet uses the gold he has brought back from the Indies to secure his marriage to a woman who can furnish him with a noble title.

As Balzac sought to capture nineteenth-century society in his fiction, so Epstein and Ingram were equally concerned that their films should present spectators with an authentic vision of reality. Despite Mathis's decision to update *Eugénie Grandet*, principally by dressing the actors in modern costume, Ingram worked to retain some of the authenticity of his source text and its geographical setting. During production, he required the actors to speak only in French. Valentino, meanwhile, read Balzac's novel and before shooting practised for days with a monocle that he felt suited the dandified appearance of Charles.[15] In *L'Auberge rouge*, Epstein went further still in his pursuit of authenticity. Whereas earlier Balzac adaptations had commonly used theatrical backcloths to represent exterior settings, Epstein obtained permission to shoot Magnan's execution at La Caponnière military base at the Château de Vincennes. The choice of location added another layer of authenticity to the production, since it was here in 1917 that the dancer Mata Hari had gone before the firing squad convicted of espionage, a crime of which she, echoing the fate of the fictional Magnan, may have been innocent. Six years before portraying Magnan in *L'Auberge rouge*, Léon Mathot had been present at the execution of the infamous dancer, a fact which, according to one reviewer, reinforced the credibility of the actor's performance: 'On l'adossa à un poteau tout neuf (qui doit servir pour la prochaine exécution) et le peloton le fusilla. Jean Epstein était enchanté de son interprète, qui n'avait jamais si bien joué.'[16]

Like Balzac, however, Epstein used his medium not to imitate, but to present his own perspective on reality. As a cinematographer, he explored the ways in which film could express psychological states. In particular, he insisted that the actors in *L'Auberge rouge* should remain slow and deliberate in their movements in order to build suspense, and to convey 'un rythme psychologique convenable au roman de Balzac'.[17] The film also reflects the influence of Epstein's concept of *photogénie*, which the director defined as 'tout aspect des choses, des êtres et des âmes qui accroît sa qualité morale par la reproduction cinématographique'. According to Epstein, the medium of cinema invested objects and people with a sublime quality that transcended the boundaries of everyday reality. As he explains in his essay 'De quelques conditions de la photogénie', 'un gros plan de revolver, ce n'est plus un revolver, c'est le personnage-revolver, c'est-à-dire le désir ou le remords du crime, de la faillite, du suicide'.[18] The close-ups of Taillefer's face in *L'Auberge rouge* reflect this hyper-reality that for Epstein is the essence of *photogénie*. The old man's wrinkled appearance metaphorises the suffering he has endured since the night of the robbery, and in so doing identifies him to the audience as the likely perpetrator.

While Epstein and Ingram plundered reality as Balzac had done before them, silent filmmakers also recognised the need to entertain spectators with thrilling plots and emotive stories. At a time when cinema had still to develop its own stock of narrative material, early cinematographers turned readily to the theatre for artistic inspiration. The result, claims Anne Hollander, was that 'many early movies were stagey . . . In those early days, movement was the point, not camera imagery'.[19] In Alice Guy's 1906 adaptation of Balzac's play *La Marâtre*, the actors face the camera as if performing to a theatre audience, and then stop at the end of scenes, apparently uncertain of whether to leave the set as they might the stage. The reliance on theatre that Hollander implies was a shortcoming in early cinema must nevertheless be considered in light of the innovative ways in which the medium appropriated themes and techniques from its dramatic heritage. Silent filmmakers exploited the resources of vaudeville and, in the notable case of Georges Méliès, theatrical magic, to create ever more elaborate visual effects.[20] At the heart of their determination to thrill and stir the emotions of spectators, however, was melodrama. In both nineteenth-century theatre and its subsequent incarnations in cinema, melodrama employed sudden plot twists, acute suspense and tales of good versus evil to generate a 'nervous charge' in the audience.[21] The genre also favoured highly sentimental narratives and tales in which romance blossoms in the face of adversity.

Viewed through this lens, early cinema proves especially valuable to our understanding of Balzac, since melodrama was itself a central component of the novelist's aesthetic. As Peter Brooks and Christopher Prendergast have shown, Balzac eschewed the banality of popular fiction and melodrama while simultaneously appropriating themes and narrative conventions from them.[22] The texts studied in this chapter reflect his use of the melodramatic to excite readers 'whose taste', writes Brooks, 'had been formed by the theatre'.[23] *L'Auberge rouge* begins in an atmosphere of familial intimacy that was a stock feature of the genre, before one of the fictional dinner guests asks to hear 'une histoire allemande qui nous fasse bien peur' (xi, p. 90). A moment of pure melodrama also triggers the action in *Eugénie Grandet.* The unexpected arrival of Charles on a dark winter's night startles the members of the Grandet household, interrupting their card game and creating suspense both for them and the reader: 'Au moment où Mme Grandet gagnait un lot de seize sous . . . un coup de marteau retentit à la porte de la maison, et y fit un si grand tapage que les femmes sautèrent sur leurs chaises' (iii, p. 1053). Although Balzac subverts the melodramatic expectation of a happy ending for Charles and Eugénie, the theatrical qualities of *Eugénie Grandet* ensured that a stage version appeared in Paris within a year of the novel's publication, enjoying a run of more than three hundred performances.[24]

Epstein and Ingram continue Balzac's enthusiasm for exploiting a range of theatrical techniques. The opening sequence of *The Conquering Power* gestures explicitly towards the theatrical origins of early cinema as Ingram shows Charles celebrating his twenty-seventh birthday. The audience first glimpses the lavish party in a long shot bordered by the folds of an Arabian tent that resemble heavy theatrical drapes. In an allusion to the performance acts typical of vaudeville, a dancer sways provocatively on a small platform held aloft by a group of servants. As Ingram situates his film within a stage framework, he, like Balzac, adapts themes and narrative devices gleaned from melodrama. A range of melodramatic conventions can be observed in *The Conquering Power.* A defining feature of the genre, both on stage and in early cinema, was its tendency to classify characters as either morally good or evil. Ingram fits Grandet within this dichotomy by emphasising the cruelty that goes hand in hand with the old man's greed. In the first scene in which Grandet appears, one of his tenant farmers asks for more time to pay his rent. An inter-title voices his landlord's terse reply: 'I cannot wait – and it will do you no good to appeal to my wife. She knows better than to interfere with my business.' *The Conquering Power* reflects, moreover, the melodramatic topos of frustrated romance as Grandet, played by the seasoned character actor Ralph Lewis, asserts his determination to keep Charles and Eugénie apart. On the night that Eugénie gives away her gold, Ingram shows her father stalking the house with a shotgun, a weapon that reflects his status as a dangerous obstacle to the couple's affection for each other. In no less theatrical a manner, *L'Auberge rouge* bears witness to the influence of the melodramatic mode through the strategies that Epstein uses to excite his spectators. As the story of the murder begins to unfold, the director jolts us out of the genteel opulence of the Parisian dinner party, cutting away swiftly to a shot of horses pounding towards the camera as Magnan and Taillefer race to reach their destination. In addition to exploiting the sensationalism inherent in melodrama, Epstein's screenplay heightens the pathos of Balzac's story by incorporating the subplot of a doomed romance between Magnan and the fictional innkeeper's daughter. Ben Singer defines another common feature of the genre as a powerful sensation of pity 'triggered by the perception of moral injustice against an undeserving victim'.[25] In keeping with the aesthetic requirements of melodrama, Epstein invites his audience to feel pity not only for Magnan, but for the innkeeper's daughter, who through no fault of her own loses her beloved and is left to tend his grave.

If Balzac's enthusiasm for melodrama ensured that *L'Auberge rouge* and *Eugénie Grandet* would be well suited to adaptation for the silent screen, the novelist's use of silence provides further evidence of the strong aesthetic connections between his work and early cinema. At repeated intervals in the mass of words, allusions, digressions and passages of description that make up *La Comédie humaine*, Balzac's texts fall silent. In *Eugénie Grandet*, the novelist evokes the stillness of Saumur, establishing a contrast between the small-town setting and the domestic drama that ensues. 'La vie et le mouvement y sont si tranquilles', the narrator informs us of the town's streets, 'qu'un étranger les croirait inhabitées' (iii, p. 1027). Similarly, in *L'Auberge rouge*, Balzac's allusions to silence reinforce the dramatic tension of the scene in which Magnan contemplates murder. Knowing that the slightest sound could awaken his roommates and with them the rest of the inn, Magnan prepares his escape with slow and deliberate care:

> Prosper se leva lentement et sans faire aucun bruit. Certain de n'avoir réveillé personne, il s'habilla, se rendit dans la salle commune; puis . . . il dévissa les barres de fer, les sortit de leurs trous sans faire le plus léger bruit, les plaça près du mur, et ouvrit les volets en pesant sur les gonds afin d'en assourdir les grincements (xi, p. 102).

In tandem with the literal silences that recur in these texts, both *L'Auberge rouge* and *Eugénie Grandet* contain instances of metaphorical silence. The murder of Walhenfer, in particular, is a crime shrouded in silence. There are no witnesses to this cold-blooded act, a lacuna maintained by the text itself, which neglects to show the moment at which the killer strikes. These omissions transform *L'Auberge rouge* into a detective fiction that ends in another textual silence as Balzac, frustrating our desire for an unambiguous solution to the mystery, refuses to confirm the identity of the murderer. As Aline Mura-Brunel has argued, *L'Auberge rouge* further reflects the ways in which Balzac uses silence to invest his fiction with a powerful sense of immediacy. By silencing his own omniscient voice, the novelist exposes his reader to two narrators who are implicated directly in the tale: an anonymous frame narrator, who attends the dinner party, and Hermann, the businessman who befriended Magnan in prison and who recounts his story to the assembled guests. According to Mura-Brunel, the suppression of a third-person voice fits the requirements of a narrative that depends on an interplay of perspectives and possible interpretations of the crime. 'Chez Balzac en l'occurrence,' she writes, 'le silence est avant tout régi par les exigences de la narration.'[26] In *L'Auberge rouge*, narrative silence invites the reader to enter into a direct relationship with the fictional protagonists, and in so doing to question the reliability of the evidence that would otherwise seem to point to Taillefer's guilt.

As silence sometimes threatens to envelop the Balzacian text, early cinema teaches us to be attentive to those actions that unfold in the very midst of silence. Although pre-dialogue films were usually screened to music, cinematographers relied heavily on visual communication to express what spoken language would otherwise convey. 'As he [the actor] cannot speak,' explains Aaron

Sultanik, 'he must channel the techniques of mime acting.'[27] A medium that operates in and through the absence of dialogue, silent film gives voice to Balzac's own conviction that movement and gesture are loaded with meaning. The novelist claimed in *Théorie de la démarche* that both of these features of human behaviour 'sont d'une effrayante signification . . . Un simple geste, un involontaire frémissement de lèvres peut devenir le terrible dénouement d'un drame caché longtemps entre deux cœurs' (xii, p. 280). Perhaps anticipating the role of the audience in silent cinema, Balzac eagerly interprets those movements that produce no sound. In *Eugénie Grandet*, the narrator tells us that even a twitch of Grandet's muscles is enough to send shockwaves through the district of Anjou: 'ses gestes, le clignement de ses yeux faisaient loi dans le pays . . . "L'hiver sera rude, disait-on, le père Grandet a mis ses gants fourrés"' (iii, p. 1034). By extension, in *L'Auberge rouge*, Taillefer's gestures of covering his eyes with his hand and reaching desperately for the carafe – gestures replicated by the actor David Evremond in Epstein's film – seem to offer irrefutable evidence that he committed the murder. As Dorothy Kelly argues, however, the presumption of Taillefer's guilt is based not only on his outer movements, which may or may not confirm an inner reality, but on the interpretations of the frame narrator, who hears and then writes up the story 'à [s]a guise' (xi, p. 92).[28] Silence in *La Comédie humaine* does not always speak volumes, therefore, but instead foreshadows the challenge that early cinema audiences would face in attempting to construct meaning from the evidence of gestures and movements performed on screen.

Balzac's use of silence to trigger a range of emotional and intellectual responses in the reader provided early cinematographers with a template for overcoming the constraints of unvoiced narration. Coupled, moreover, with the novelist's exploitation of reality and melodrama, these silences rendered his work particularly well suited to the screen. The ways in which silent filmmakers plundered Balzac's fiction in order to create new artistic products nevertheless warrants further analysis. That silent filmmakers have been accused repeatedly of stealing from, and undermining, the artistic value of *La Comédie humaine* is neither surprising nor entirely without justification. As an industry, silent cinema was riddled with acts of plagiarism and the outright theft of intellectual property. A lack of rigorous copyright law meant that filmmakers not only stole material from literary sources, but often simply remade each other's films without fear of being pursued through the courts. As William K. Everson writes in reference to early American cinema:

> The infringements of copyright in this period were many, but basically the industry was still too small for the losses or profits involved to be worthy of lawsuits. The greatest losers were the writers, whose work was pillaged, 'borrowed', altered, or literally stolen, with no payment to them.[29]

The factor that appraisals of early Balzac films have neglected to consider, however, is that the novelist himself engages with theft as both a theme and a creative impulse in his own fiction.

Stealing takes multiple forms in *L'Auberge rouge*. The fictional Prosper Magnan, whose name ironically evokes the adjective 'prosperous', contemplates theft as a means of fulfilling his ambitions. As the young doctor settles down to sleep after dining at the inn, images of the gold tucked beneath his roommate's pillow begin to pervade his mind: 'il s'arrangeait avec cette somme toute une vie de délices, et se voyait heureux, père de famille, riche, considéré dans sa province, et peut-être maire de Beauvais' (xi, p. 102). In addition to the theft that Magnan is tempted to carry out, the text also alludes, however, to other acts of real and figurative theft. In interpreting Taillefer's actions at the dinner table as a sign of guilt, the frame narrator believes that he has been robbed of the chance of marrying the old man's daughter with a clear conscience: 'Ce dîner, cette soirée, exercèrent une cruelle influence sur ma vie et sur mes sentiments. J'aimai Mlle Taillefer, précisément peut-être parce que l'honneur et la délicatesse m'interdisaient de m'allier à un assassin' (xi, p. 118). Moreover, the text recalls the stealing that was endemic during the Revolution, when many aristocrats were dispossessed of their property and murdered. As Laura Poulosky has argued, the clinical murder in *L'Auberge rouge*, in which the head of the victim falls onto the floor while his torso remains in the bed, resembles an execution by guillotine.[30] Through the position of the dead man's body, the royalist Balzac evokes the memory of the Terror, and invites his reader to view theft not merely as an isolated and opportunistic act, but as one that is socially destructive and harmful to the country as a whole.

If stealing manifests itself in a variety of forms in *L'Auberge rouge*, then Epstein's version of the story reveals the artistic profit that he gains from Balzac's text. In his film, the director proves adept at appropriating fragments of the source narrative and reorienting them towards a new aesthetic purpose. His approach is illustrated by the scenes in which Magnan struggles against the temptation to steal from his roommate. In Balzac's text, the fictional doctors arrive at the inn under a cloudless sky. By nightfall, however, a storm begins to rage inside Magnan's head: 'Tout en rêvant la mort du négociant, il voyait distinctement l'or et les diamants. Il en avait les yeux éblouis. Son cœur palpitait' (xi, p. 102). Alighting on this image of a mental thunderstorm, Epstein resolved to create an actual storm for the night of the murder. In June 1923, Jean Eyre, a reviewer for *Mon Ciné*, described visiting the studio to watch the director shoot the film's visual centrepiece. As Eyre observed a team of firemen soaking Mathot and Evremond, he reported that 'une énorme hélice d'avion chassait la pluie factice en rafales et agitait les feuilles des arbres d'un vent de tempête. C'était très . . . américain.'[31] Signalling his intention to rival the kind of lavish special effects favoured by early American filmmakers, Epstein claimed to have spent 500,000 francs on this scene alone.

While giving physical form to the mental storm that Magnan experiences in the source narrative, Epstein uses this act of textual plundering, however, as a basis for applying aspects of his own cinematic theory. Announced by the inter-title 'Tentation', this section of the film shows rain lashing the outside of the inn and waking Magnan. The storm conveys visually the shifts in the protagonist's mental state as he oscillates between the idea of committing the crime and disgust at his own thoughts. As the camera switches between the storm outside and close-ups of Magnan's tormented face, Epstein cuts in a dream image of diamonds that multiply like drops of rain. Just as the would-be assailant draws his scalpel, a bolt of lightning brings him to his senses, and he backs out of the room. A series of quick fades slash across the screen, accentuating both his murderous desires and the nightmarish nature of the experience.[32] As Richard Abel has noted, this thunderstorm contains one of the earliest examples of Epstein's use of camera and editing to merge objective and subjective viewpoints. At first, the storm seems to awaken Magnan to the possibility of committing the crime, only for the lightning to deter him from his plan as the memory of his mother flashes into his mind. Even as Magnan rushes outside in horror at himself, the rain appears to function as a cleansing water of repentance while metaphorising the character's fate as a victim of forces outside of his control.[33] The factor that Abel omits from his commentary, however, is that Epstein continues Balzac's strategy of enriching and reorienting his own source material. In the text, as in the film, we never witness the moment at which the blade falls. By focusing instead on Magnan's torment and the bloody scene the next morning, Balzac exploits a romantic obsession with the macabre while simultaneously distancing himself from it. Appealing to the reader's memory of novels such as Janin's *L'Ane mort ou la femme guillotinée*, which overflowed with murders, executions and other grisly deaths, Balzac's omission reminds us that the interest of his own text lies in its philosophical reflection on the nature of crime and guilt. By the same token, Epstein asserts his originality by plundering the image of the thunderstorm and using it to advance his conception of cinema as an amalgam of shifting and unstable perspectives. In so doing, he demonstrates that adaptation does not amount merely to theft or plagiarism, but, in the words of Linda Hutcheon, 'is an act of appropriating or salvaging [that] is always a double process of interpreting and then creating something new'.[34]

As Epstein sought to extract material of artistic value from *L'Auberge rouge*, so Balzac's characters strive to enrich themselves by plundering and hoarding gold. In keeping with Christopher Prendergast's characterisation of gold as an 'object of cupidity' in *La Comédie humaine*, this precious currency tempts Prosper Magnan like no other.[35] The lure of gold is so strong that, bidding Walhenfer goodnight, the young doctor appears to forget that his roommate is also carrying diamonds. 'Nous dormirons tous deux sur notre fortune,' he tells him, 'vous, sur votre or; moi, sur ma trousse!' (xi, p. 101). Magnan is subsequently condemned by the suspicion that he has buried Walhenfer's gold in the countryside, a metaphorical reflection of the way in which this currency enriches a fictional landscape that silent cinema would later excavate. As gold fades from the plot of *L'Auberge rouge*, the currency retains a more visible presence, however, in *Eugénie Grandet*. A thirst for gold drives the career of the fictional Grandet, who, in the wake of the Revolution, uses his wife's dowry to purchase an abbey and 'les plus beaux vignobles de l'arrondissement' (iii, p. 1030). Under the Consulate, he levers himself into the position of town mayor, and quietly abuses his authority to build roads leading to and from his farms. With the return of the Bourbons in 1815, he turns to finance, investing in new government bonds and purchasing a château and its parkland.[36] Grandet is a silent predator who believes that the tides of history will simply deliver gold to him: 'Financièrement parlant, M. Grandet tenait du tigre et du boa: il savait se coucher, se blottir, envisager longtemps sa proie, sauter dessus; puis il ouvrait la gueule de sa bourse, y engloutissait une charge d'écus, et se couchait tranquillement' (iii, p. 1033).

While Grandet's talent for speculation earns him a vast fortune, the character is also a miser whose passion for gold dominates every aspect of his existence. In physical appearance, he seems to personify both the colour and coldness of the metal: 'ses cheveux jaunâtres et grisonnants étaient blanc et or' (iii, p. 1036). Moreover, he delights in being able to gaze upon his coins, and treats them with the kind of paternal affection that he fails to show Eugénie. At night, he retreats to his strongroom while the rest of the household sleeps in order to 'choyer, caresser, couver, cuver, cercler son or' (iii, p. 1070). When he can no longer climb the stairs, he asks his daughter to lay coins on the table so that he can derive physical satisfaction from being in their presence: 'il demeurait des heures entières les yeux attachés sur les louis . . . "Ça me réchauffe!" disait-il quelquefois' (iii, p. 1175). In conceiving of gold as a living entity, Grandet invests the yellow metal with healing properties. As his wife nears death, his first thought is to spread gold over the bed covers. To have no gold is for the miser akin to death itself. Thus, after Eugénie gives her collection of gold coins to Charles, her father reacts as if he has been robbed: 'Comment! ici, dans ma propre maison, chez moi, quelqu'un aura pris ton or!' (iii, p. 1155). The enraged cry that follows Grandet's initial bewilderment reflects his conception of gold as the source of his own vital energy, the loss of which he avenges by imprisoning Eugénie in her room and subjecting her to a social death.

The plundering of gold that functions as a key theme in *Eugénie Grandet* also lies at the heart of Rex Ingram's concerns in *The Conquering Power*. In a further reflection of Mathis's desire to modernise the source text, the film suppresses the historical circumstances behind Grandet's rise, focusing instead on the character's greed and the moral lesson that, in further deference to melodramatic convention, Ingram seeks to draw from it. Ingram's Grandet retains the gold-lust of his literary predecessor. He invests his currency with Eugénie only to demand it back, and admires her beauty merely because she has 'hair to match the precious metal'.

While recognising Grandet's avarice, Ingram dwells for longer, however, on the character's dishonesty. As in the source text, Grandet has Charles renounce any claims over his father's estate without telling him of his plans to avert the bankruptcy. Moreover, in a sensational twist that has no direct equivalent in the novel, the old man keeps from Eugénie the secret that he is not her biological father and, therefore, has no rights over his late wife's fortune. By portraying Grandet as a thief in both the legal and moral sense of the term, Ingram prepares for the comeuppance that is due to the villain in melodrama by having Grandet's tenant farmer warn the miser that he will be crushed by his gold. The film's climactic scene repeats this warning as the spirits of Eugénie's mother and Charles's father materialise in Grandet's strongroom to accuse him of stealing from their offspring. As the old man attempts to escape, hammering at the door and smashing a window to no avail, a monstrous personification of gold warns, before the walls of the strongroom close in and Grandet is buried beneath his fortune, 'I am gold. All your life you have sought me – now you are mine!'.

Through this hallucinatory sequence, Ingram appears to give cinematic form to his own anxiety that the artistic treasure he has coveted will turn against him. In a film driven by commercial imperatives, the gold might be seen to articulate the director's unspoken fear that Balzac, like the gold that breathes and then bursts into life, will punish him with critical and commercial failure, and the death of his own career. Any such fears would be realised in part by the mixed critical reception of *The Conquering Power* upon its release in the United States, where *The New York Times* praised the director's use of lighting and close-ups but lamented that the film retained 'much of the nature of a novel. Despite its many expressive scenes, a good part of its actual story is told in words. Without its subtitles it would be incomprehensible.'[37] If the anxiety of influence weighs heavily over this scene, Ingram nevertheless makes a more positive statement of his own filmmaking credentials and the growing artistic confidence of his medium. The element that is particularly significant in this sequence is the rocking cradle in which Grandet keeps his fortune. The cradle, together with the shaft of light that streams down through the window, link this scene to a shot from D. W. Griffith's 1916 film *Intolerance.* Ingram reuses this shot, but makes it his own by packing the cradle with gold. In so doing, he creates a metonym for greed and the avarice that has replaced

Grandet's love for his daughter. Moreover, he offers a mocking tribute to Griffith himself, for whom *Intolerance* not only proved a financial disaster but eventually bankrupted his Triangle Film Corporation.[38] The shot confirms that Ingram's ability to generate an artistic profit from Balzac's text was by no means impaired by his commercial ambitions. More importantly, it shows that early film-makers readily appropriated material from each other. As this scene demonstrates, Ingram not only recreated his artistic heritage like Balzac, but was capable of doing so without him.

While reshaping the artistic currency of *Eugénie Grandet* and *Intolerance*, Ingram also exploits the commercial potential of his star, Valentino. As Ginette Vincendeau has argued in her study of stardom in French cinema, actors are key to the critical and commercial success of a film. 'The star's persona', writes Vincendeau, 'is a commodity positioning the performer and his/her work in the market-place and attracting finance: the name in huge letters on the posters and the marquee. The importance of stars is economic, cultural and ideological.'[39] Hollywood was central to developing this model of stardom, and the growing star power of Valentino certainly dominated production of *The Conquering Power*. Following his success in *The Four Horsemen of the Apocalypse*, the Italian was increasingly aware of his own commercial value, and had reportedly become difficult to manage. As Emily Leider notes in her biography of Valentino, the atmosphere on the set of *The Conquering Power* was undermined early in the film's production by the actor's demands of a salary increase, which would have taken his earnings with Metro to $450 a week.[40] After Ingram refused, the pair argued constantly over the production, and in particular what clothes Valentino should wear on screen. Noel Botham elaborates: 'The film dragged on in an atmosphere of almost constant hostility, and Ingram, who was known to loathe stars who insisted on behaving like stars and not like actors, eventually found Valentino's daily temper tantrums too much and walked out.'[41]

Nevertheless, *The Conquering Power* plays self-consciously on Valentino's star persona, and in particular on his reputation as a man of fashion. The actor appears in a succession of different outfits in the film. In the opening scene, he dons an elegant tuxedo, and later arrives in the provinces in a travelling suit that prompted one contemporary critic to ask why the actor was dressed 'like a Broadway fashion plate'.[42] Valentino's array of costumes are in fact a perfect fit for the dandified attire of the fictional Charles Grandet, who takes notable care over his hair and clothing in Balzac's text: 'A Tours, un coiffeur venait de lui refriser ses beaux cheveux châtains; il y avait changé de linge, et mis une cravate de satin noir combinée avec un col rond de manière à encadrer agréablement sa blanche et rieuse figure' (iii, p. 1057). Similarly, Ingram presents Valentino as an object of beauty and fragility to be admired by female spectators. In the scene in which Eugénie creeps into Charles's bedroom and finds him asleep in the chair, Ingram's lighting emphasises the unblemished whiteness of the actor's skin as Eugénie watches her sleeping cousin and then wraps his embroidered dressing gown around him for warmth. Her actions metaphorise the desiring gaze of the female audience to which Valentino films sought typically to appeal. Miriam Hansen explains: 'As Hollywood manufactured the Valentino legend, promoting the fusion of real life and screen persona that makes a star, his female admirers became part of that legend . . . never again was spectatorship so explicitly linked to the discourse on female desire.'[43] During Charles's subsequent voyage to Martinique, the film casts Valentino as a heroic adventurer who writes to his beloved without compromising his masculinity as he throws an object to wake his sleeping servant. Exploiting the combination of effeminate beauty and brooding strength that defined Valentino's film persona, Ingram utilised his star as an asset with which to sell the film to the largest possible audience.

As *The Conquering Power* trades in the cinematic currency of Valentino, so Balzac's characters engage in their own acts of real and figurative commerce. Breaking with the tradition of hoarding gold with which Balzac associated the provinces, the fictional Grandet ensures that his coins circulate and yield a profit. 'Les écus', he claims, once again investing gold with anthropomorphic qualities, 'vivent et grouillent comme des hommes: ça va, ça vient, ça sue, ça produit' (iii, p. 1153). The extent to which Grandet remains alert to opportunities to swell his fortune is further illustrated by the trip that he makes to Angers. Having heard that gold is in short supply, he loads eighteen hundredweight of coins into wooden casks and transports them to the docks for sale. Emphasising the clandestine nature of this operation, Balzac has the old cooper avoid unwanted attention from his neighbours by undertaking the journey at night. In financial terms, Grandet's willingness to trade his coins proves a stunning success. He sells the contents of his barrels for a profit of 14,000 francs, eventually earning 600,000 francs in interest over the course of his lifetime.[44] This achievement mirrors, in a legitimate manner, that of Taillefer in *L'Auberge rouge*, who if he does indeed steal from Walhenfer, increases the original amount from 100,000 francs to 'un million en fonds de terre' (xi, p. 91) by trading military supplies across Europe. As Balzac makes clear, however, Grandet's actions also strengthen his attachment to the gold that he believes remains in his possession in the form of Eugénie's coins. The fire that his daughter thinks she sees under her door on the night he travels to Angers, which in fact is the light of a single candle, represents metaphorically both the increase in Grandet's fortune and the inferno of rage that will consume the household once he realises that the last of his gold has disappeared.

While Grandet and Taillefer delight in their commercial trading at the level of plot, silent cinema calls attention to the anxiety with which Balzac depicts the act of exchange. When the critic Montchanin interviewed a selection of filmmakers in 1923 to establish why more of them had not adapted Balzac, one anonymous director cited the difficulty of conveying the dense psychological realism of *La Comédie humaine*; 'Il y a là-dedans des choses qui sont au-dessus de moi,' he explained, 'j'ai peur de ne pas être à la hauteur des caractères'.[45] Balzac's own fiction anticipates this fear of communicative failure and frustrated exchange. When the eponymous heroine gives away her dowry in *Eugénie Grandet*, Charles in return gives her his gold-decorated travelling case. On the same night as Grandet trades his own gold for monetary gain, Eugénie exchanges hers for love: 'Depuis la scène de nuit pendant laquelle la cousine donna son trésor au cousin, son cœur avait suivi le trésor' (iii, p. 1135). The gold coins provide Charles with a basis to begin trading in the Indies. Grandet's nephew travels onwards from there to the coast of Africa, Portugal and the United States. However, as his financial wealth increases with each transaction, his youthful innocence and identity are gradually eroded: 'A force de rouler à travers les hommes et les pays, d'en observer les coutumes contraires, ses idées se modifièrent et il devint sceptique' (iii, p. 1181). Through repeated commerce, Charles forgets his former self, his cousin and the exchange that had once bonded them together. By exposing Balzac's suspicion of the damaging effects of monetary trade, *Eugénie Grandet* continues the patterns of destructive exchange that afflict the characters in *L'Auberge rouge*. With Walhenfer's fortune, Taillefer might have expected to purchase a lifetime of prosperity. If he trades his moral conscience for gold, however, the pain he endures afterwards leads the reader to question whether the crime was worth such torment. And the story highlights other instances of failed exchange. Magnan's mother dies, a victim of consumption, without ever receiving the letter in which her son had protested his innocence, but also, perhaps, without knowing of the small-town gossip that Magnan suggests would be enough to kill her. The story of the murder, exchanged over dinner for the purpose of entertainment, also fails to achieve its objective when one young woman becomes so upset that she begs to hear no more: 'Si j'apprenais aujourd'hui qu'il a été fusillé, je ne dormirais pas cette nuit' (xi, p. 112). The structure of the text itself further replicates the theme of frustrated and incomplete exchange, with Balzac interrupting his narrative in order to return to Taillefer's reactions at the dinner table, and the gestures that appear to communicate, but never confirm, his guilt.

Epstein's adaptation of *L'Auberge rouge* echoes the failed exchanges represented by Balzac's text. A prominent symbol of exchange in the film is that of the playing card. Following his arrival at the inn, Magnan warms himself by the fire, his back turned to the conversation between Taillefer and the Dutchman, in another example of blocked exchange. In this scene, which has no counterpart in the source text, an old woman approaches the table and persuades Magnan to have his fortune told. The transaction seems to point towards his future prosperity when the fortune teller identifies the first of the cards, the ace of diamonds, as signifying gold. The prediction of wealth is quickly undermined, however, by the next two cards: the seven of diamonds ('crime') and the ten of clubs ('death'). As Richard Abel observes, Epstein returns to the image of the cards throughout the film. When the Dutchman reveals to Magnan and Taillefer that he is carrying diamonds in his purse, the ace of diamonds dissolves over a close-up of a single large diamond. On the morning after the murder, the seven of clubs appears over a shot of Magnan's face, and as the judge passes the death sentence we see the ten of clubs. 'This pattern of rhetorical figuring', writes Abel, 'somewhat conventionally suggests a fatalistic force beyond the control of any character.'[46] However, Epstein's use of the playing cards also links this theme of predestination to failure and death. In the film's climactic episode, the banker's son André (here replacing Balzac's frame narrator) attempts to expose Taillefer as the murderer during a game of cards. Already troubled by having listened to Hermann's story, Taillefer reaches a peak of agitation when André deals him the very same sequence of cards as Magnan had drawn years before. Epstein invites his audience to recall the failed exchange of Magnan's earlier fortune-telling by dissolving an image of the dead man's face over the cards now held by Taillefer, followed by a shot of the fortune teller herself. Confronted by the memory of his supposed crime, Taillefer rises to his feet and then collapses to the floor. But, rather than confirm that the old man is dead, the scene maintains the structure of incomplete exchanges that underpins Balzac's narrative. Instead, Epstein cuts away to a shot of André and Victorine who, mirroring the perspective of the audience, reflect on the significance of Taillefer's fall while remaining uncertain of his eventual fate.

Blocked and incomplete exchanges also feature prominently in *The Conquering Power*. In Ingram's film, Grandet attempts to thwart the romance between Charles and Eugénie by withholding the letters that his nephew sends from Martinique. Moreover, the film underscores the recurrence of looks and glances that remain unreciprocated. As in the novel, Grandet watches Eugénie as she walks in the garden with Charles. The camera replicates the miser's position in the window and gestures towards the hidden voyeur in the audience as we glimpse this scene through the bushes. Windows assume particular importance in the film as lenses through which characters see without being seen in return. In contrast to Balzac's text, in which Eugénie and her mother sit at their parlour window watching the occasional stranger pass by, Ingram emphasises Eugénie's own status as an object of contemplation. In the closing scene of the film, we witness her again in the garden as Charles returns from Martinique to propose marriage. While it is a melodramatic ending that wholly inverts the conclusion of the source text, the sequence highlights the failure of the rival families who had competed for Eugénie's hand, who look on through the window and open door as Charles and Eugénie embrace. At its end, *The Conquering Power* unblocks the love that the couple had been determined to share with each other, and that Grandet, in his relentless avarice, had been no less determined to frustrate. That Ingram ends the sequence of failed and incomplete exchanges in his film is doubly significant. By reuniting Charles and Eugénie, he does not, as Emily Leider claims, turn 'literary gold into Hollywood corn'.[47] Instead, he asserts on screen his capacity for appropriating Balzac's fiction and creating a new artistic product from the source text. Moreover, his choice of ending returns us to Balzac's own conceptualisation of authorship, and to the literary currency that the novelist does not simply plunder, but sends back into fictional circulation.

References to other authors and texts circulate widely in *L'Auberge rouge* and *Eugénie Grandet*. Foremost among these sources is the Bible. As Anne-Marie Baron has shown, Balzac knew and studied the Bible from childhood, and its stories remained a powerful stimulant to his creative imagination. Baron explains: 'La Bible n'est plus pour les écrivains du dix-neuvième siècle un livre d'autorité, mais surtout un vivier de représentations auréolées de mystère, disponibles pour la littérature qui, si souvent, interprète et réécrit les textes de la tradition.'[48] In *Eugénie Grandet*, Balzac engages with a variety of biblical references. The narrative describes Grandet as a godlike figure who sees everything that takes place in his home, while the old man's deathbed pledge to Eugénie ('Aie bien soin de tout. Tu me rendras compte de ça là-bas', iii, p. 1175) is clearly reminiscent of the Bible's promise that Christ will one day return to call the people of the Earth to account. In addition to reminding us of these well-known parallels, Allan Pasco sees a reflection of the Holy Trinity in this novel.[49] If Balzac models Père Grandet after the Father, Pasco suggests, then Nanon, who brings Eugénie food during her domestic imprisonment, parallels the comforting role of the Holy Spirit. As the third member of this trinity, Charles, who trades under the pseudonym Carl Sepherd, recalls the image of Jesus as a shepherd. However, Balzac does not merely steal or plunder the textual resources of the Bible without investing further thought in the creative profit that he can gain from them. As Pasco indicates, such allusions are useful to him precisely because he can channel them towards a new aesthetic purpose.[50] Through his portrayal of Charles, in particular, Balzac employs a well-known Bible story as a springboard for his own originality. The young man's sudden impoverishment and financial resurrection echo the tale of Lazarus, the beggar whom Jesus raised from the dead after his body had lain in its tomb for four days. Unlike Lazarus, however, who accepted his poverty without bitterness, Charles's resurrection merely fuels his greed. Upon hearing that Eugénie has settled his outstanding debts and is to marry, the cynical dandy can think only of the fortune he has lost: 'Mais, reprit-il frappé tout à coup par une réflexion lumineuse, elle est donc riche?' (iii, p. 1195). While our reading of the text does not simply collapse if we fail to recognise the source being adapted, knowledge of the Bible enhances our sensitivity to the individualism that Balzac treats as endemic in nineteenth-century society. A close reading of *L'Auberge rouge*, for example, reveals that when Walhenfer arrives at the inn, he finds not only that the establishment is packed, but that there is not even any room to sleep outside, 'les écuries étant pleines de monde' (xi, p. 99). The situation resembles that of the Nativity, but only those readers who recognise this allusion will appreciate fully the contrast between the innocence of Christ's birth and the murderous events that Balzac proceeds to relate. As the narrative switches direction to evoke another biblical intertext, *L'Auberge rouge* shows Walhenfer enjoying his own last supper before tempting the reader to conclude that Taillefer, like Judas Iscariot, betrays his friend for money and sends him to his execution.[51]

Echoes of Balzac's appropriation of these biblical intertexts can be seen in Epstein's *L'Auberge rouge*. The story of the Nativity, most especially, is discernible in the film. As Magnan and Taillefer race through the Bavarian countryside on horseback, Epstein shows a single light at the window of the storm-lashed inn, guiding the men towards their destination like the Star of Bethlehem. Once the men are inside, their clothes dripping wet, Epstein playfully emphasises the packed nature of the inn by panning around the room using a medium close-up of the innkeeper's hand to point to each of the tables. Like Balzac, Epstein proceeds to evoke the image of the Last Supper as Taillefer and the Dutchman converse jovially and share what remains of the innkeeper's food and wine. The presence of the fortune teller, however, coupled with the set of pistols that the Dutchman places carefully on the bench next to him, foreshadow the violence of the ensuing night and the execution of Magnan who, like Jesus, goes to his death soon afterwards. If *L'Auberge rouge* maintains and, indeed, extends Balzac's appropriation of these Christian intertexts, Ingram's use of the Bible is more oblique. *The Conquering Power* makes vague reference to the protective qualities of the Holy Mother, whose statue stands in the garden of the Grandet house and, according to Charles, watches over a bird's nest while the mother bird is away. The scene that culminates in

Grandet's death also evokes the calling to account of God's people as Grandet, having made money his god, faces punishment at the hands of his own gold.

However, the Bible is by no means the only source text appropriated by Balzac. Most notably, *L'Auberge rouge* borrows from nineteenth-century melodrama, and in particular the 1823 play *L'Auberge des Adrets.* The representation of crime-ridden inns and drinking-houses, claims Anne-Marie Meininger, was already commonplace in French literature before Balzac utilised this setting in his own writing.[52] A collaboration between at least three authors writing under the pseudonyms Benjamin Antier, Saint-Amant and Paulyanthe, *L'Auberge des Adrets* nevertheless reinvigorated this tradition by introducing audiences to the fictional villain Robert Macaire. In the 1823 play, Macaire, using the false name Rémond, arrives at a provincial inn with his accomplice Bertrand. Having recently escaped from prison in Lyon, the two are quick to begin plotting their next crime. After learning that one of their fellow guests is carrying 12,000 francs, Macaire steals the money during the night, only to be killed as he tries to make his escape the next morning. Balzac certainly knew the story of Robert Macaire, who returned to the stage in a sequel to *L'Auberge des Adrets* in 1832, the same year as the publication of *L'Auberge rouge.*[53] *L'Auberge rouge* borrows elements both of theme and of plot from this theatrical source. Taillefer's jocularity following his arrival in Andernach mirrors the black humour with which Macaire contemplates his victims. However, the confidence that Balzac's protagonist shares with Robert Macaire is by no means the only similarity between the two texts. In *L'Auberge des Adrets,* Macaire cannot rid himself of the thought of stealing the contents of another man's wallet. Anticipating the temptation that Magnan experiences in *L'Auberge rouge,* the unscrupulous criminal reveals that 'ces 12,000 fr. me trottent par la tête!'.[54] As in Balzac's story, there are no witnesses to the subsequent crime. The unfortunate victim, like Walhenfer, is 'frappé presque dans son sommeil, il n'a rien pu voir, reconnaître personne'.[55] In a reflection of the possible innocence of Prosper Magnan, *L'Auberge des Adrets* also sees Bertrand wrongfully accused of the murder before Macaire is exposed as the real killer. Both texts, then, are set in a provincial inn, where a large amount of money excites criminal desires and leads to a rich man being murdered in his bed. More subtly, *L'Auberge rouge* echoes the greed and hypocrisy practised by Robert Macaire, whom Balzac and his contemporaries readily came to interpret as a symbol of French society under the July Monarchy.[56] *L'Auberge rouge* portrays the ruthlessness of the escaped convict as typical of a wider pattern of social behaviour that had already begun to emerge in the aftermath of the Revolution. Thus, when the narrator's friends vote against his marriage to the daughter of a presumed murderer, the young man recognises immediately the selfish motives behind their public show of morality. 'Il y a unanimité secrète pour le mariage', he concludes, 'et unanimité pour me l'interdire!' (xi, pp. 120–1).

However, while Balzac borrows discreetly from the personality of Robert Macaire, he also recreates *L'Auberge des Adrets* by trading the drama against his own authorial concerns. Unlike the source text, which leaves no doubt as to Macaire's responsibility for the crime, *L'Auberge rouge* prompts us to consider whether guilt can always be determined easily, and whether an individual should be punished for his actions alone. Significantly, when Balzac incorporated *L'Auberge rouge* into *La Comédie humaine*, he classified the text among his *Etudes philosophiques*, and the second part of the narrative, entitled 'l'Idée et le fait', explores the contrast between committing a murder in thought and in deed. Although the fictional Magnan refuses to believe that he killed Walhenfer in a fit of somnambulism, he does acknowledge that contemplating murder was a sin in and of itself. As he tells Hermann from his prison cell, 'je sens que j'ai perdu la virginité de ma conscience' (xi, p. 108). Magnan views his death sentence as wrongful punishment for a crime of which he is not actually guilty, but he is also prepared to accept this fate in order to atone for his murderous thoughts. 'Cette injustice', he declares, 'm'a rendu tout entier à mon innocence. Ma vie aurait toujours été troublée, ma mort sera sans reproche' (xi, p. 109). As this philosophical reflection on the meaning of guilt shows, Balzac does not limit himself to plundering themes and character traits from *L'Auberge des Adrets*, but instead reconfigures his source in order to enrich a textual landscape of his own design.

As Epstein appropriates conventions from melodrama, so he continues Balzac's interest in somnambulism and the workings of the unconscious mind. The filmmaker was, in particular, an enthusiastic reader of Freud. In his 1922 essay 'Freud ou le nick-cartérianisme en psychologie', Epstein expressed a mixture of admiration and amusement at Freud's theories. Listing an array of symbols (knives, swords, revolvers) that Freud associated with the phallus, he admitted to feeling suspicious of the value and integrity of psychoanalysis.[57] His depiction of the night of the murder in *L'Auberge rouge* illustrates, however, the extent to which he engaged with Freudian thought. At the outset of this sequence, Epstein references the phallic symbol of the scalpel, which we see in a medium close-up as Magnan prepares to kill the Dutchman before recoiling in horror at his own actions. If the emphasis on this surgical instrument is coincidental, however, the rest of the scene gives cinematic form to several key tenets of Freud's *The Interpretation of Dreams.* In his 1899 work, Freud considers dreams to be 'fragmentary reproductions' of previous experiences.[58] Epstein conveys Magnan's own dream and subsequent temptation in fragmented images. Shots of the storm outside alternate with images of the diamonds and a close-up of the Dutchman's hands pulling the jewels out of his travelling case. As Magnan sits up in bed, Epstein further postulates that the character's semi-conscious state has awakened a suppressed desire for the precious stones. The notion of the dream as wish fulfilment taps into another aspect of Freudian theory. 'Unconscious wishes', writes Freud, 'are always alive, ready at all times to seek out expression if the opportunity offers, always ready to ally themselves with some impulse from the conscious.'[59] Freud's theory that dreams could activate the desires of the unconscious mind was a particular source of fascination for Epstein, who records in his notes, in distinctly Freudian terms, that 'le rêve est la réalisation d'un désir refoulé'.[60] As well as suggesting that Magnan's slumber alerts his conscious mind to the possibility of stealing, *L'Auberge rouge* playfully extends the dream motif. As in Balzac's story, Magnan faints as soon as he realises that his roommate is dead. Throughout the subsequent court martial, Léon Mathot interprets Magnan's distress as a barely conscious state in which, his eyes half-closed, he appears on the brink of fainting or falling asleep. As Epstein makes clear, Magnan's dream of stealing the diamonds is also a nightmare from which the young doctor never seems to awake.

Alongside the interest in the unconscious mind that he shared with Epstein, Balzac drew upon the resources of Gothic fiction and the fantastic. From the outset of his literary career, the novelist showed particular enthusiasm for the works of Ann Radcliffe and Charles Maturin. As exponents of the *roman noir,* both writers achieved widespread influence over prose fiction and the theatre in France, where Radcliffe's novels began to appear in 1797, followed by a translation of Maturin's *Melmoth the Wanderer* in 1821. Balzac reserved special affection for Maturin's text, in which the protagonist sells his soul to the devil in return for 150 years of life, and produced his own version of the story, *Melmoth réconcilié*, in 1835.[61] While this novel stands as the most obvious indication of Balzac's artistic debt to Maturin, *Eugénie Grandet* reflects, in a more understated manner, his earlier borrowings from Gothic fiction. The passage describing the Grandet house, first, recalls the eerie and unwelcoming sight of Melmoth's lodge, which shows 'signs that penury had been aggravated and sharpened into downright misery'.[62] In a similar state of disrepair, Grandet's home is 'froide, silencieuse, située en haut de la ville, et abritée par les ruines des remparts' (iii, p. 1039). Physically, Grandet evokes the 'spiteful sneer' of Melmoth, 'which the attraction of approaching death stiffened into a hideous grin'.[63] The old cooper's own features are equally grosteque: 'Son nez, gros par le bout, supportait une loupe veinée que le vulgaire disait, non sans raison, pleine de malice' (iii, p. 1036). Furthermore, Grandet's strongroom appears to generate gold with supernatural ease, causing those who do business with him to speculate that 'il avait à ses ordres une fée ou un démon' (iii, p. 1070).[64] However, the fortified room, which no one but the miser himself is allowed to enter, also functions as a metaphor for the way in which Balzac adapts elements of the Gothic novel tradition. In confining the overtly supernatural element of the story to the representation of the strongroom, *Eugénie Grandet* emphasises its own status as a realist text that chooses when and how to exploit the wealth of other fictional modes.

The Conquering Power picks up on Balzac's adaptation of the Gothic novel, and in particular the demonic aspects of Grandet's personality. Like his Balzacian model, Ingram's Grandet is quick to anger. When he learns that Eugénie has given away her gold, the old man raises his hand to his daughter (a shot that featured in publicity posters for the film) before dragging her violently to her room. Captured in profile, Grandet's face is contorted with rage as he demands to know if someone has stolen Eugénie's gold. However, the scene in which Grandet is attacked by his gold provides the most visible indication of Ingram's own artistic debt to the Gothic and, more broadly, horror genres. The appearance of the spirits of those Grandet has cheated, together with the long-fingered hands that reach out menacingly from the cradle, infuse this scene with elements of the supernatural more obvious than those Balzac had envisaged in his own portrait of the strongroom. More specifically, and as befits an American production, this scene, in which the walls close in, resonates with echoes of the work of Edgar Allan Poe. In Poe's story 'The Pit and the Pendulum', an unidentified man is thrown into a dungeon during the Spanish Inquisition. After spending a night grasping around in the darkness, the prisoner realises that the walls of his cell are closing in, pushing him ever closer to a deep pit. 'The room had been square,' writes Poe. 'In an instant the apartment had shifted its form into that of a lozenge . . . I shrank back – but the closing walls pressed me resistlessly onward.'[65] For the unnamed prisoner in Poe's tale, salvation comes as the French enter Toledo and the walls of the dungeon rush back. By contrast, the strongroom walls in *The Conquering Power* continue to push towards Grandet, who is crushed beneath his gold in a punishment that, unlike the religious persecution of 'The Pit and the Pendulum', Ingram suggests is well deserved.

Silent cinema had a key role in reinterpreting Balzac's literary legacy. Before the onset of sound film in 1927, cinematographers eagerly exploited the textual riches of *La Comédie humaine.* Many critics have denigrated these films repeatedly, accusing them of pillaging Balzac's work merely for commercial gain. Through their own interest in stealing and financial plundering, Epstein's *L'Auberge rouge* and Ingram's *The Conquering Power* nevertheless invite us to reconsider the relationship between theft and the adaptive process. At the level of plot, these films throw into relief the multiple acts of stealing and financial plundering at work in their source texts. Moreover, Epstein and Ingram use these themes as conduits through which to explore the possibilities of their medium. In *L'Auberge rouge,* Epstein appropriates the mental thunderstorm of Balzac's story to articulate his own vision of cinema as an interplay of objective and subjective viewpoints. Similarly, in *The Conquering Power,* Ingram can be seen to adopt Grandet's plundering of gold as a basis for confronting his own adaptive anxieties on screen. Foreshadowing de Certeau's concept of reading as poaching, *L'Auberge rouge* and *The Conquering Power* illustrate the artistic gains that are to be had not simply in plundering an array of literary sources, but in reinvesting this textual currency in new creative endeavours. Extending Balzac's adaptation of the melodramatic mode, Epstein connects the fictional experience of somnambulism to Freudian psychoanalysis and the suppressed desire for diamonds that Magnan's dream reawakens. Ingram, for his part, shares in Balzac's enthusiasm for the Gothic novel. By reaching, moreover, into the fiction of Edgar Allan Poe, he endows his version of *Eugénie Grandet* with a conclusion that both thrills his audience and punishes the fictional Grandet for his own acts of theft and monetary greed. In so doing, Epstein and Ingram reveal themselves, like Balzac, as participants in a naturally recurring process of textual appropriation. In the final analysis, neither they, nor the author they adapt, can be considered merely thieves or plagiarists. They present themselves as legitimate artists and, as a result, challenge us to modify how we see and describe them. As Julie Sanders writes, 'we need to view literary adaptation and appropriation from [a] more positive vantage point, seeing it as creating new cultural and aesthetic possibilities that stand alongside the texts which have inspired them, enriching rather than "robbing" them'.[66] Epstein and Ingram did not rob or devalue the artistic currency of *La Comédie humaine.* As filmmakers, they recognised the creative affinities between Balzac and their own medium, and helped to bring the nineteenth-century novelist to the attention of a new, twentieth-century audience.

Notes

1 Laure Doumens, 'Répertoire des adaptations cinématographiques et télévisuelles des œuvres de Balzac' (Maison de Balzac, unpublished, 2008).

2 Richard Abel, *French Cinema: The First Wave, 1915–1929* (Princeton, NJ: Princeton University Press, 1984), pp. 98–100, 351–9.

3 Anne-Marie Baron, *Balzac cinéaste* (Paris: Klincksieck, 1990), and *Romans français du dix-neuvième siècle à l'écran: problèmes de l'adaptation* (Clermont-Ferrand: Presses Universitaires Blaise-Pascal, 2008), pp. 35–42.

4 René Jeanne, 'Balzac au cinéma', *Cinémagazine*, 46 (2 December 1921), 5–8 (6).

5 Linda Hutcheon, *A Theory of Adaptation* (New York and London: Routledge, 2006), p. 4.

6 Honoré de Balzac, *La Comédie humaine*, ed. Pierre-Georges Castex, 12 vols (Paris: Gallimard, Bibliothèque de la Pléiade, 1976–81), i, p. 10. All subsequent references to this edition are parenthesised in the main text and accompanied by the relevant volume and page number(s).

7 Marcel Lapierre, *Les Cent Visages du cinéma* (Paris: Grasset, 1948), p. 159.

8 Jean Eyre, '*L'Auberge rouge*', *Mon Ciné*, 85 (4 October 1923), 18–19 (19).

9 Liam O'Leary, *Rex Ingram: Master of the Silent Cinema* (Dublin: Academy Press, 1980), p. 87.
10 '*The Conquering Power* starring Rudolph Valentino and Alice Terry', *New York Times*, 10 July 1921, *www.silentsaregolden.com/conqueringpower-review.html*, accessed 9 April 2011.
11 M. P., 'Avant *La Cousine Bette*: quelques minutes avec Max de Rieux', *Cinémagazine*, 27 (6 July 1928), 13.
12 Brian J. Robb, *Silent Cinema* (Harpenden: Kamera, 2007), p. 29.
13 Laure Surville, *Balzac: sa vie et ses œuvres d'après sa correspondance* (Paris: Jaccottet, Bourdilliat, 1858), p. 103.
14 Albert Béguin, *Balzac lu et relu* (Paris: Seuil, 1965), p. 49.
15 On Valentino's preparations for playing the role of Charles, see Emily W. Leider, *Dark Lover: The Life and Death of Rudolph Valentino* (London: Faber and Faber, 2003), p. 143.
16 'Comment Léon Mathot fut fusillé', *Mon Ciné*, 73 (12 July 1923), 19.
17 Jean Epstein, 'Rythme et montage', in *Ecrits sur le cinéma*, 2 vols (Paris: Seghers, 1974–5), i, pp. 121–3 (p. 121).
18 Jean Epstein, 'De quelques conditions de la photogénie', in *Ecrits sur le cinéma*, i, pp. 137–42 (p. 137 and p. 141).
19 Anne Hollander, *Moving Pictures* (London and Cambridge, MA: Harvard University Press, 1991), p. 50. On the relationship between early cinema and the theatre, see also Ben Brewster and Lea Jacobs, *Theatre to Cinema: Stage Pictorialism and Early Film* (Oxford: Oxford University Press, 1997).
20 For further discussion of the techniques with which early filmmakers sought to excite their audiences, see Tom Gunning, 'An aesthetic of astonishment: early film and the (in)credulous spectator', *Art and Text*, 34 (1989), 31–45.
21 Ben Singer, *Melodrama and Modernity: Early Sensational Cinema and Its Contexts* (New York: Columbia University Press, 2001), p. 40.
22 Peter Brooks, *The Melodramatic Imagination: Balzac, Henry James, Melodrama, and the Mode of Excess* (New Haven and London: Yale University Press, 1976), and Christopher Prendergast, *Balzac: Fiction and Melodrama* (London: Edward Arnold, 1978).
23 Brooks, *The Melodramatic Imagination*, p. 111.
24 For a list of theatrical adaptations of Balzac's work, see Linzy Erika Dickinson, *Theatre in Balzac's 'La Comédie humaine'* (Amsterdam: Rodopi, 2000), pp. 344–9.
25 Singer, *Melodrama and Modernity*, p. 44.
26 Aline Mura-Brunel, *Silences du roman: Balzac et le romanesque contemporain* (Amsterdam and New York: Rodopi, 2004), p. 78.
27 Aaron Sultanik, *Film: A Modern Art* (New York, London, Toronto: Cornwall, 1986), p. 77.
28 Dorothy Kelly, 'Balzac's *L'Auberge rouge*: on reading an ambiguous text', *Symposium*, 36 (1982), 30–44.
29 William K. Everson, *American Silent Film* (New York: De Capo, 1998), p. 102.

30 Laura J. Poulosky, *Severed Heads and Martyred Souls: Crime and Capital Punishment in French Romantic Literature* (New York: Peter Lang, 2003), pp. 180–1.
31 Jean Eyre, 'Comment on tourne un orage la nuit', *Mon Ciné*, 70 (21 June 1923), 7–8 (7).
32 For a detailed appraisal of the shots used in this sequence, see Abel, *French Cinema: The First Wave*, p. 354.
33 Ibid., p. 355.
34 Hutcheon, *A Theory of Adaptation*, p. 20.
35 Prendergast, *Balzac: Fiction and Melodrama*, p. 67.
36 For an extended discussion of the role of history in shaping Grandet's career, see Andrew Watts, *Preserving the Provinces: Small Town and Countryside in the Work of Honoré de Balzac* (Oxford: Peter Lang, 2007), pp. 157–66.
37 '*The Conquering Power* starring Rudolph Valentino and Alice Terry', *www.silentsaregolden.com/conqueringpowerreview.html*, accessed 9 April 2011.
38 For further background on the financial disaster that enveloped Griffith as a result of *Intolerance*, see William M. Drew, *D. W. Griffith's 'Intolerance': Its Genesis and Vision* (Jefferson, NC and London: McFarland, 1986), pp. 118–19.
39 Ginette Vincendeau, *Stars and Stardom in French Cinema* (London and New York: Continuum, 2000), p. viii. On the actor as 'auteur' with special reference to Jean Gabin's role in Renoir's adaptation of *La Bête humaine*, see also Kate Griffiths, *Emile Zola and the Artistry of Adaptation* (Oxford: Legenda, 2009), pp. 113–14.
40 Leider, *Dark Lover*, pp. 142–3.
41 Noel Botham, *Valentino: The First Superstar* (London: Metro, 2002), pp. 140–1.
42 Cited by Leider, *Dark Lover*, p. 145.
43 Miriam Hansen, *Babel and Babylon: Spectatorship in American Silent Film* (London and Cambridge, MA: Harvard University Press, 1991), p. 254.
44 For an extended discussion of the financial detail behind the sale of Grandet's gold, see Jean-Luc Seylaz, 'Une scène de Balzac: le transport de l'or dans *Eugénie Grandet*', *L'Année balzacienne* (1980), 61–7.
45 Montchanin, 'Balzac à l'écran', *Mon Ciné*, 67 (31 May 1923), 10–11 (10).
46 Abel, *French Cinema: The First Wave*, p. 354.
47 Leider, *Dark Lover*, p. 144.
48 Anne-Marie Baron, *Balzac et la Bible: une herméneutique du romanesque* (Paris: Champion, 2007), p. 14.
49 Allan H. Pasco, *Allusion: A Literary Graft* (Charlottesville, VA: Rockwood, 1994), pp. 114–16.
50 Ibid., p. 113.
51 For an extended discussion of Balzac's allusions to the Nativity and the Last Supper in *L'Auberge rouge*, see Poulosky, *Severed Heads*, pp. 177–8 and p. 181.

52 Anne-Marie Meininger, Introduction to *L'Auberge rouge*, in Balzac, *La Comédie humaine*, xi, p. 81.
53 For a complete list of references to the figure of Robert Macaire in Balzac's fictional output, see *La Comédie humaine*, xii, p. 1813.
54 Benjamin, Saint-Amant and Paulyanthe, *L'Auberge des Adrets* (Paris: Pollet, 1823), i.13, p. 13.
55 Benjamin, *L'Auberge des Adrets*, iii.1, p. 32.
56 On the character of Robert Macaire as a reflection of social and political corruption during the July Monarchy, see Gabriel Louis Moyal, 'Retranslation and ideological unravelling: Balzac's *conte philosophique* takes a return trip', *www.umass.edu/french/people/profiles/documents/Moyal.pdf*, 7, accessed 20 August 2011.
57 Jean Epstein, 'Freud ou le nick-cartérianisme en psychologie', in Jacques Aumont (ed.), *Jean Epstein: cinéaste, poète, philosophe* (Paris: Cinémathèque française, 1998), p. 145.
58 Sigmund Freud, *The Interpretation of Dreams*, ed. Ritchie Robertson and trans. Joyce Crick (Oxford: Oxford University Press, 2008), p. 20.
59 Ibid., p. 362.
60 Jean Epstein, 'Notes de lecture: résumés, citations, notes personnelles', notes held at the Paris Cinémathèque, EPSTEIN9 B 1 (packet 1 of 10, no date, no pagination).
61 For an overview of Balzac's interest in Radcliffe, Maturin and the Gothic novel, see Geneviève Delattre, *Les Opinions littéraires de Balzac* (Paris: Presses Universitaires de France, 1961), pp. 227–30.
62 Charles Maturin, *Melmoth the Wanderer*, ed. Douglas Grant and Chris Baldick (Oxford and New York: Oxford University Press, 1989), p. 9.
63 Ibid., p. 15.
64 For an alternative perspective on Balzac's exploitation of Gothic fiction, see Janet Gurkin, 'Romance elements in *Eugénie Grandet*', *L'Esprit créateur*, 7, 1 (1967), 17–24.
65 Edgar Allan Poe, 'The Pit and the Pendulum', in *The Collected Tales and Poems of Edgar Allan Poe* (London: Wordsworth, 2009), p. 200.
66 Julie Sanders, *Adaptation and Appropriation* (London and New York: Routledge, 2006), p. 41.

Chapter Three
Fragmented Fictions: Time, Textual Memory and the (Re)Writing of *Madame Bovary*

ANDREW WATTS

Since its publication in 1856, *Madame Bovary* has continued to fascinate writers, dramatists and filmmakers, who have shown a compulsive enthusiasm for recreating the novel in their own media. The film adaptations by Renoir (1933), Minnelli (1949) and Chabrol (1991) have attracted much scholarly attention.[1] However, rewritings of *Madame Bovary* in fiction have been largely neglected.[2] Over the past thirty years, literary homages to Flaubert's text have appeared in both French and English. A select bibliography compiled by the Centre Flaubert at the Université de Rouen lists twenty-four such works, eight of them published since the turn of the millennium.[3] Like adaptations of *Madame Bovary* for the screen, however, these fictions have often struggled to be recognised as having any artistic merit. 'Les phénomènes de réécriture et de suite ont le don d'agacer les puristes admirateurs des textes dont ils s'inspirent', writes Lionel Archer .[4] As works derived from a canonical source, literary recreations of *Madame Bovary* are particularly susceptible to being labelled copies because they exploit a novel that epitomises Flaubert's ideal of stylistic perfection. This accusation of inferiority is, not surprisingly, prevalent among certain French critics who remain anxious to protect a symbol of their country's cultural prestige. 'Il suffit de relire le chef-d'œuvre de Flaubert', wrote Astrid de Larminat in reviewing Philippe

Doumenc's *Contre-enquête sur la mort d'Emma Bovary* in 2007, 'pour être persuadé que toute copie fait pâle figure'.[5]

Analysis of Doumenc's novel and a second case study, Posy Simmonds's *Gemma Bovery* (1999), suggests, however, that contemporary fiction offers insights that deepen our understanding of the creative process as both portrayed and used by Flaubert.[6] As the present chapter will demonstrate, these 'hypertexts', to use Gérard Genette's term, throw into relief the importance of time and temporality in *Madame Bovary.*[7] More specifically, they share with their source novel an interest in how fiction rewrites earlier texts, and how these antecedents, following the Latin verb *adaptare,* meaning 'to fit', can themselves be refitted for a new era. Both of these reincarnations of *Madame Bovary* reach into the textual past, appropriating elements of Emma Bovary's story and achieving a sometimes paradoxical originality by combining them with more recent social, cultural and artistic discourses. In so doing, *Gemma Bovery* and *Contre-enquête sur la mort d'Emma Bovary* invite us to explore Flaubert's notion of time as a fragmented construct that destabilises the identity of his fictional heroine while simultaneously rethinking the creative materials from which he assembled his own novel.

Twentieth- and twenty-first-century fiction has routinely exploited time as a resource for rewriting *Madame Bovary.* In 'The Kugelmass Episode' (1975), a short story set in contemporary New York, Woody Allen links past and present by inserting his protagonist directly into the pages of Flaubert's novel. The eponymous Kugelmass seduces Emma before bringing her back to twentieth-century Manhattan, prompting readers of *Madame Bovary* to notice her sudden disappearance from the text:

> 'I cannot get my mind around this,' a Stanford professor said. 'First a strange character named Kugelmass, and now she's gone from the book. Well, I guess the mark of a classic is that you can reread it a thousand times and always find something new.'[8]

While Allen reflects playfully on the appeal of *Madame Bovary* to readers in different times and places, other writers have retraced the chronology of Flaubert's narrative in an attempt to make sense of Emma's disillusionment and eventual suicide. Sylvère Monod's *Madame Homais* (1988) and Laura Grimaldi's *Monsieur Bovary* (1991) replay the action of the source text, but suppress Emma's point of view in favour of the perspectives of her husband and their provincial neighbours. In this vibrant adaptive industry, writers have also extended the temporal boundaries of Flaubert's novel. Raymond Jean's *Mademoiselle Bovary* (1991) presents itself as a sequel to *Madame Bovary* in which Emma's daughter Berthe emerges from the cotton mill on the eve of her twentieth birthday to confront Flaubert about the fate he inflicted on her parents. A further category of texts illustrates what Genette terms 'un mouvement de translation proximisante', an updating of the novel's temporal setting aimed at reflecting the modernity of Flaubert's characters and thematic concerns.[9] As early as 1933, Odette Pannetier's 'Un drame de la vie provinciale', part of a collection of five short fictions entitled *Les Incarnations de Madame Bovary*, adopted this adaptive approach, recasting Emma as an alcoholic with a love of bars and nightlife, and Rodolphe as a seductive idol of the silver screen.

That each of these works engages with questions of time and memory is by no means coincidental. As Robert Stam and Alessandra Raengo have argued in relation to reinventions of classic novels in film, time is central to the adaptive act. Time in adaptation, they suggest, is doubly revealing, exposing 'facets not only of the novel and its period and culture of origin, but also of the time and culture of the adaptation'.[10] The time in which the reader or spectator consumes the new work, by definition later than the period in which the adaptation itself was produced, operates as a further prism through which adaptations reflect, and refract, the concerns and sensibilities of a new era. As well as informing our knowledge of sources, adaptations and the temporal contexts that surround them, time is also integral to understanding the myriad ways in which texts remember and recreate earlier texts. As specific theorists have shown, writing itself is an adaptive act that requires authors to contend with the work of their predecessors, and to situate themselves in relation to their literary inheritance. According to Bloom, this dialogue with the past manifests itself as an 'anxiety of influence' in which originality depends on the writer's self-conscious acknowledgement that our 'precursors flood us'. He asserts that 'Our imaginations can die by drowning in them, but no imaginative life is possible if such inundation is wholly evaded'.[11] Intertextual theory has firmly cemented this concept of textual memory. Writing, Genette claimed, is a 'palimpsestuous' activity anchored in the principle that 'tout texte [est] dérivé d'un texte antérieur'.[12] In a metaphor that will serve as a central reference point for this chapter, Kristeva further compared textual production to building a mosaic: 'tout texte se construit comme mosaïque de citations, tout texte est absorption et transformation d'un autre texte'.[13] As the temporal image of the mosaic suggests, texts anticipate the adaptations based upon them by fragmenting the artistic resources of the past and rearranging them to create new works in the present.

Gemma Bovery and *Contre-enquête sur la mort d'Emma Bovary* offer compelling insights into *Madame Bovary* by exposing the processes through which Flaubert uses time and textual memory to rework his own literary heritage. Serialised in the British newspaper *The Guardian* before its publication in book form in 1999, Simmonds's graphic novel resonates with memories of its source text, reinventing Emma as a freelance illustrator whose worldly expectations are conditioned by glossy lifestyle magazines. The fictional Gemma, whose name recalls both that of her nineteenth-century counterpart and Flaubert's first initial, is perpetually disappointed by the failure of reality to match her dreams and ambitions.[14] In an ironic reversal of Emma's contempt for small-town life, Gemma abandons her career in London for a new life in Normandy, only to fall into a cycle of debt and marital infidelity. As Liz Constable shows in her astute reading of *Gemma Bovery*, however, Simmonds does not simply overwrite her source text, but actively resituates Emma Bovary in a 'new historical situation: middle-class, forty-something, Brits in London . . . in the late twentieth century'.[15] Having devoted much of her career to satirising contemporary British society, Simmonds perceives Emma as a type still present in modern life. Indeed, a chance encounter during a holiday to Italy, where the author noticed a woman who reminded her of Flaubert's heroine, sparked her enthusiasm for rewriting, and redrawing, *Madame Bovary*: 'She was treating her lover in such a disgraceful way', Simmonds recalls, 'and she was surrounded by Prada bags and expensive shoe bags. She looked so bored and so miserable and she just exuded a kind of "Alas, what might have been."'[16]

While Simmonds's observations on her own time inspired *Gemma Bovery*, *Contre-enquête sur la mort d'Emma Bovary* reflects Philippe Doumenc's more systematic exploration of the cultural past. Doumenc came to prominence in France after his first novel, *Les Comptoirs du Sud*, a semi-autobiographical account of French naval life during the Algerian War, won the coveted Prix Renaudot in 1989. After revisiting this painful episode in French history,

Doumenc turned to focus on his country's literary heritage, alighting on *Madame Bovary* in a detective fiction that re-examines the reasons behind Emma's death. *Contre-enquête* opens with the image of Emma on her deathbed as a final convulsion grips her body and she falls, lifeless, to the mattress. Like the first instalment of *Gemma Bovery*, which reveals that Gemma has been dead for three weeks, Doumenc invites the reader to participate in recalling the events that led his soon-defunct heroine to the grave. Andreas Huyssen claims that 'the temporal status of any act of memory is always the present'.[17] Echoing the opening pages in *Madame Bovary*, in which Charles's first day at a new school is recalled by one of his former classmates, Doumenc takes the narrative present as his point of departure, speculating that Emma did not commit suicide, but was in fact murdered. The task for the fictional detectives Delévoye and Remi is to work backwards from this present position, building a picture of Emma's final hours that they hope will lead them to her killer. Through the act of retracing time, Simmonds and Doumenc also encourage their readers to remember the plot of *Madame Bovary* in order to compare source and adaptation, and to enhance the pleasure of the reading experience.

The link between these hypertexts is further strengthened by the way in which they mirror Flaubert's notion of authorship as an exercise in reassembling the past. During the composition of *Madame Bovary* in 1852, Flaubert described his creative praxis to Louise Colet as that of a literary archaeologist 'qui fouille et creuse le vrai tant qu'il peut', digging down through time in search of truths which could be moulded into new works of art.[18] Excavating the past appears as a key theme in *Gemma Bovery*. After relocating to France, Simmonds's heroine struggles in vain to infuse the present with the atmosphere of a bygone age. Gemma's 'mania . . . for the patina of Time' leads her to decorate her Normandy home in a faux-peasant style, only to find that the random display of cider jugs and gelding irons gives her living room the appearance of an antiques shop.[19] By contrast, Doumenc's protagonists Remi and Delévoye are more successful in their attempts to piece together the clues they need to solve Emma's supposed murder. As the fictional Doctor Larivière declares in summarising their mission, 'la question est de savoir qui l'aurait fait et pourquoi'.[20] As well as its thematic importance to these works, the process of reassembling time also underpins their authors' common approach to adaptation. Simmonds's graphic novel, a fractured format which combines verbal narration with a variety of drawing styles, reinvents *Madame Bovary* by borrowing not only from its nineteenth-century source, but from other graphic novels and contemporary cultural trends such as the 1990s British vogue for owning a second home in France. For Doumenc, recreating *Madame Bovary* as a detective novel also involves rewriting earlier works, engaging with celebrated exponents of French crime fiction, foremost among them Georges Simenon. By placing time at the heart of their thematic concerns and adaptive methods, these works thus provide a unique and illuminating framework through which to examine Flaubert's own interest in time and the textual past.

Equally, the case for studying *Madame Bovary* in relation to literary adaptation is strong. One of the most compelling reasons for undertaking such an analysis is that the relationship between fiction and adaptation is a core theme in the novel itself. As a girl in the convent, Emma develops a voracious appetite for reading, her taste for sentimental novels and popular romances nourished by the books she borrows from the laundry maid who visits once a month. The washerwoman's role is to clean and repair the girls' bed linen, but she sullies Emma by filling her with outdated romantic imagery. Of these novels, Flaubert wrote in a memorable parody: 'Ce n'étaient qu'amours, amants, amantes, dames persécutées s'évanouissant dans des pavillons solitaires, postillons qu'on tue à tous les relais . . . Pendant six mois, à quinze ans, Emma se graissa donc les mains à cette poussière des vieux cabinets de lecture.'[21] The narrator's association of fiction with dirt contrasts sharply with the idealised visions that Emma gathers from her reading. Later she discovers Walter Scott, and imagines herself living in a Highland cottage, awaiting the return of her gallant knight. Once married, she fuels her dreams of living in Paris by devouring the works of Balzac and Eugène Sue. The tragedy of Emma's existence, however, is not merely that she is obsessed by these earlier literary models, but that she is unable to match the world she has read about in fiction with the reality of her existence. Emma is a woman who adapts badly, struggling hopelessly to fit the expectations she derives from novels to the boredom and mediocrity of her provincial surroundings.

As Christophe Ippolito has shown, Emma is by no means the only character in *Madame Bovary* to view the world through the lens of fiction. He writes: 'An undeniable aspect of Flaubert's characters is the importance their readings have in the course of their destiny.'[22]

What Ippolito neglects to consider is that the impact of literature in *Madame Bovary* is closely intertwined with the process of adaptation. In Léon, Emma finds a mirror image of her own Romantic sensibilities, but his stories of Swiss lakes and mountains have, he admits, merely been passed on to him by his cousin. Léon's landlord Homais, for his part, boasts of having an extensive library stocked with the works of Voltaire, Rousseau and Scott, and selects the names for two of his children from literary fashions and Racinian tragedy: 'Irma, peut-être, était une concession au romantisme; mais Athalie, un hommage au plus immortel chef-d'œuvre de la scène française' (p. 92). While inviting us to mock this choice of names as inconsonant with the real world, especially that of a provincial backwater, Flaubert's portrayal of Rodolphe reveals another aspect of his suspicion of literary adaptation. By recycling the clichés of sentimental fiction, the virile landowner succeeds in seducing Emma for his own pleasure, and then in ridding himself of her just as brutally, by means of a farewell letter smudged with fake tears. As portrayed by Flaubert, such acts of adaptation cause lasting damage to those who are exposed to them. Even Charles, whose lack of interest in reading is evidenced by the uncut copy of the *Dictionnaire des sciences médicales* that sits on his shelf, feels their effect. After Emma's death, the fantasies she has spun from fiction will continue to haunt him as he, too, falls into debt to support his newfound penchant for trinkets and luxuries: 'il adopta ses prédilections, ses idées [d'Emma]; il s'acheta des bottes vernies, il prit l'usage des cravates blanches. Il mettait du cosmétique à ses moustaches, il souscrivit comme elle des billets à ordre' (p. 349). Like Emma before him, Charles fails to reconcile fiction and reality. By ignoring the basic truth that he is a rural health officer rather than an aristocratic dandy, he continues Emma's adaptation of literary models as badly and inappropriately as she had done when alive.

In contrast to the plot of *Madame Bovary*, which reflects an authorial sensitivity to the dangers of adaptation, Flaubert's own adaptive method demonstrates the potential for rewriting an array of earlier texts and sources. Like the fictional Remi in *Contre-enquête sur la mort d'Emma Bovary*, Flaubert embraced the challenge of working back through time to uncover hidden truths that could then be incorporated into his text. The inspiration for *Madame Bovary*, as has frequently been noted, stemmed in part from the tale of Eugène Delamare, a health officer in the Normandy village of Ry whose young wife Delphine was rumoured to have had a series of adulterous affairs before her premature death in 1848. Flaubert knew of the scandal, but was not content to base his novel solely on local gossip, despite the story's evident literary potential. He scoured medical dictionaries for the symptoms of female hysteria and the corrosive effects of arsenic poisoning. In preparation for describing Hippolyte's failed club-foot operation, he read Duval's 1839 *Traité pratique du pied-bot*, and visited an agricultural fair before writing the famous 'comices agricoles' episode. As Timothy Unwin observes, Flaubert adopted research as a standard part of novel writing. Unlike Dumas and, later in the century, Verne, who used research to accelerate production, Flaubert viewed writing as an 'exacting task accompanied by constant self-criticism, and involving repeated redrafting and reworking'.[23] The painstaking hours he spent procuring factual material for *Madame Bovary* were exceeded only by the time needed to weave these details into the fabric of the novel itself.

While mining the documentary resources of the past, Flaubert also drew extensively on his predecessors in fiction. Classical mythology, Renaissance comedy, Shakespearean drama, Spanish Golden Age literature, in addition to works by his contemporaries, all shaped his conceptualisation of writing as an adaptive act which involved selecting materials from previous texts, genres and literary traditions in order to redeploy them in his own work. In *Par les champs et par les grèves*, his account of the journey he made across France, mostly on foot, in 1847, Flaubert reflects on the possibility of exploiting the literary past and finding originality in these sometimes unpromising resources. In particular, he recalls the stereotypical figure of *la femme de trente ans*. The idea that women are most attractive after the age of thirty had been popularised by Balzac over a decade before, but the cliché appeals to Flaubert's imagination precisely because of its familiarity and capacity for renewal. 'Exhumer dans ce qu'on rejetait comme hors d'usage des trésors nouveaux,' he asks, 'cela n'est-il pas spirituel et sublime?' Extending the analogy between writing and digging, he promises to return to these creative riches in the future: 'on y reviendra plus tard comme à tout ce qui est vrai, comme à tout ce qui est bon; . . . on verra ce qu'on n'a qu'entrevu, on soudera ce qu'on n'a qu'effleuré, la mine est neuve encore, la veine profonde'.[24] This desire to adapt the fragments of earlier works anticipates the way in which *Madame Bovary* has been appropriated by twentieth- and twenty-first-century writers, who have elevated Emma's debts, sensuality and death to the status of myth while continuing to create new fictions from the novel's familiar thematic components.

To what extent, then, can the processes of rewriting and adaptation help us to understand the representation of time in *Madame Bovary*? Part of the answer to this question stems, first, from a recurrent perception of Flaubert's novel as a 'timeless' text. When Fay Weldon's play *Breakfast with Emma* enjoyed a revival on the London stage in 2009, the author attributed the success of this new production to the ease with which *Madame Bovary* transcends temporal boundaries. Emma's story, she declared, 'is not really about infidelity. It is about shopping and guilt and compulsive behaviour, themes of our times.'[25] Because Emma's taste for material luxuries reflects the acquisitive instincts of a capitalist economy, subsequent adaptations have readily associated the novel with a society still recognisable as our own. That *Madame Bovary* remains pertinent today, however, is by no means a temporal accident. On the contrary, timelessness and the immobility of time are features which Flaubert built self-consciously into his text. Although the narrative unfolds between 1828 and Homais's receipt of the *Légion d'honneur* in 1856, the events of what was a tumultuous period in French history receive little attention. As Stephen Heath observes, the revolutions of 1830 and 1848 are mentioned nowhere in the text, and there are few signs of the country's burgeoning strength in industry and commerce, except for the factory chimneys that Charles sees from the window of his student lodgings in Rouen: 'There is no longer any *history*, and the provincial world, its cities included, figures a reality of stasis.'[26] Flaubert emphasises that this is a world outside of time by substituting precise historical markers for abstractions such as 'tous les jours, à la même heure' (p. 66), which convey a sense of sameness and crushing monotony. The historical indeterminacy of *Madame Bovary* is a key consideration in adapting the novel for a new era, since writers must strike a balance between, on the one hand, creating an original work and, on the other, not effacing the memory of the source text entirely.[27] The reader's enjoyment in discovering the adaptation lies precisely in remembering *Madame Bovary* while at the same time perceiving two distinct works. As Alain Buisine explains in reference to the challenge of reinventing the character of Emma specifically: 'tel est le paradoxe d'un nom propre quand il devient emblématique: le type doit rester identique à lui-même tout en disposant d'une véritable plasticité'.[28]

Both *Gemma Bovery* and *Contre-enquête* appeal to the reader's memory of their source text by repeating elements of Emma's story in a new time and situation. Simmonds's heroine shares with her fictional counterpart a tendency towards dreaming and disillusionment. *Contre-enquête*, meanwhile, perpetuates the image of Rodolphe as a serial adventurer who has enjoyed liaisons with women throughout Normandy. The interest in repetition that characterises recreations of *Madame Bovary* is consonant with Flaubert's own use of repetition as a thematic motif. At the level of plot, repetition in *Madame Bovary* metaphorises the emptiness of human existence. As a young medical student, Charles goes through the same routine every week: 'Sa mère lui envoyait, par le messager, un morceau de veau', the narrator informs us, in an imperfect tense which underscores the habitual nature of the action. 'Ensuite il fallait courir aux leçons, à l'amphithéâtre, à l'hospice, et revenir chez lui, à travers toutes les rues' (p. 10). While Charles is content to replay time, Emma's aspirations towards a more varied and fulfilling life make repetition a constant source of torment. The monotonous sound of Binet's lathe gives an unwanted soundtrack to her frustrated ambition. Homais's daily interruption of the Bovarys' evening meal, during which the pharmacist trots out a stream of *idées reçues*, further illustrates what Roger Huss describes as a 'sense of déjà vu and tedium' consistent with Flaubert's 'inability to believe in the originality of any event'.[29] As Rosemary Lloyd points out, the structure of the novel replicates this 'temporal stammer', not least in the description of Emma's wedding day.[30] In the first part of the novel this appears to conclude at the end of chapter three, only for the celebrations to start all over again at the beginning of chapter four.

Temporal repetition in *Madame Bovary* is closely aligned with memory. Moreover, memory underpins the very act of rewriting Flaubert's work. According to Kristeva, texts remember and repeat earlier texts: 'l'écriture lit une autre écriture, se lit elle-même et se construit dans une genèse destructrice'.[31] The memory of *Madame Bovary* as a canonical work of literature has both inspired and intimidated writers in their attempts to recreate the novel. Having discovered *Madame Bovary* at school, Posy Simmonds claims that she read the text again before starting work on *Gemma Bovery*, but then felt compelled to lock her copy of the book in a drawer, fearing that her own version of the story would replicate its source too closely.[32] The way in which readers remember earlier fiction is a central concern in *Madame Bovary*, in which Emma's memories of a back catalogue of texts operate as a filter through which she perceives and evaluates every subsequent experience. Her tendency to measure her actual circumstances against fiction is particularly evident in her reflections on marriage. As she walks her greyhound Djali (named, in another act of literary adaptation, after Esmeralda's goat in *Notre-Dame de Paris*), she pauses to consider what kind of man she might have married: 'Il aurait pu être beau, spirituel, distingué, attirant, tels qu'ils étaient sans doute, ceux qu'avaient épousés ses anciennes camarades du couvent' (p. 46). Tellingly, Flaubert connects Emma's mental portrait of her ideal husband to the convent, the place in which she was first exposed to literature, and to the friends she imagines must now be enjoying more glamorous lives: 'A la ville, avec le bruit des rues, le bourdonnement des théâtres et les clartés du bal, elles avaient des existences où le cœur se dilate, où les sens s'épanouissent' (p. 46). As she seeks comfort in nostalgia for the past, Emma succeeds only in creating new fictions that make her own present seem even more intolerable. 'Memories', writes William Vanderwolk, further echoing the interrelatedness of time and adaptation, 'serve only to destroy any possibility of Emma adapting to her present, and in this capacity, contribute significantly to her demise'.[33]

The extent to which Emma's memories of fiction shape her attitude towards the present is further illustrated by her visit to the ball at La Vaubyessard. Evoking the sumptuous dinner of lobster and exotic fruits, Flaubert shows how his heroine's gaze is drawn repeatedly towards the Marquis's elderly father-in-law, the Duc de Laverdière. The old man appears exhausted from having led 'une vie bruyante de débauches, pleine de duels, de paris, de femmes enlevées'. After one of the servants speaks loudly in his ear, the aged aristocrat stutters his choice of dish, his 'lèvres pendantes' (p. 50) suggestive of the dribbling that follows as he consumes his meal. The figure who captivates Emma, however, is not merely the wreckage of an earlier time, but an embodiment of the kind of dashing heroes she has read about in her keepsakes. Her gaze settles on the Duc 'comme sur quelque chose d'extraordinaire et d'auguste. Il avait vécu à la Cour et couché dans le lit des reines!' (p. 50). In a passage not included in the final manuscript, Flaubert emphasised that Emma rarely sees things for what they really are. The morning after the ball, she pauses at one of the château's stained-glass windows, and finds that each segment of colour alters her perspective on the countryside beyond: 'à travers les bleus tout semblait triste – une buée d'azur répandue dans l'air allongeait la prairie et reculait les collines'.[34] Significantly, as R. J. Sherrington noted, the one window she does not look through is made up of clear glass.[35] As well as confirming the highly subjective nature of Emma's reality, the window also functions, however, as a temporal metaphor. Like mosaics, stained-glass windows consist of fragments of earlier material, broken up and reassembled to create a new design. When Emma contemplates the Duc de Laverdière, therefore, she does not simply fictionalise his biography, even though what she sees appears wholly disconnected from the truth. Instead she selects from his richly varied past, a past that the narrative elusively implies is known to others ('l'ancien favori du comte d'Artois . . . avait été, *disait-on,* l'amant de la reine Marie-Antoinette' (my italics), p. 50), and arranges the resultant fragments into a more appealing image of his present.

Flaubert juxtaposes time and fragmentation with the destabilising effect these elements have on Emma's identity. At La Vaubyessard, when a servant breaks a window to let air into the room, the act of shattering the glass reveals the faces of the peasants outside, reminding Emma of her childhood on the farm: 'Elle revit la ferme, la mare bourbeuse, son père en blouse sous les pommiers, et elle se revit elle-même, comme autrefois . . . Mais, aux fulgurations de l'heure présente, sa vie passée, si nette jusqu'alors, s'évanouissait tout entière, et elle doutait presque de l'avoir vécue' (p. 53). As memories rush in, Emma finds herself unable to reconcile two moments in her life that to her seem far removed from each other. Her visit to the opera in Rouen, where she enthuses over the performance of the tenor Lagardy in *Lucie de Lammermoor,* replays this struggle to exert control over the memories that, in a pre-Proustian manner, involuntarily pervade her consciousness. As the curtain rises to reveal a wooded landscape, Emma remembers once again the books she read as a girl: 'Elle se retrouvait dans ses lectures de jeunesse, en plein Walter Scott' (p. 228). While the memory of fiction enhances her sensibility to the music (and, in particular, the chorus, in what Diana Knight correctly identifies as one of the few instances of pleasurable repetition in the novel) Emma also perceives the scene as a fragmented spectacle, too varied for her to capture with a single glance.[36] Seeking a focal point for her imagination, she fantasises over an impossible future in which she tours the capitals of Europe with Lagardy, 'brodant elle-même ses costumes' (p. 231).

Tony Tanner highlights the importance of sewing in *Madame Bovary*, focusing especially on the scene in which Emma pricks her finger during Charles's first visit to Les Bertaux. Tanner argues:

> By marking her imperfect mastery of this distinctly and distinguishingly human activity from the start, Flaubert can make us aware of a continuity and relatedness between all Emma's uncertainties, instabilities and incompetencies – in marriage, in money, in language, in love. She cannot sew them together in a coherent way.[37]

Emma's difficulty with sewing, however, is not restricted to her inability to piece together the various threads of her life in the present; it also extends to the memories she is unable to stitch together into seamless contentment. Flaubert illustrates this problem during the meeting between Emma and Léon in her hotel room in Rouen, the day after the opera. Both are selective in recounting what has happened to them since they were last together. Emma does not mention her affair with Rodolphe, and Léon does not admit to having forgotten about her until the previous evening. Their conversation clutches instead at memories of an earlier time, when they enjoyed an unconsummated affection for each other. Léon recalls 'le berceau de clématite, les robes qu'elle avait portées, les meubles de sa chambre', and the day he followed Emma through Yonville, not wanting to be separated from her. Flaubert punctures the nostalgia of these reminiscences, however, by having Emma announce that the cactus plants Léon once gave her are dead: 'Le froid les a tués cet hiver' (p. 240). Tersely undercutting the couple's desire to rediscover their happiness in the fragmented recollections of the past, Flaubert asserts his pessimism that time, once elapsed, can never be recaptured in a form untainted by subsequent experience.

While Emma's struggle to reassemble the past ends in failure and disappointment, her creator explores the processes through which the fragmented resources of earlier fictions can be shaped into a new artistic product. Alison Finch points out that recent scholarship has focused increasingly on Flaubert's exploitation of his literary precedents, rather than on the subsequent writers he has influenced.[38] The intertextual presence of Balzac, Stendhal,

Cervantes, Austen and numerous other writers from Antiquity to the nineteenth century, is certainly discernible in *Madame Bovary*. Any discussion of these sources, however, requires us not only to assess what Flaubert adapts and appropriates from them, but to consider the ways in which he employs literary history to engage with his own era. What artistic value do these antecedents hold for him in the 1850s, when he is writing *Madame Bovary*? How does he reinvigorate age-old themes and narrative conventions, many of which were already familiar to the reading public? And, most importantly, what message does he use these earlier texts to convey about the role played by literature in his own time? As we have seen, Flaubert's borrowings have a chronological span that this chapter cannot accommodate in its entirety. Nevertheless, by examining a small sample of his fictional sources, it is possible to demonstrate that *Madame Bovary* is underpinned by an adaptive method more commonly associated with its hypertexts, which as Julie Sanders has explained in a different context, involves 'assembling found items to create a new aesthetic object'.[39] Analysed through this framework, *Madame Bovary* appears as a textual mosaic that selects from and rewrites earlier fictions, resulting in a work that is simultaneously past and present.

At the heart of Flaubert's engagement with literary history is Romanticism, a mode that had itself sought to create new art by borrowing from other texts and traditions. *Madame Bovary* reflects the contemporary status of Romantic fiction as a genre whose time had passed, but which for Flaubert continued to represent a fertile source of artistic innovation. Among the antecedents who feature most prominently in the novel is Walter Scott, whom Flaubert mentions in his summary of the authors read by Emma as a girl, and in the chapter recounting her visit to the theatre, where the opera that enthrals her is itself a dramatic adaptation of Scott's *The Bride of Lammermoor* (1819). Like many of his contemporaries, Flaubert counted the *Waverley* novels among his own youthful readings. These historical fictions, set mostly in the Scottish Highlands during the Middle Ages, abound in clichés and clumsy plot devices that Flaubert treats as ripe for mockery. The parodic effects he generates from these conventions are appropriately evident in his description of the performance of *Lucie de Lammermoor*. When Charles leaves the box in search of refreshments, he happens unexpectedly upon Léon, in an already packed corridor. This meeting sparks the subsequent affair between Emma and Léon, which is also beset by unlikely coincidences.[40] A notable example occurs in Flaubert's portrayal of the boat trip taken by the couple during their 'honeymoon' in Rouen. As the lovers recline in the vessel, Emma's happiness is swiftly punctured by the oarsman's revelation that he transported Rodolphe along the river just a few days before. The scene contains an implicit criticism of Scott's enthusiasm for driving his narratives with sudden twists of fortune, a parody Flaubert subtly conceals behind the boatman's inability to remember whether his passenger was in fact called Adolphe or Dodolphe (p. 263). By maintaining this uncertainty over whether or not the coincidence really occurred, Flaubert ultimately frustrates any attempt to determine what attitude he requires us to adopt towards Scott. While gently ridiculing this earlier material, *Madame Bovary* displays a residual affection for Scott's novels through the very act of parodying them.

As well as his interest in specific writers, Flaubert also targets the sentimental imagery which dominates Emma's convent reading, and marks his ironic distance from these time-worn stereotypes by listing them, thereby emphasising their mundane nature: 'forêts sombres, troubles du cœur, serments, sanglots, larmes et baisers, nacelles au clair de lune, rossignols dans les bosquets, *messieurs* braves comme des lions' (p. 38). Flaubert mocks not only the kind of material that Emma reads, however, but the selective way in which she reads. After devouring Chateaubriand's *Génie du christianisme* (1802), Emma appreciates only those aspects of the world which correspond to her romanticised sensibilities:

> Elle n'aimait la mer qu'à cause de ses tempêtes, et la verdure seulement lorsqu'elle était clairsemée parmi les ruines. Il fallait qu'elle pût retirer des choses une sorte de profit personnel; et elle rejetait comme inutile tout ce qui ne contribuait pas à la consommation immédiate de son cœur. (p. 37)

The narrative warns against extracting imagery from previous fictions merely because they offer consolation for one's present circumstances. What makes this passage relevant in the context of literary adaptation is that Flaubert appears to ridicule exactly the kind of activity in which he engages as a novelist, adapting earlier works in order to derive his own creative profit from them. Unlike Emma, however, whose enthusiasm for literature sows the seeds of her destruction, Flaubert employs his memory of literary history as a basis for constructing his own artistic identity.

Of crucial importance to understanding this adaptive method is a writer who bridges the gap between romantic and realist fiction: Balzac. Just as twentieth- and twenty-first-century writers have been scorned for daring to reinvent *Madame Bovary*, Flaubert attracted criticism in his own time for producing what some considered a second-rate copy of Balzacian novel writing. As the journalist Charles de Mazade wrote disdainfully in the *Revue des Deux Mondes* in May 1857, 'Flaubert imite M. de Balzac dans son roman'.[41] With its apparently everyday subject, and a subtitle, *Mœurs de province*, that echoed Balzac's own *Etudes de mœurs*, *Madame Bovary* invited readers to associate the novel with *La Comédie humaine*.[42] Equally, as Graham Falconer has shown, Flaubert's determination not to imitate Balzac caused him to engage in 'un travail de débalzaciénisation', by which he sought to remove from his manuscript any trace of the didactic conventions beloved of his predecessor.[43] *Madame Bovary* also admits a third position, however, which suggests that Flaubert neither imitates nor rejects Balzac entirely, but rewrites him, appropriating themes and plotlines from *La Comédie humaine* for the very purpose of differentiating his own work from them. Flaubert's technique is neatly illustrated by a comparison of two passages from *Madame Bovary* and *Le Curé de village*. The protagonist of Balzac's 1839 novel, Véronique Graslin, is a provincial whose discovery of sentimental fiction awakens her to new emotional possibilities. Having persuaded her father to buy her a copy of *Paul et Virginie*, Véronique quickly starts to dream of innocent love and exotic shores:

> Mais la chaleur des tropiques et la beauté des paysages, mais la candeur presque puérile d'un amour presque saint avaient agi sur Véronique. Elle fut amenée par la douce et noble figure de l'auteur vers le culte de l'Idéal, cette fatale religion humaine! Elle rêva d'avoir pour amant un jeune homme semblable à Paul.[44]

In *Madame Bovary*, Flaubert describes Emma's enthusiasm for Bernardin de Saint-Pierre's novel in strikingly similar terms: 'Elle avait lu *Paul et Virginie* et elle avait rêvé la maisonnette de bambous, le nègre Domingo, le chien Fidèle, mais surtout l'amitié douce de quelque bon petit frère, qui va chercher pour vous des fruits rouges dans des grands arbres' (p. 36). The fantasies inspired by *Paul et*

Virginie, particularly in the minds of female readers, was as much a literary cliché by Balzac's time as it was later in the century for Flaubert. Whereas Balzac employs *Paul et Virginie* to support his deterministic analysis of Véronique's melancholy state, Flaubert's use of the novel, however, is coloured by his further reading of *Le Curé de village*. By remembering both Bernardin de Saint-Pierre and Balzac's reading of him, Flaubert works through the stereotype of dangerous fiction while simultaneously asserting his own originality. Avoiding, unlike Balzac, any subjective condemnation of Romantic idealism as 'cette fatale religion humaine', he demonstrates instead that fiction only partially explains Emma's psychological condition, which itself has no single or straightforward cause.

While Flaubert absorbs *Le Curé de village* almost imperceptibly into his textual mosaic, his adaptation of earlier fictions is by no means, however, an exclusively private activity. *Madame Bovary* also appeals to the reader's memory of the sources being reworked, and requires us to participate actively in decoding its traffickings between past and present. Adopting Charles Perrault's fairy tale *La Belle au bois dormant* (1697) as another base text, Flaubert manipulates our expectations of his own novel by inviting us to share in his retelling of an age-old narrative in a new time and situation. The well-known story of Sleeping Beauty recounts the tale of a princess who falls into a hundred-year sleep after pricking herself on a spindle. The king and queen lay their daughter in a bed crafted from gold and silver, while the girl's fairy godmother surrounds the castle with a forest of thorns, shielding her from curious eyes until a prince arrives to awaken her from her sleep. *La Belle au bois dormant* was a recurrent obsession for Flaubert, who clearly appropriated elements of Perrault's story with a view to recreating them in *Madame Bovary*. The parallels between the two works, as Juliette Frølich and Anne Green have shown, are established by the opening pages of the novel, in which Charles sets out for Les Bertaux.[45] As the *officier de santé* slumbers in his saddle, we learn that his progress is slowed by the 'trous d'épines' which punctuate the Normandy landscape, and that he is forced to lower his head 'pour passer sous les branches' (p. 14). As he enters the farmhouse, the scene inside continues to mirror the fairy tale discreetly. Distracted by attending to her father, Emma pricks her finger while sewing, prompting Charles to notice the whiteness of her fingernails as she sucks blood from the wound.

Père Rouault (whose name clearly evokes that of Perrault, the father of the fairy tale genre) then expresses his gratitude to Charles by inviting him to stay for breakfast, at a table laid with silver goblets, 'au pied d'un grand lit à baldaquin revêtu d'une indienne à personnages représentant des Turcs' (p. 16).[46]

The fragments of Perrault's story – the thorns, the ornate bed and the sewing injury – are certainly recognisable in *Madame Bovary*. Foreshadowing Kristeva's assertion that texts transform other texts, it is equally clear, however, that Flaubert adapts these images to fit a new aesthetic purpose. Through the act of pricking her finger, Emma excites the desire of a man who, far from being her prince, is a dull and unsuitable match. Flaubert adds further weight to this irony when Emma pricks her finger for the second time in the novel, on the dried-up wedding bouquet that symbolises her marital disappointment. Shortly afterwards she meets Rodolphe, a lover she hopes will rescue her from a life of temporal stasis and mediocrity, but who coldly abandons her at the hour of their planned elopement. While employing *La Belle au bois dormant* to subvert any expectation we might have that Emma's story will have a happy ending, Flaubert remains fully aware, however, that Perrault's text also produces irony by thwarting readerly expectations. A feature of the fairy tale which contemporary culture has striven resolutely to forget is that the story contains a second part, in which the prince, by now married and having fathered two children by the princess, goes to war, leaving his family in the care of his mother.[47] The former queen, whom the story reveals is an ogress, instead abuses this maternal role by attempting to eat the princess and her children for supper, and then plotting to throw them into a vat of serpents. According to Green, the story concludes on a 'satisfactorily gruesome' note when the ogress submits herself to this fate.[48] The ending to the fairy tale also suggests, however, that Flaubert's portrayal of Emma, who angrily pushes her young daughter to the ground and dies a gruesome death of her own, exploits an irony of expectation already present in Perrault's text. Viewed through this adaptive lens, *Madame Bovary* encourages the reader to remember *La Belle au bois dormant* in order to appreciate fully Flaubert's own message that disillusionment is a permanently recurring state.

Just as Flaubert sought to rewrite his literary predecessors, Simmonds's *Gemma Bovery* and Doumenc's *Contre-enquête sur la mort d'Emma Bovary* share a determination to recreate *Madame Bovary* in the popular formats of their own time. As a graphic novel, *Gemma Bovery* exemplifies the aesthetic possibilities of a medium that during its seventy-year history has matured into a complex instrument of cultural expression.[49] Engaging the reader's ability to process both verbal and visual narration, Simmonds's prose switches, as Flaubert's does in *Madame Bovary*, between multiple perspectives. The voice of the fictional baker, Joubert, predominates, his name underscoring his role as narrator (Flau-/Jou-bert) and, by recalling the stem of the verb 'jouer', the playfulness of the text as a whole. The illustrations, meanwhile, drawn in grey pencil and black ink, are as attentive to the details of setting as they are to physical appearance and facial expressions, in particular the range of emotions conveyed by Gemma's eyes. In a more understated though no less innovative manner, Doumenc's reinvention of *Madame Bovary* exploits a genre which currently accounts for one in every four sales of novels in France: detective fiction. *Contre-enquête* despatches a grizzled detective, Delévoye, to Yonville on his final case before retirement. Accompanied by his young assistant Remi, Delévoye must investigate a claim that Emma Bovary's last words were 'assassinée, pas suicidée' (*CE*, p. 15). The mystery having been established in the time-honoured tradition of detective writing, Doumenc's narrative gathers clues and recollections from the key protagonists in the case, including Charles, Homais, Lheureux, Rodolphe and the Bovarys' maid, Félicité. At the same time, Doumenc operates a game of repetitions and reversals with *Madame Bovary* which challenges our own memory of the source text, exposing the fictional Larivière, whom Flaubert had declared 'irréprochable' (p. 327), as Emma's killer. Neither *Gemma Bovery* nor *Contre-enquête* simplifies *Madame Bovary*, therefore; rather, both problematise the novel by filtering it through the prism of current artistic modes.

Time functions as a key mechanism in these re-imaginings of *Madame Bovary*, and in their contrasting remembrance of the novel. In a manner reminiscent of adaptations of Zola for radio, Simmonds and Doumenc fragment Flaubert's artistic personality, highlighting those aspects of *Madame Bovary* that continue to resonate in their own era. *Gemma Bovery* recalls Flaubert's social satire, and his contempt for the French bourgeoisie. Simmonds turns this satirical spotlight on the British middle classes, mocking their rampant materialism, social vanity and emotional insensitivity. When Gemma makes her first appearance in the text, it is through the unflattering recollections contained in her diary. At the outset she vents her anger towards her former lover, Patrick, and her jealousy of his new wife Pandora, whom she despises for 'her bag, her tiny underwear, her smart background, her Cambridge degree, her ambition' (*GB*, p. 17). In describing Gemma's London lifestyle, Simmonds parodies the middle-class pretensions with which her heroine decorates her apartment in a 'Pre-Raphaelite-y style' (*GB*, p. 18). A further instalment reveals Gemma's snobbery as she discovers mouse droppings in Charlie's kitchen cupboards but delights nonetheless in the 'real eighteenth-century dust' (*GB*, p. 19) between his floorboards. Simmonds's reflections on contemporary life also run deeper, however, incorporating a feminist satire on the place of women in late twentieth-century society. Gemma, like Emma Bovary, is a woman of her times, enjoying a social mobility that remains forever beyond the reach of her nineteenth-century predecessor. As well as having her own career, she purchases the house in Bailleville without a mortgage, and with only a small financial contribution from her husband. Nevertheless, Gemma's independence also disguises the physical and emotional suffering she endures at the hands of the men in her life. Patrick betrays her, Charlie fails to understand her emotional needs, while Joubert, to whose obsession with *Madame Bovary* this chapter will return, manipulates her in the belief that her life will parallel that of her near-namesake Emma. Finally, when Gemma chokes on the bread that symbolises her affection for France, it is two men who are responsible for the accident – Patrick, who surprises her with a kiss while she is eating, and Charlie, who fights his rival instead of saving his wife. In her remembrance of *Madame Bovary*, Simmonds evokes Flaubert the class satirist, but also the writer who empathised with the situation of women in a patriarchal society.

If *Gemma Bovery* gives a new temporal context to the nineteenth-century class and gender criticism formulated by *Madame Bovary, Contre-enquête*, on the other hand, mirrors Flaubert's conceptualisation of writing as a means of understanding and reinvigorating the past. As a detective novelist, Doumenc, like his canonical predecessor, digs through time to uncover truths that can then be shaped into new fictions. As a thematic motif, this search for truth is initiated in the first part of the novel, when Remi and Delévoye, recently arrived from Rouen, begin their investigation by viewing Emma's body. After peeling back the sheet, they find that the autopsy has already been carried out, but that the corpse has still to be stitched up. 'L'incision de l'abdomen était précise,' writes Doumenc, 'montrant les principaux organes, préparés ou plutôt *parés* comme pour l'exposition dans quelque vitrine de boucherie de luxe' (*CE*, p. 35). The scene immediately recalls Achille Lemot's 1869 caricature of Flaubert, which depicted the novelist holding the heart of Emma Bovary on the point of his scalpel. For the realists, *Madame Bovary* was a work of medical precision that exposed the truths of the human heart. Having viewed Emma's body, which apparently hides no part of her anatomy from view, Remi and Delévoye must seek to uncover a criminal truth, sifting though evidence just as Flaubert himself had poured over documents and factual sources in order to produce a realist or 'true' fiction. The link between writing and detection is further reflected in the list of equipment that Delévoye instructs his assistant to bring with him to Yonville. As Remi asks whether there is anything he might have forgotten, his irascible superior reminds him of the essential tools of his trade: 'ton écritoire, tes plumes ou tes encres, tes rames de papier, enfin ce qu'il faut pour traiter la moindre affaire, puisque aujourd'hui c'est ainsi qu'on travaille!' (*CE*, p. 24). While the two detectives scour the town and its environs for clues, Doumenc excavates *Madame Bovary* in a manner that blurs the divide between fiction and reality. In a postface entitled 'Flaubert a-t-il menti?', the author speculates that Flaubert hid the fact of Emma Bovary's existence and the criminal investigation prompted by her death. 'Pour la véracité de son récit,' writes Doumenc, 'le malheur voulut qu'il [Flaubert] emprunta ses éléments non à de vrais témoins comme Delévoye ou Remi, mais aux articles faux ou hyprocrites publiés par le père Homais dans *Le Fanal de Rouen*' (*CE*, p. 183). *Contre-enquête* accuses Flaubert of having stumbled across Emma's story too late, and *Madame Bovary* of rewriting actual events that had themselves already been fictionalised. In ludic fashion, Doumenc redramatises the more serious truth that Flaubert adapted his own earlier sources.

While Simmonds and Doumenc remember different facets of Flaubert's creative aesthetic, both echo their source text by representing time as a fragmented construct. At the textual level, the illustrated format of *Gemma Bovery* breaks time into multiple units. As Scott McCloud explains, the use of sequential panels, in particular, a convention typical of comics but widely appropriated by graphic novelists including Simmonds, demands that the reader follow a series of distinct frames which together comprise the story: 'Comics panels fracture both time and space, offering a jagged, staccato rhythm of unconnected moments.'[50] The blank spaces, or 'gutters', between the panels emphasise the fragmented nature of the cartoon format, with the reader drawing on his or her imagination in order to fill in the gaps and follow the chronological thread of the narrative. By essence a fragmented text, *Gemma Bovery* reflects no less explicitly, then, on the processes through which time can be reconstructed. The opening page of the novel begins with an example of this authorial concern with reassembling the past. 'Gemma Bovery has been in the ground three weeks', sighs Joubert. 'People have begun to forget . . . But I – I never stop thinking of her. The nights are worst. If I sleep, I dream of her dead eyes which are the blue of stained glass' (*GB*, p. 2). By starting her novel with the announcement of Gemma's death, Simmonds states her intention to project backwards in time, piecing together the events that culminated in her heroine's demise. The metaphor of stained glass highlights both the reconstructive nature of this task, and Simmonds's desire to create a new story from the aesthetic materials provided by *Madame Bovary*. Moreover, this determination to rebuild the past invites immediate comparison with *Contre-enquête*, which as a detective novel focuses on making connections between the traces of an earlier crime. Alternating between third-person narration and fictional witness statements (some of which, such as Charles's first grief-stricken deposition, are themselves incomplete), Doumenc self-consciously repeats the noun 'fragments' in describing the clues to Emma's final hours. The autopsy on the young woman's body removes 'fragments de l'œsophage, de l'estomac, du duodénum', while the last dress she wore exhibits 'des fragments de ronces et d'épines' (*CE*, p. 37). Thus, Delévoye and Remi are engaged in what John Scaggs, referring to the principles of detective fiction as a genre, terms 'a quest to make sense of a fragmented, disjointed and largely unintelligible world' by connecting a crime committed in the past to a perpetrator who remains unidentified in the narrative present.[51]

Both Simmonds and Doumenc reflect on the difficulties of recreating time after it has elapsed. At the root of Gemma Bovery's disillusionment is her inability, like Emma, to stitch together the fragmented memories of the past into present happiness. As she furnishes the house in Bailleville, Simmonds's heroine attempts to 'recreate the atmosphere of a hundred years ago, as if peasants still lived there' (*GB*, p. 5). According to Constable, Gemma's subsequent frustration at living in a home that resembles an agricultural museum stems from a nostalgia 'for things she has never lost'. The past cannot be resurrected wholesale, Constable argues, when that which is supposedly authentic is, in fact, 'fake'.[52] As an extended flashback to her life in London demonstrates, however, Gemma also has a stock of personal memories and lived experiences that undermine her relationships with the present. In the chapter entitled 'Gemma's Past', Simmonds brings together seventeen instalments in which she recounts her heroine's biography prior to her departure for France. These episodes establish a pattern in which involuntary memories continue to impact negatively upon Gemma's attitude towards her physical environment. After her affair with Patrick ends, her apartment in Shepherd's Bush becomes intolerable to her as a place she associates with 'love sickness, crying, sitting about trying not to phone bloody Patrick' (*GB*, p. 18). Moving in with Charlie introduces her to Hackney, which her diary describes as 'really buzzy and full of artists, a great deli down the road and a pub where you can play *boules* outside' (*GB*, p. 19). However, just as Emma Bovary cannot erase the memory of Charles's first marriage simply because he removes his wife's bridal bouquet to the attic, Gemma, similarly, finds that she cannot cleanse the spaces she inhabits of unwanted reminders of previous times. The memory of Charlie's own first wife, Judi, who berates her ex-husband constantly over his relaxed parenting style and late maintenance payments, remains ever present, despite Gemma's attempts to distance herself from their squabbles. The Boverys' move to Normandy replays this struggle to exert control over the past. In Bailleville, Gemma discovers that unwelcome memories are as persistent as they were in London, not least in the form of the random reminders of British life with which her fellow expatriates Mark and Wizzy Rankin punctuate the local landscape, from their poolside red telephone boxes, to Wizzy's 'crappy "Bundles from Britain" – Marmite, Weetabix, last week's *Sunday Times*' (*GB*, p. 43). Unable to adapt to the present or reconcile herself with the past, Gemma finds herself trapped in the very space in which she had once identified the promise of fulfilment.

The fictional detectives in *Contre-enquête* prove more accomplished at harnessing the resources of time and memory. In keeping with the genre, Doumenc involves his reader in reconstructing the criminal's motive and movements. 'A condition of all classic detective fiction', writes Peter Brooks, is 'that the detective [should] repeat, go over again, the ground that has been covered by his predecessor.' The sleuth, adds Brooks, engages in 'a repetition and rehearsal . . . of what has already happened'.[53] An unseasonal snowfall facilitates this process of temporal repetition in *Contre-enquête*, preserving a set of footprints which lead across the fields, and which appear to match Emma's ankle boots. The retracing of these steps functions as a unifying metaphor in the text, connecting the investigation of the crime to the author's own adaptation of *Madame Bovary*. By revisiting, through interviews and witness statements, each of the key protagonists in Flaubert's story, Doumenc appeals to the reader's presumed familiarity with the source text, recalling, in particular, the defining personality traits of each of its characters. The rapacious Lheureux, for example, shows no remorse for triggering the seizure of the Bovarys' possessions, while Charles remains as baffled as ever by the reasons for his wife's death. 'Je l'adorais, je travaillais, je lui donnais tout ce qu'elle voulait,' he cries. 'Que pouvais-je de plus?' (*CE*, p. 58) Doumenc also follows Flaubert's example, however, by rewriting rather than imitating, retracing the narrative thread of *Madame Bovary* so as better to highlight the difference between his adaptation and the source text. As Remi and Delévoye conduct their interviews, the author playfully suggests that Flaubert selected too deliberately from actual events, omitting those details which did not fit with his ambition to '*faire mesquin* dans un roman qui, à la mode de l'époque, se voulait "naturaliste"' (*CE*, p. 185). By returning to focus on those moments in time which he claims Flaubert elided, Doumenc purports to offer a new perspective on the events and characters behind the 'real' story. As a result, the investigation reveals that Larivière, alone with Emma for a few short minutes while her neighbours went to fetch the priest, killed her by pressing on the carotid arteries under her jawline, thereby cutting off the blood supply to her brain. With an adaptive dexterity that returns us to the Kristevan image of the mosaic, Doumenc asserts the independence of his new work by interlocking this crime with another 'unseen' fragment of Flaubert's narrative. Exposing Larivière's motive, Remi discovers that the respected doctor killed

Emma because she fell pregnant by him during an orgy held at La Huchette. Appropriately in a novel predicated on the convention of repeating time, the mystery is solved using the footprints in the snow, and by the confession of Homais's eldest daughter Marie (a character invented by Doumenc), who reveals that she had borrowed Emma's boots in order to attend one of Rodolphe's debauched gatherings.

Anticipating Doumenc, Simmonds employs repetition as a strategy for asserting her own artistic independence. As Danielle Wargny has shown, *Gemma Bovery* replays, and in so doing modernises, numerous themes and plotlines from *Madame Bovary*, in particular Emma's marital boredom, and Charles's contentment with an existence his wife perceives as mediocre. In Simmonds's transposition of the novel to the 1990s, Gemma becomes similarly irritated with Charlie for spending hours happily ensconced in his workshop, where she imagines him 'playing Doom, Minesweeper and Solitaire on his computer . . . playing tunes on his teeth . . . and doing crosswords in the papers the Rankins save for him' (*GB*, p. 40). Wargny neglects to mention, however, that Simmonds also challenges her reader to remember *Madame Bovary* in order to engage fully with her reinvention of the text. In an interview with *The Comics Journal* in 2007, Simmonds stated that 'it shouldn't matter if the reader didn't know Flaubert's book, but if he or she did, they'd get just a little extra out of it [*Gemma Bovery*]'.[54] A closer reading suggests, in fact, that *Gemma Bovery* purposefully continues a trajectory initiated by Flaubert, who had demanded that readers apply their memory of sentimental fiction as a key to understanding the clichéd nature of Emma's fantasies. By the same token, Simmonds exploits the possibilities of her visual format to invoke the memory of *Madame Bovary*, but also to flag the differences between her text and its Flaubertian template. This tension between repetition and innovation is exemplified by one of the largest illustrations in the text, which depicts Gemma's vision of a future in which she at last finds happiness. The combination of elements, which include a successful interior design business and clients throughout Paris, aligns Gemma's fantasies with Emma's romantic longings. At the same time, Simmonds makes clear that this is a new textual landscape by representing her heroine's dreams as a bespoke tree. As Julie Sanders has noted, it is precisely in such departures from a given source that the 'most creative acts of adaptation and appropriation take place'.[55] In a drawing that reflects Simmonds's powerful sense of originality, the illustrated tree dominates a page of the text, requiring the reader to trace its various branches, each bearing the fruit of another fantasy, and the whole topped with a nest containing the child that Gemma imagines she might have with her current lover Hervé.

Simmonds's desire to situate *Madame Bovary* in a new time extends further, however, with the author casting Flaubert's novel as a protagonist in her own text. As soon as Gemma and Charlie arrive in Bailleville, the interfering Joubert announces to his wife: 'Martine! Martine! Dévines [*sic*] quoi! Guess what! Madame Bovary's next door!!! I mean it! They're English, but they're called BOVARY! BOVARY! . . . incroyable, non?' (*GB*, p. 32). Joubert's obsession with *Madame Bovary* drives the plot of *Gemma Bovery*, taking the form of what Lucile Farnoux, in her reading of this graphic novel, describes as 'la sur-fictionnalisation, qui installe une fiction première explicitement au cœur de la fiction seconde, non plus seulement comme modèle abstrait, mais comme élément agissant'.[56] Curious about his neighbour's spending habits, and then witnessing one of her meetings with Hervé, Joubert believes Gemma's life will take an identical course to Emma's, ending ultimately in her death: 'A bit of casual sex, a bit of overspending on one's Amex card, does that drive one to take arsenic? The idea was so mad, it's hard for me to explain why I feared it might be possible' (*GB*, p. 80). With each successive attempt at diverting Gemma's life narrative, however, he merely strengthens the parallels between her and her fictional counterpart. In the hope of precipitating an end to her affair with Hervé, Joubert sends Gemma a photocopy of the letter in which Rodolphe breaks off his elopement with Emma. The letter, however, serves only to weaken Gemma's emotional resistance to the renewed advances of Patrick, just as Emma's abandonment by Rodolphe makes her more receptive to Léon after they meet again unexpectedly at the theatre. Although Farnoux is correct to point out that *Madame Bovary* functions as a motor of Simmonds's plot, the crucial factor she omits from her discussion, however, is the selective nature of this remembrance. Despite Joubert's boasts that he is a man of culture, his own memory of the novel is fragmented. He conceives of *Madame Bovary* in terms of clichés – debts, adultery and death – and tries to persuade Gemma to read the text in the same terms. When Charlie rushes for help as his wife lies dead on her kitchen floor, Joubert's reaction betrays his failure to understand the situation outside of these narrow categories. 'I knew it!', he exclaims. 'Elle a pris de l'arsenic!!? . . . de la mort-aux-rats?' (*GB*, p. 95). The fictional baker's incomplete understanding of both fact and fiction (which itself evokes the memory of another baker, Rodolphe *Boulanger*, and his equally selective understanding of Emma's life narrative) nevertheless returns us to Simmonds's conceptualisation of the adaptive process. The task of recreating *Madame Bovary* involves her, too, in a selective remembrance of the novel. Mocking the extent to which our own era remembers *Madame Bovary* as an assortment of clichés, Simmonds also demonstrates that these thematic fragments are indispensable to exposing the originality of the new work that she constructs from them.

While *Madame Bovary* functions as the core reference in *Gemma Bovery* and *Contre-enquête*, both works borrow from across a wide temporal span. Simmonds and Doumenc adapt an array of earlier texts and traditions and, like Flaubert, encourage their readers to share in remembering the material being reworked. *Contre-enquête* belongs to a genre whose origins are rich and well established. As Jacotte Dugelet-Chignac suggests in her appraisal of the novel for *L'Express*, there is one antecedent, however, who stands out in this fictional investigation: 'Remi [est] plongé dans une ambiance à la Simenon, mène un jeu de pistes, dérange de soi-disant notables, perturbe le pouvoir hiérarchique de Rouen . . . à la recherche d'une vérité dissimulée parmi les suspects revêtus de masques divers.'[57] Doumenc reactivates themes, narrative devices and character types that had preoccupied Simenon throughout his career. At the heart of the mystery is the figure of the 'médecin assassin', and a crime that recalls Simenon's 1947 novel *Lettre à mon juge*, in which a doctor writes to the judge in his case to explain the circumstances that drove him to take, rather than save, another life.[58] A clearer indication of Doumenc's artistic debt to Simenon is the hostile small-town atmosphere that *Contre-enquête* has in common with the provinces as they are represented in the Inspector Maigret mysteries. In *L'Affaire Saint-Fiacre* (1932), one of the earliest of the seventy-five novels in this series, the fictional Maigret is confronted by a community riven by petty jealousies and class hatreds which have spilled over from earlier times, and in which families close ranks to protect their own interests. Doumenc's Yonville, which betrays the influence of its Flaubertian model as well as Simenon's own affection for Balzac's *Scènes de la vie de province*, fits clearly into this mould, as each of the characters attempts to stall the investigation. The resultant alibis and false accusations endow the plot with moments of suspense that are staples of the detective genre, and of the Maigret novels. Testing the boundaries of his own playfulness, Doumenc exploits these familiar plot devices in Remi's interview with Madame Homais, who confesses to murdering Emma because she was having an affair with her husband. 'Monsieur,' she declares, 'inutile de continuer ce jeu: j'avoue tout. Depuis longtemps je savais que mon mari entretenait une liaison coupable avec Mme Bovary. C'est moi qui l'ai tuée' (*CE*, p. 124). While exposing a psychological motive for the crime, another recurrent feature of Simenon's texts, this confession drives the second temporal plane on which detective fiction operates, urging the reader to race to solve the mystery before the 'narrative clock' runs out and the detective casts us back in time once more to explain how the murder was committed.[59]

Simmonds's borrowings, as befits the more recent origins of the graphic novel, have a much narrower temporal range. At the level of its illustrations, *Gemma Bovery* reflects the visual techniques of Japanese manga comics, an influence suggested by the oversized proportions of Gemma's eyes. In rewriting the sources that comprise her own intertextual mosaic, however, Simmonds also captures a specific moment in time, the 1990s, and engages with the cultural trends of that decade. The expatriate lifestyle, and the appeal of France in particular, had received fresh impetus in 1989 with the publication of Peter Mayle's *A Year in Provence.* This travel diary, in which a former marketing executive recounted his experience of moving to the Lubéron mountains with his wife, remained a best-seller throughout the 1990s. The central theme of the text, which Simmonds clearly appropriates, is the difficulty encountered by a British couple in adapting to the idiosyncracies of French life. The Mayles, like their fictional counterparts Gemma and Charlie, seek to build a new life from the fragmented materials of the past. The text focuses in large part on the restoration of their farmhouse, and the delays that, among other inconveniences, reduced their kitchen to rubble for months on end, and forced the couple to eat outside in sub-zero temperatures. With relentless good humour, Mayle shows every such problem being overcome. Describing Provençal builders, he writes: 'Despite their genial contempt for punctuality and their absolute refusal to use the telephone to say when they were coming or when they weren't, we could never stay irritated with them for long . . . In the end, they were worth waiting for.'[60] With similar aspirations towards a contented, stress-free lifestyle, Gemma conceives of France as a paint-by-numbers picture in which she stands smiling with Charlie, glass of wine in hand, as a brush fills in the image of the house behind them. This dream, however, like the paint-by-numbers, remains fragmented and incomplete, as Gemma considers the property 'too small, too dark. There was a brownish light, like living in a pencil box. There was no privacy. You heard people in the WC and when guests stayed the drains blocked' (*GB*, p. 36). The resultant stench serves as a reminder of another unwanted past, as Gemma is forced to sit in her rustic-style living room with a handkerchief pressed to her face. In satirical contrast to *A Year in Provence*, in which the Mayles become more settled in their new life as time progresses, Gemma's expatriate idyll disintegrates with each passing season. After her arrival in Normandy in June, when she delights in being able to buy fresh food in the village, Simmonds's heroine gradually becomes more disillusioned. By October, she is already shopping at a supermarket in Rouen, and in her diary entry for January complains bitterly about the lack of privacy in this 'bloody one-eyed place' (*GB*, p. 35). *Gemma Bovery* plays out *A Year in Provence* in reverse, satirising a British middle-class obsession with owning a second home abroad which for Simmonds had become a time-worn cliché ripe for parodic reinvention.

Simmonds and Doumenc continue Flaubert's adaptive technique, then, by fusing their own artistic concerns with the multiple resources of the textual past. In so doing, however, both of these recreations must defy time and challenge the finality of Emma's first literary death. That *Gemma Bovery* and *Contre-enquête* are linked by their fascination for a dead heroine is not surprising given that images of death and decay are so prevalent in *Madame Bovary*. Flaubert's Yonville is named after an abbey 'dont les ruines n'existent même plus' (p. 71), while the church, rebuilt towards the end of the reign of Charles X, has a wooden arch that has already begun to rot away. Outside in the cemetery, Lestiboudois grows potatoes that, like the literary adaptations whose artistry is nourished by *Madame Bovary*, are fertilised by the dead. This is a town in which time and history are forever being reduced to putrefying nothingness, a 'temporal logic', observes Elissa Marder, seen in the 'cotton factory that is rusted before it is finished and in Hippolyte's gangrenous leg that must be amputated after his ill-advised clubfoot operation'.[61] By the end of the novel, death threatens to consume the entire narrative as its eponymous heroine is followed to the grave by her husband. Emma's daughter Berthe, meanwhile, suffers another death, when her grandmother dies, condemning the orphaned child to the hardships of the cotton mill. Both Simmonds and Doumenc are haunted by the numerous ghosts produced by *Madame Bovary*. As Gemma succumbs to the temptations of debt and adultery, her creator draws the spectre of Emma Bovary closing in menacingly on the house in Bailleville. In *Contre-enquête*, Flaubert himself makes a ghostly appearance on a street corner in Yonville, only to vanish as Remi considers whether to approach him. A more obvious spectre in Doumenc's text is the mysterious carriage named the *Chasse Hellequin*, which the locals believe carries the souls of the previous year's dead. As interpreted by Richard Saint-Gelais, these apparitions reflect the extent to which *Madame Bovary* haunts the cultural consciousness of our own era. 'Le texte de Flaubert,' writes Saint-Gelais, 'ce texte lu, relu et réécrit sans cesse, . . . hante, non seulement une part de notre imaginaire, mais les univers fictifs qui s'y logent.'[62] In raising the spectre of *Madame Bovary*, however, Simmonds and Doumenc go further, asserting the value of their works as original creations in their own right. By bringing Emma back to life, they do what Flaubert's nineteenth-century novel cannot, and in so doing claim an artistic superiority over the source that provides their base material.

This chapter has sought to demonstrate the close relationship between fiction and adaptation in *Madame Bovary*. Flaubert's novel places adaptation at the heart of its thematic concerns, and that may in turn be one of the reasons why it has inspired numerous rewritings and recreations in literature. Emma is a woman who adapts badly, and whose failure to reconcile fiction and reality contrasts sharply with Flaubert's ability to exploit his literary inheritance. Time and temporality enable us to problematise the aesthetic implications of this dichotomy. At the level of plot, Emma finds herself not only trapped in a world of repetition and temporal stasis, but unable to piece together the fragmented memories from which she might otherwise construct a stable sense of identity. Foreshadowing the Kristevan image of the mosaic, Flaubert also engages himself in the task of reassembling the past. *Madame Bovary* repeats the assorted clichés and conventions of earlier fictions, but with a view to refitting them for a new era in which their effects range from the parodic to the satirical and purely literary. *Gemma Bovery* and *Contre-enquête sur la mort d'Emma Bovary* re-dramatise the functions of time in their source text. The fictional Gemma, like her nineteenth-century predecessor, struggles in vain to impose order on the fragmented recollections of the past, a skill in which the fictional detectives Remi and Delévoye prove more accomplished, as they retrace the steps that, in Doumenc's novel, lead to Emma's murder. Exploiting the popular fictional modes of their own time, Simmonds and Doumenc remember and adapt contrasting aspects of *Madame Bovary*. Combining her admiration for Flaubert's class satire with the more recent intertext of *A Year in Provence*, Simmonds ridicules the expatriate lifestyle that during the 1990s became a British middle-class obsession. By digging further into literary history, Doumenc connects Flaubert's archaeological search for hidden truths to the process of detection, highlighting, with a mixture of humour and seriousness, the adaptive process that spawned *Madame Bovary*. In the final analysis, however, these hypertexts and their canonical source return us to the question of what it means to create an original work of art. As Antoine Compagnon has shown, defining the 'new' was a recurrent preoccupation in nineteenth-century French culture.[63] Applied to the writing and rewriting of *Madame Bovary*, time and textual memory expose the ideal of an original creation as a myth. Instead, Flaubert, Doumenc and Simmonds share a conceptualisation of art as a series of open-ended connections between past and present, source and adaptation, in which the role of the novelist is to renew and make sense of what has come before.

Notes

1 For a recent critical appraisal of cinematic adaptations of the novel, see Mary Donaldson-Evans, *'Madame Bovary' at the Movies: Adaptation, Ideology, Context* (Amsterdam and New York: Rodopi, 2009).

2 For an exception to this critical neglect, see Richard Saint-Gelais, 'Spectres de *Madame Bovary*: la transfictionnalité comme remémoration', in Susan Harrow and Andrew Watts (eds), *Mapping Memory in Nineteenth-Century France* (Amsterdam: Rodopi, 2012), pp. 97–111.

3 '*Madame Bovary*: réécritures et expansions', *http://flaubert.univ-rouen.fr/derives/mb_reecri.php*, accessed 4 March 2010.

4 Lionel Archer, 'Réécritures et suites de *Madame Bovary*', *http://flaubert.univ-rouen.fr/derives/artic.php*, accessed 9 January 2010.

5 Astrid de Larminat, 'Rebondissement dans l'affaire Bovary', *www.lefigaro.fr/livres/2007/05/24/03005-20070524ARTFIG90242-rebondissement_dans_l_affaire_bovary.php*, accessed 6 January 2010.

6 Early versions of my analysis of these texts have been expanded considerably for this chapter. See Andrew Watts, 'Cracks in a cartoon landscape: fragmenting memory in Posy Simmonds's *Gemma Bovery*', *Essays in French Literature and Culture*, 48 (2011), 45–65, and Andrew Watts, 'Footsteps in the snow: piecing together time in *Madame Bovary* and *Contre-enquête sur la mort d'Emma Bovary*', *South Carolina Modern Language Review*, 10, 1 (2011), 13–34.

7 Gérard Genette, *Palimpsestes: la littérature au second degré* (Paris: Seuil, 1982), p. 16.

8 Woody Allen, 'The Kugelmass Episode', in *Side Effects* (New York: Ballantine, 1991; first published 1975), p. 72.

9 Genette, *Palimpsestes*, p. 431.

10 Robert Stam and Alessandra Raengo, *Literature and Film: A Guide to the Theory and Practice of Film Adaptation* (Oxford: Blackwell, 2005), p. 45.

11 Harold Bloom, *The Anxiety of Influence: A Theory of Poetry* (London, Oxford and New York: Oxford University Press, 1973), p. 154.

12 Genette, *Palimpsestes*, p. 16.

13 Julia Kristeva, *Semeiotikè: recherches pour une sémanalyse* (Paris: Seuil, 1969), p. 85.

14 On the use of names in *Gemma Bovery*, see Danielle Wargny, 'Emma, version BD, version GB', in Nicole Terrien and Yvan Leclerc (eds), *Le Bovarysme et la littérature de langue anglaise* (Rouen: Université de Rouen, 2004), pp. 209–18 (p. 209).

15 Liz Constable, 'Consuming realities: the engendering of invisible violences in Posy Simmonds's *Gemma Bovery*', *South Central Review*, 19, 4 (2002–3), 63–84 (64).

16 Paul Gravett, 'The Posy Simmonds interview', *The Comics Journal*, 286 (November 2007), 26–67 (58–9).

17 Andreas Huyssen, *Twilight Memories: Marking Time in a Culture of Amnesia* (New York and London: Routledge, 1995), p. 3.

18 Gustave Flaubert, *Correspondance*, ed. Jean Bruneau, 4 vols (Paris: Gallimard, Bibliothèque de la Pléiade, 1973–98), ii, p. 30.

19 Posy Simmonds, *Gemma Bovery* (London: Jonathan Cape, 2001), p. 36. All subsequent references to *Gemma Bovery* are parenthesised in the main text using the abbreviation *GB* followed by the relevant page number.

20 Philippe Doumenc, *Contre-enquête sur la mort d'Emma Bovary* (Arles: Actes Sud, 2007), p. 17. All subsequent references to this novel are parenthesised in the main text using the abbreviation *CE* followed by the relevant page number.

21 Gustave Flaubert, *Madame Bovary*, ed. Claudine Gothot-Mersch (Paris: Garnier, 1971), p. 38. All subsequent references to this edition are parenthesised in the main text with the relevant page number.

22 Christophe Ippolito, *Narrative Memory in Flaubert's Works* (New York: Peter Lang, 2001), p. 41.

23 Timothy Unwin, 'Gustave Flaubert, the hermit of Croisset', in Timothy Unwin (ed.), *The Cambridge Companion to Flaubert* (Cambridge: Cambridge University Press, 2004), pp. 1–13 (p. 5).

24 Gustave Flaubert and Maxime du Camp, *Par les champs et par les grèves,* in Gustave Flaubert, *Œuvres complètes,* ed. Jean Bruneau and Bernard Masson, 2 vols (Paris: Seuil, L'Intégrale, 1964), ii, p. 475.

25 Fay Weldon, 'Dying? I don't want to do that again', *Daily Telegraph,* 12 March 2009, *www.telegraph.co.uk/culture/4980926/Fay-Weldon-Dying-I-dont-want-to-do-that-again.html,* accessed 4 January 2010.

26 Stephen Heath, *Flaubert: 'Madame Bovary'* (Cambridge: Cambridge University Press, 1992), p. 55.

27 While Flaubert excises specific historical markers, Larry Duffy points out that, in its treatment of medicine and pharmaceutical practice, *Madame Bovary* is very much a work of the July Monarchy period. On this point, see Larry Duffy, '*Madame Bovary* and the institutional transformation of pharmacy', *Dix-Neuf,* 15, 1 (2011), 70–82.

28 Alain Buisine, 'Emma, c'est l'autre', in Alain Buisine (ed.), *Emma Bovary: figures mythiques* (Paris: Autrement, 1997), pp. 26–51 (p. 35).

29 Roger Huss, 'Some anomalous uses of the imperfect and the status of action in Flaubert', *French Studies,* 31 (1977), 139–48 (146).

30 Rosemary Lloyd, *Flaubert: 'Madame Bovary'* (London: Unwin Hyman, 1990), p. 132.

31 Kristeva, *Semeiotiké,* p. 98.

32 Gravett, 'The Posy Simmonds interview', 59.

33 William Vanderwolk, 'Memory and the transformative act in *Madame Bovary*', in Harold Bloom (ed.), *Emma Bovary* (New York and Philadelphia: Chelsea House, 1994), pp. 174–88 (p. 187).

34 Gustave Flaubert, Brouillons de *Madame Bovary,* vol. 1, folio 243v, *http://lettres.ac-rouen.fr/francais/BOVARY_6/accueil-0.html,* accessed 3 October 2010.

35 R. J. Sherrington contends that Flaubert suppressed this passage 'partly, no doubt, because it does not really fit Emma's experience'. R. J. Sherrington, *Three Novels by Flaubert: A Study of Techniques* (Oxford: Clarendon Press, 1970), p. 123.

36 Diana Knight, *Flaubert's Characters: The Language of Illusion* (Cambridge: Cambridge University Press, 1985), p. 58.

37 Tony Tanner, 'The "morselization" of Emma Bovary', in Harold Bloom (ed.), *Gustave Flaubert's 'Madame Bovary'* (New York and Philadelphia: Chelsea House, 1994), pp. 43–60 (p. 52).

38 Alison Finch, 'The stylistic achievements of Flaubert's fiction', in Timothy Unwin (ed.), *The Cambridge Companion to Flaubert,* pp. 145–64 (p. 147).

39 Julie Sanders, *Adaptation and Appropriation* (London and New York: Routledge, 2006), p. 4.

40 For an alternative discussion of these coincidences as a reflection of Scott's interest in chivalric romance, see Soledad Fox, *Flaubert and 'Don Quijote': The Influence of Cervantes on 'Madame Bovary'* (Brighton and Portland: Sussex Academic Press, 2010), pp. 140–2.

41 Charles de Mazade, 'Chronique de la quinzaine', *Revue des Deux Mondes*, 9 (1857), 211–23 (217–18).
42 For a discussion of these parallels, see Alan Raitt, 'Le Balzac de Flaubert', *L'Année balzacienne* (1991), 335–61.
43 Graham Falconer, 'Le travail de "débalzaciénisation" dans la rédaction de *Madame Bovary*', *Revue des Lettres Modernes*, 865–72 (1988), 123–56.
44 Honoré de Balzac, *La Comédie humaine*, ed. Pierre-Georges Castex, 12 vols (Paris: Gallimard, Bibliothèque de la Pléiade, 1976–81) ix, p. 654.
45 Anne Green, 'Flaubert and the Sleeping Beauty: an obsessive image', in Tony Williams and Mary Orr (eds), *New Approaches in Flaubert Studies* (Lewiston, Queenston, Lampeter: Edwin Mellen, 1999), pp. 65–80, and Juliette Frølich, 'Charles Bovary et *La Belle au bois dormant*', *Revue Romane*, 12, 2 (1977), 202–9.
46 Frølich points out the similarity of the two names in 'Charles Bovary et *La Belle au bois dormant*', 209.
47 Walt Disney's 1959 animated film *Sleeping Beauty* ends, for example, with the eponymous heroine awakened by the prince and reunited with her parents.
48 Green, 'Flaubert and the Sleeping Beauty', p. 66.
49 For a broader perspective on the evolution of the graphic novel as a genre, see Roger Sabin, *Comics, Comix and Graphic Novels: A History of Comic Art* (London and New York: Phaidon, 1996).
50 Scott McCloud, *Understanding Comics: The Invisible Art* (New York: HarperPerennial, 1994), p. 67.
51 John Scaggs, *Crime Fiction* (Abingdon: Routledge, 2005), p. 72.
52 Constable, 'Consuming realities', 71–2.
53 Peter Brooks, *Reading for the Plot: Design and Intention in Narrative* (New York: Knopf, 1984), pp. 24–5.
54 Gravett, 'The Posy Simmonds interview', 59.
55 Sanders, *Adaptation and Appropriation*, p. 20.
56 Lucile Farnoux, '*Gemma Bovery*: une adaptation de Flaubert en bande dessinée?', *Actas do Congresso Internacional da Associação de Literatura Comparada*, 3 (May 2001), *www.eventos.uevora.pt/comparada/VolumeIII/GEMMA%20BOVERY.pdf*, 10, accessed 1 September 2010.
57 Jacotte Dugelet-Chignac, 'La deuxième mort d'Emma', *www.lexpress.fr/culture/livre/fiches-de-lecture-sur-italique-contre-enquete-sur-la-mort-d-emma-bovary-italique_822218.html*, accessed 1 April 2011.
58 For a discussion of the 'médecin assassin' as a recurrent character type in Simenon's work, see Didier Gallot, *Simenon ou la comédie humaine* (Paris: France-Empire, 1999), pp. 102–7.
59 Charles J. Rzepka, *Detective Fiction* (Cambridge: Polity, 2005), p. 25.
60 Peter Mayle, *A Year in Provence*, illus. Leslie Forbes (London and New York: BCA, 1991; first published 1989), p. 41.
61 Elissa Marder, *Dead Time: Temporal Disorders in the Wake of Modernity (Baudelaire and Flaubert)* (Stanford, CA: Stanford University Press, 2001), pp. 158–9.
62 Saint-Gelais, 'Spectres de *Madame Bovary*', p. 111.
63 Antoine Compagnon, *Les Cinq Paradoxes de la modernité* (Paris: Seuil, 1990), pp. 15–45.

Chapter Four
Les Misérables, Theatre and the Anxiety of Excess

ANDREW WATTS

While theatre has had a key role in sustaining the cultural legacy of Hugo's work, some critics have treated stage adaptations of *Les Misérables* with contempt. This is particularly true of reactions to Alain Boublil and Claude-Michel Schönberg's West End musical, which on the one hand has been labelled 'overlong, overcomplex, [and] overdifficult'.[1] On the other hand it has been ridiculed for condensing Hugo's novel into a three-hour show: 'Toute violence dans la contestation et toute réflexion sérieuse en sont bannies,' writes Jean Gaudon disdainfully, 'la comédie musicale ayant pour fonction de remplacer le livre-action . . . par un divertissement lénifiant'.[2] Focusing on Boublil's and Schönberg's musical and José Pliya's 2001 play *Le Complexe de Thénardier*, the present chapter aims to show that there is more to theatrical adaptations of *Les Misérables* than these arguments suggest. At the level of plot, both works rearticulate Hugo's fascination with the theme of excess, and in particular his anxieties over the crime and lawlessness that *Les Misérables* associates with the chronically poor. Moreover, *Le Complexe de Thénardier* and the musical *Les Misérables*, in a manner reminiscent of the Diana Griffiths radio adaptation discussed in chapter one, call attention to the textual cropping that was integral to their own composition and that of their source text. In his 1936 essay 'The work of art in the age of mechanical reproduction', Walter Benjamin claimed that every original work of art has an aura of authenticity that is gradually stripped away by the processes of copying and reproduction.[3] As Boublil and Schönberg and Pliya strive to accommodate the vastness of *Les Misérables* within their own medium, they, too, strip away the novel's famous digressions and tendency towards narrative excess. However, while paring down this canonical source, both dramas reproduce the adaptive aura of Hugo himself, who in *Les Misérables* trims and refines the work of his predecessors in an attempt to resolve his anxiety over the multiple forms of excess that his novel represents.

Le Complexe de Thénardier and *Les Misérables* provide valuable case studies through which to explore the relationship between adaptation and excess. Having originated as a French concept album in 1980, the English-language version of Boublil's and Schönberg's musical opened at the Barbican Theatre in London in October 1985. Like its source text, the musical *Les Misérables* recounts the tale of the former convict Jean Valjean, who after stealing from the kindly priest Myriel resolves to transform himself into an honest man. As Edward Behr observes, the musical functions as 'a leaner . . . version of Hugo's plot'.[4] Working in tandem with producer Cameron Mackintosh and a team drawn in part from the Royal Shakespeare Company (RSC), Boublil and Schönberg recreated the novel in twenty-nine musical numbers, omitting or reducing substantially Hugo's discussions of politics and religion, the Battle of Waterloo and the state of the Paris sewers. However, while deeming these aspects of the narrative largely superfluous to the needs of plot and character development, Boublil and his collaborators also indulged their own appetite for creative excess. Under the guidance of Mackintosh, whose earlier production credits include Lionel Bart's *Oliver!* and Andrew Lloyd Webber's *Cats*, *Les Misérables* combines spectacular stage effects with powerful orchestration and mass choral numbers. Moreover, since transferring to the West End and Broadway, Boublil's and Schönberg's production has exceeded the boundaries of its own medium by impacting upon other spheres of social, political and cultural life. As Paul Prece and William A. Everett point out, songs from *Les Misérables* have been adapted for a variety of different contexts. During the 1992 US presidential elections, the American Democratic Party reworked 'One Day More' as its campaign song, while in the 1980s 'Empty Chairs at Empty Tables' featured as a poignant soundtrack for the work of AIDS charities.[5] As these examples demonstrate, *Les Misérables* is not only a musical steeped in artistic excess, but an adaptation that continues to transcend the theatrical purpose for which it was first conceived.

While excess characterises the production values and wider cultural impact of the musical, *Le Complexe de Thénardier* focuses on excess as a dramatic theme. Born in Benin, José Pliya embarked on a career as a teacher before *Le Complexe de Thénardier* won the Prix du Jeune Théâtre awarded by the Académie française in 2003. A straight drama rather than a musical, the play depicts the relationship between a servant girl, Vido, and La Mère, the mistress of the household in which she works. Pliya has claimed that the situation of his two protagonists 'n'a aucune appartenance à l'œuvre de Victor Hugo', and that he chose the title of his work long before realising its artistic implications.[6] The title nevertheless recalls the rapacious innkeepers of *Les Misérables* and their exploitation of the innocent child Cosette. *Le Complexe de Thénardier* can be seen to rework this single strand of Hugo's plot, which Pliya transposes to an unspecified time and place. La Mère cultivates an obsessive attachment to Vido, whom she has rescued from a war-torn landscape and the threat of genocide. When the servant announces her intention to leave, La Mère resolves to prevent her from doing so. Exhibiting none of the lavish staging of its musical counterpart, *Le Complexe de Thénardier* reflects upon the other forms of excess – violence, selfishness and the desire for power and control – that overshadow human relationships. In so doing, Pliya demonstrates, in a much more understated fashion than Boublil and Schönberg, the potential for breaking what Benjamin termed the ties of 'parasitical dependence' linking a reproduction to its original.[7] Since the first stage production of *Le Complexe de Thénardier* opened at the Théâtre du Rond-Point in Paris in 2002, critics have praised Pliya for dramatising the questions raised by *Les Misérables* independently of the context of nineteenth-century France. As Henri Scepi writes, with specific reference to the example of *Le Complexe de Thénardier*, 'il [le théâtre] s'est emparé de cette œuvre [*Les Misérables*] pour en faire varier les résonances politiques et en décentrer les perspectives poétiques'.[8] In its engagement with the extreme violence of war and genocide, *Le Complexe de Thénardier* exceeds the original context and time of the source novel to address new social and political concerns.

The interest in excess that Pliya shares with Boublil and Schönberg extends to the adaptive strategies that all three dramatists employ in reinventing *Les Misérables*. *Le Complexe de Thénardier* and the West End musical throw into relief Hugo's own understanding of authorship as a cumulative activity that involved trimming and refining earlier texts and genres. In *William Shakespeare* (1864), Hugo described the novel as a hybrid form: 'L'épique, le lyrique et le dramatique amalgamés,' he claimed, 'le roman est ce bronze'.[9] Evoking the image of the metal alloy, Hugo's statement further invites us to contemplate the novelist as a sculptor who shapes existing material and smoothes away its rough edges to create a new work of art. Boublil and Schönberg echo this creative praxis in their own version of *Les Misérables.* In addition to cropping elements of the source text, their production engages with an abundance of literary and theatrical reference points. In particular, the co-directors of the original London production, Trevor Nunn and John Caird, appropriated techniques borrowed from their own previous work for the RSC. Indeed, it was the pair's collaboration on another large-scale project, a nine-hour adaptation of *The Life and Adventures of Nicholas Nickleby* in 1980, which persuaded Mackintosh that Nunn and the RSC could cope with the demands of bringing Hugo's novel to the stage. 'The whole production', wrote Sheridan Morley in response to the opening of *Les Misérables* in 1985, 'reflects what Nunn and his co-director have learnt from *Nickleby* and *Cats* and their Shakespeare-based musicals'.[10] For Pliya, the challenge of creating a drama based on the suffocating relationship between master and servant required him to draw upon literary sources of his own, among them the fairy tale of Cinderella and Perrault's treatment of domesticity and exploitation. Viewed through this adaptive lens, it is clear that *Le Complexe de Thénardier* and the Boublil and Schönberg musical both elide substantial portions of Hugo's plot while simultaneously refining the artistic materials of earlier authors, texts and theatrical productions.

In reworking *Les Misérables* for their own medium, Pliya, Boublil and Schönberg are connected by a novel that proves especially well suited to the stage. The relationship between *Les Misérables* and the theatre is a long-standing one. While Charles Hugo produced the earliest known dramatic adaptation of the work in 1863, other recreations have since followed, spanning a range of theatrical genres. Among those fields to have shown particular enthusiasm for *Les Misérables* is opera. In Ukraine, Stanislaw Duniecki adapted the text under the title *Nedznicy* in 1864, while Camillo Bonsignore's *Les Misérables* (US, 1925) and Vincenzo Michetti's and Emidio Mucci's *La Vagabonda* (Italy, 1933) confirm that others recognised the potential for setting the novel to music before Boublil and Schönberg. It is tempting to assume that *Les Misérables* is an obvious target for theatrical adaptation, as it has been for film, television and radio.[11] The novel is well known, and continues to sell in large numbers. According to Guy Rosa, 'c'est même [le livre] le plus lu de notre littérature, non seulement à l'étranger mais en France, où aucun autre n'atteint le chiffre de son tirage'.[12] However, while the enduring popularity of *Les Misérables* is clear, theatrical interest in the novel has not been motivated solely by commercial imperatives. On the contrary, the connections between *Les Misérables* and the theatre run much deeper, to a vision of art and its potential for combating the excesses of contemporary society that Pliya and Boublil and Schönberg share with Hugo himself, one that extends beyond the desire to attract paying audiences to the theatre.

One of the foremost reasons for which *Les Misérables* lends itself so readily to the stage is the fact that drama and theatricality function as key themes in the novel itself. Anne Ubersfeld writes that 'le théâtre est partout présent dans *Les Misérables*'.[13] At the level of plot, the theatre provides an important source of entertainment for several of the characters. While the fictional Gillenormand prefers opera and classical drama, his grandson Marius, together with the student members of the A.B.C. Society, enjoy the popular melodramas of the day, not least *L'Auberge des Adrets*. The street urchin Gavroche shares their affection for the stage villain Robert Macaire and the actor who had made the role his own. 'Je vous mènerai à Frédérick Lemaître,' Gavroche tells his brothers. 'J'ai des billets, je connais des acteurs, j'ai même joué une fois dans une pièce.'[14] However, theatricality in *Les Misérables* is by no means restricted to the physical confines of the stage. The world of the theatre spills over into Hugo's representation of everyday life. Masks, disguises and multiple identities abound in the text. Jean Valjean becomes a mere number, 24601, when he enters prison, and following his release works his way through a succession of aliases, from Monsieur Madeleine to Ultime Fauchelevent and Monsieur Leblanc.[15] Hugo's depiction of Thénardier and the Patron-Minette gang further illustrates the extent to which theatre permeates the wider world in *Les Misérables*. At his inn in Montfermeil, Thénardier plays the role of genial host in order to separate his customers from their money. The landlord's appetite for drama increases when he relocates to Paris under another pseudonym, Jondrette. Out of a mixture of greed and desperation, he sends a begging letter to Valjean, signing himself 'Fabantou, artiste dramatique' (p. 541), and attempts to elicit further sympathy for his plight by having his daughter Azelma smash a window in the family's apartment in order to heighten the impression of poverty and excessive squalor. As Ubersfeld explains, 'masque, déguisement, tragi-comédies aident les misérables à manger, tout en les amusant: le théâtre est à la fois leur culture et leur pain quotidien; ils le voient et ils le font'.[16] Theatricality in *Les Misérables* not only exceeds the boundaries of the stage, but functions as an instrument with which Hugo's protagonists confront the extremes of crime, poverty and injustice that surround them.

If drama and theatricality are central to the plot of *Les Misérables*, they also underpin the author's creative aesthetic. Hugo's ambitions as a dramatist were largely exhausted by the time he began work on *Les Misérables* in 1845. His most well-known known plays, *Hernani* (1830), *Lucrèce Borgia* (1833) and *Ruy Blas* (1838), were behind him, while *Les Burgraves*, a drama about the ancient robber barons of the Rhineland, had closed in April 1843 after only thirty-three performances. *Les Misérables* reflects Hugo's disappointment at this failure, as well as his interest in adapting theatrical conventions to an extent that could no longer be accommodated by the stage. Kathryn Grossman has shown that the text 'invokes many schemas, practices and techniques' of the theatre, 'and then plays off them in surprising ways'.[17] Much of the novel's dramatic impact stems from its exploitation of tragedy. While the character of Jean Valjean represents a departure from the high-born protagonists favoured by classical Greek tragedy, *Les Misérables* conforms in other respects to Aristotle's definition of the genre as one that should inspire a mixture of fear and pity in its audience.[18] Fantine's descent into poverty, marked by the sale of her hair, teeth and then the rest of her body into prostitution, is clearly capable of arousing such emotions. At the same time, Hugo lightens the darkness of his narrative with moments of comedy, the majority of which are provided, as in the West End and Broadway musical, by Thénardier. Cast in the traditional burlesque role of the *trompeur trompé*, the innkeeper exhibits an unshakeable belief in his own sense of cunning, only to be outwitted in each of his encounters with Valjean.[19] As we have seen in the case of Balzac, however, the most visible indication of Hugo's artistic debt to the theatre is his dexterity in adapting the conventions of melodrama. As characterised by

Peter Brooks in his seminal discussion of this 'mode of excess', melodrama involves 'the use of coups de théâtre, of the unexpected and the fortuitous, the hyperbolic and grandiloquent'.[20] *Les Misérables* is replete with precisely such moments of shock, exaggeration and intense pathos. Among the scenes in which Hugo seeks to create 'une émotivité qui réenracine le lecteur dans des passions vitales et simples', Fantine's arrest for retaliating against a bourgeois who mocks her in the street and Valjean's sudden appearance to rescue Cosette on Christmas Eve both fit this melodramatic mould.[21] For the author, however, melodrama is rarely an end in itself, but an instrument with which to create new artistic effects. The ending of the novel, to which this chapter will return, is notable in this regard, for, while the wedding of Marius and Cosette appears to fulfil the melodramatic requirement of a happy ending, the couple soon forget Valjean, who lies in a corner of Père-Lachaise cemetery that no one visits, 'parce que l'herbe est haute et qu'on a tout de suite les pieds mouillés' (p. 997). Familial harmony is restored in keeping with the conventions of melodrama, but is tainted by selfishness and neglect. As this final chapter of the novel makes clear, Hugo does not simply adapt the melodramatic mode, but does so in ways that are often subtle, and that form part of his engagement with a much broader array of theatrical genres.

While the inherent theatricality of *Les Misérables* makes the text a highly suitable candidate for dramatic adaptation, theatre also provides a natural home for Hugo's sensitivity to the social excesses of crime and poverty. In the epigraph to *Les Misérables*, the novelist formulated a plea on behalf of those who lived beyond the margins of French society. 'Tant qu'il y aura sur la terre ignorance et misère,' he declared, 'des livres de la nature de celui-ci pourront ne pas être inutiles' (p. 49). Earlier, in the 1832 preface to *Le Dernier Jour d'un condamné*, Hugo warned the privileged against indifference to 'ces misérables que vous regardez à peine . . . dans la rue', while his visits to the prisons of Brest and Toulon, in 1834 and 1839 respectively, sharpened his awareness of the cyclical relationship between poverty and the desperation that caused many to break the law.[22] If Hugo is well known as a champion of the poor, only recently, however, have the links between his social conscience and musical theatre begun to receive critical attention. According to Paul Prece and William A. Everett, the West End and Broadway show melds Hugo's long-standing belief in the educative value of art with the traditions of French grand opera. In the first half of the nineteenth century, grand operas such as Meyerbeer's hugely successful *Les Huguenots* (1836) established a format predicated on relating 'some sort of socio-political message through a grandiose medium that combined music, drama, dance, lavish costumes and set designs and special effects'.[23] The musical *Les Misérables* appears as a modern incarnation of this genre, as Boublil and Schönberg use their own blend of music and lyrics to rail against social injustice and class oppression. Thus, when the factory workers at Montreuil gather to sing 'At the End of the Day', their words express bitter frustration at the harsh conditions they are forced to endure: 'At the end of the day you're another day older, / And that is all you can say for the life of the poor.' Other songs voice more optimistic hopes for the future. On the eve of the 1832 uprising, Enjolras and the student rebels declare their faith in the possibility of a better tomorrow: 'Every man will be a king', state the lyrics of 'One Day More'. 'There's a new world for the winning, / There's a new world to be won.' In both numbers, Hugo's social sensibility coincides with Boublil and Schönberg's own reinvention of the grand opera genre, according to which the audience should be equipped with a lesson that can be carried over into life beyond the theatre.

Like the musical *Les Misérables, Le Complexe de Thénardier* presents its audience with the vision of a better world and, in particular, one that is free of the violent excesses of war and genocide. While refusing to give his work a precise temporal or geographical setting, Pliya makes pointed references to the mass killings provoked by conflicts throughout the twentieth century, and the loss of individual and collective freedom that these caused for certain ethnic and religious groups. 'Le "complexe de Thénardier" existe,' reads the epigraph to the play. 'On a pu le recontrer au cours du siècle dernier, dans l'Europe occupée, au Rwanda, dans l'ex-Yougoslavie . . . Et chez moi, dans la maison de mon enfance.'[24] Having been rescued from the threat of such extreme violence, the fictional Vido talks compulsively of wishing to find her parents, and of savouring the peace that she wants to believe has now been restored: 'Dans ma vie de recluse, c'est un bien bel espoir. Il me faut sortir. Voir le soleil en face. Voir les fleurs. Il me faut m'en aller' (*CT*, p. 20). One of the most striking and recurrent images through which the character expresses her desire for freedom is that of the 'homme aux cheveux bleus' (*CT*, p. 18) from whom she claims to have learned that her homeland is no longer at war. In an interview with Philippa Wehle, who translated *Le Complexe de Thénardier* into English under the title *Trapped* in 2005, Pliya explained that children in Benin commonly refer to UN peacekeepers, with their distinctive blue helmets, as 'soldats aux cheveux bleus'. Moreover, he attributed Vido's description of the soldier as having 'le fort accent du Dakota' (*CT*, p. 11) to her thirst for independence. 'Pour une personne recluse,' Pliya suggested, '[le Dakota], c'est dehors, l'exotisme et le rêve fantasme d'une liberté'.[25] That the dramatist associates freedom with a chimera is nevertheless significant, for, while Boublil and Schönberg seek to inspire their audience to create a fairer society, Pliya is careful to undercut Vido's hopes of an end to the persecution that she and her people have endured. In her determination to retain control over the girl, La Mère warns her that the blue-haired soldier was nothing more than a dream, and that the war rages on. When Vido leaves in spite of this emotional pressure, Pliya confirms neither what kind of future awaits her beyond the suffocating walls of the house, nor whether the fighting is indeed over. Instead, the play ends with La Mère's suicide and her deeply pessimistic conclusion that 'il n'y a pas d'humanité' (*CT*, p. 48). Thus, while Pliya joins with Boublil and Schönberg in lamenting the violence of the contemporary world, it is clear that he does not automatically share their faith in the possibility of social and political harmony.

Alongside the social conscience echoed by both the West End musical and *Le Complexe de Thénardier*, Hugo's enthusiasm for artistic excess has actively facilitated the adaptation of his novel for the stage. Few descriptions of *Les Misérables* avoid making reference to the novel's physical and narrative dimensions, typically describing it as 'epic', 'vast' and 'immense'. The use of these terms is certainly justified, and not only because, as Graham Robb suggests, the work 'takes a noticeable percentage of one's life to read'.[26] *Les Misérables* is a novel that, in more than one respect, appears to strain at its own seams. The action spans eighteen years, from Valjean's release from prison in 1815, through the failed insurrection of 1832, and ends with the hero's death the following year. In this sweeping narrative, Hugo deals with a catalogue of themes that are broad both in and of themselves: crime, poverty, romance, post-Revolutionary politics and spiritual redemption, to name but the most salient. The author's penchant for engaging in digressions on most of these subjects requires a further investment of time and effort from the reader. Even after excising some of these passages, the English translation in the Penguin Classics series runs to more than 1,200 pages, including a preface in which the translator, Norman Denny, makes no attempt to disguise his irritation at Hugo's apparent verbosity: 'He [Hugo] is in many ways', writes Denny, 'the most exasperating of writers – long-winded, extravagant in his use of words (it is not uncommon to find eight or ten adjectives appended to a single noun), sprawling and self-indulgent'.[27] However, the narrative extravagance that Denny views as a defect in *Les Misérables* is also key to understanding the novel's suitability for the theatre, a medium which has thrived on Hugo's tendency towards excess. This is especially true in the case of stage musicals, and the subgenre of West End and Broadway shows to which Jessica Sternfeld has given the collective title 'megamusicals'. A trend that grew out of the success of Andrew Lloyd Webber's rock opera *Jesus Christ Superstar* in 1971 and that reached its peak in the 1980s with *Cats, Miss Saigon* and *The Phantom of the Opera*, the megamusical quickly established its own aesthetic. As Sternfeld explains:

> A megamusical . . . is usually sung-through and features an epic, historically situated, but timeless plot staged on a fancy set. Of course, the composers of megamusicals did not invent these features . . . But the megamusical is the first twentieth-century musical theatre genre to combine these factors with such consistency.[28]

Opening during a decade now synonymous with greed and financial excess, the musical *Les Misérables* represents the apogee of the megamusical genre. Sung throughout with barely a single break for applause, the West End production retains the temporal span of the source text. Moreover, original set designer John Napier provided the 'physical hugeness' that the genre demands, in the form of an interlocking barricade made from furniture and other random pieces of debris.[29] Far from being intimidated by Hugo's novel, the musical *Les Misérables* translates the source text into a medium already founded on a desire for vast scale and elaborate spectacle.

However, while Boublil and Schönberg share Hugo's appetite for creative excess, the symbiosis between *Les Misérables* and musical theatre is not restricted to their common artistic features. The advertising campaign that preceded the publication of the novel in May 1862 was relentless, and has since provided the West End and Broadway with a template for marketing the show to a global audience. Having sold the rights to *Les Misérables* to the Belgian publishers Lacroix and Verboeckhoven for the enormous sum of 300,000 francs, Hugo fuelled public interest in his work with the 'practised skill of the born media star', advising on the content of press releases and dictating which quotations from the text should be released to newspapers across Europe and the Americas.[30] When the first volume, *Fantine*, appeared in Paris, the initial run of 48,000 copies sold out within hours. According to Edward Behr, 'bookshop owners, commissionaires with horsedrawn vehicles and delivery-boys pushing carts and barrows literally fought for copies of *Les Misérables* the day the Paris printing-shop, Pagnerre, finally began distribution'.[31] The Boublil and Schönberg musical has replicated the scope and success of this marketing strategy, grossing more than £2.7 billion in worldwide ticket sales in the decade following its move from the Barbican to the West End. This achievement owes much, claims Sternfeld, to producer Cameron Mackintosh's Hugolian determination to sell the musical 'like any other product, complete with logos, theme songs and advertisements saturating newspapers, radio and television'.[32] Central to this mammoth commercial operation is the image of Cosette that has become the musical's most recognisable emblem. Based on Emile Bayard's 1862 lithograph, the logo crops an illustration that appeared in the first edition of the novel, in which the girl is shown outside Thénardier's inn dressed in rags and holding a broom that dwarfs her tiny frame. Adapted by the London advertising agency Dewynters, the image has featured on posters for the musical *Les Misérables* around the world. In publicity materials for the Norwegian production, Cosette dons a Viking helmet. In Iceland she wears a scarf and ear muffs, and in advertisements for the 1989 outdoor concert in Australia she appeared upside down. With each transformation of Bayard's image, Mackintosh has continued the mass-marketing that underpins the success of the musical, and that echoes the commercial acumen of Hugo himself.

While Mackintosh has saturated the theatrical marketplace with advertising and merchandise for *Les Misérables*, his creative contribution to the musical has nevertheless been largely undervalued. In a reversal of Hugo's orchestration of the media campaign behind his novel, Mackintosh has exceeded the role of theatrical producer to exert a powerful influence on the artistic development of the West End show. That he would be involved in every aspect of the musical was clear to Boublil and Schönberg when they met the producer in 1982 to discuss selling the rights to an English-language version of *Les Misérables*. As Boublil remembers:

> He [Mackintosh] was clever and generous enough to understand immediately that what we had written was the bulk of the musical, and to convince us at the same time that it needed some improvement . . . All the way he brought his artistic knowledge to it as well as his financial clout and managerial knowledge.[33]

Mackintosh's decision to produce *Les Misérables* at the Barbican, in particular, enabled him to access the theatrical and financial resources of the RSC, and to draw the cast from actors trained in classical theatre (among them Roger Allam, who would take the role of Javert, and Alun Armstrong as Thénardier). Between the first preview of *Les Misérables* and its official opening, Mackintosh would also press for the length of the performance to be cut by an hour, a move that resulted in the elimination of several potentially confusing scenes in which Javert pursues Valjean across Paris. As his role in the creative development of the production showed, Mackintosh was quick to tame the artistic exuberance of his collaborators in order to present the audience with a more streamlined show.

If the advertising drive that accompanied the publication of *Les Misérables* can be seen to foreshadow the ongoing – and for Jean Gaudon excessive – commercialisation of the musical, Hugo's interest in music similarly anticipates the reworking of his novel for musical theatre. Despite the persistent assumption that he disliked music – a myth fuelled by his supposed wish that none of his poetry should be set to music after his death – Hugo possessed a keen musical sensibility, and showed particular appreciation for the works of Gluck, Mozart and Beethoven.[34] In 1836, having previously rejected Berlioz's and Meyerbeer's proposals for an operatic version of *Notre-Dame de Paris*, he also wrote the libretto for Louise Bertin's grand opera *La Esmeralda*. Though the run lasted for only six performances, Hugo's willingness to collaborate in this production suggests that he was by no means hostile towards a genre that would inform the development of twentieth-century musical theatre. Analysis of his prose fiction reveals, moreover, that he punctuated his narratives with references to songs, music and the sound of musical instruments. As Arnaud Laster writes of *Notre-Dame de Paris*, 'de nombreuses pages . . . attestent une sensibilité auditive très développée et une grande attention au phénomène sonore'.[35] Songs and music feature prominently in *Les Misérables*, where they support a range of dramatic effects. After leaving Digne with the bishop's silver, Valjean hastens through an otherwise silent countryside when he hears the voice of 'un petit savoyard . . . qui chantait' (p. 124). The former convict's subsequent encounter with Petit-Gervais proves crucial to his decision to make an honest life, for, after stealing the child's treasured coin, Valjean is tormented by the sound of his victim sobbing in the distance. This episode sets the tone for Hugo's use of songs to generate pathos elsewhere in the text, not least during Fantine's struggle to regain custody of her daughter. As she lies on her deathbed, the despairing mother recalls a lullaby with which she used to sing Cosette to sleep, and whose words encapsulate her hopes for a more prosperous future: 'Nous achèterons de bien belles choses / En nous promenant le long des faubourgs' (p. 221). Upon learning of her mother's death, Cosette, in turn, sings the anguished refrain 'ma mère est morte' as Thénardier and his customers carry on drinking, wholly indifferent to her grief: 'Les ivrognes chantaient toujours leur chanson, et l'enfant, sous la table, chantait aussi la sienne' (p. 322). In addition to reinforcing these moments of high emotion, songs and musical instruments reflect the enormity of the struggles in which Hugo's characters become embroiled. Thus, in his depiction of the 1832 riots, the author represents the barricades not only as physical defences, but as walls of sound: 'on y entendait les cris du commandement, les chansons d'attaque, des roulements de tambour, des sanglots de femme et l'éclat de rire ténébreux des meurt-de-faim' (p. 823). Like the barricade, *Les Misérables* reverberates with the sound of music and song as Hugo seeks to induce a state of emotional catharsis in his reader.

Boublil's and Schönberg's version of *Les Misérables* echoes the source text in striving to overwhelm the audience with the scale of its musical effects. Sheridan Morley writes: 'There is an energy and an operatic intensity here which exists in the work of no British composer, past or present: the sense of a nation's history being channelled through trumpets and drums and violins and guitars and 'cellos.'[36] While Morley is correct to highlight the range of sounds and instruments used in the production, *Les Misérables* nevertheless offers spectators much more than a barrage of orchestral noise. Indeed, a closer reading of the score reveals that Boublil and Schönberg build complex vocal melodies and musical patterns 'which pop up in different forms, lengths and guises' throughout the show.[37] The most prominent example of this technique is the music from the Prologue, in which the prisoners at Toulon are shown working in a chain gang in the blistering heat. The low, rhythmic chords express the shame and suffering of the convicts, whose toil brings them ever closer to death: 'Look down, look down, / You'll always be a slave. / Look down, look down, / You're standing in your grave.' The same music occurs later in act I, when a chorus of beggars calls upon the privileged – and by extension the audience – to show greater consideration for the poor: 'Look down and see the beggars at your feet. / Look down and show mercy if you can.' The solemn music also intones during the building of the barricade and the subsequent fighting, while elements of the same piece, notes Sternfeld, recur at more than twenty different junctures in the show.[38] Such iterations are crucial to the cohesion of each performance as fragments of music are carried over from one section to another. Lyricist Herbert Kretzmer describes the resultant effect:

> The reverberations set in motion in the mind of the audience are that they are combining the melodic cadences of [a particular] tune into a mental, almost semi-remembered dream landscape, which they couldn't put a memory to, but something inside their recent memory is telling them that they've heard that song before.[39]

Thus, when the music that accompanies Fantine's death recurs later in Eponine's 'On My Own', the repetition is intended to link the fates of the two characters, as Fantine laments having abandoned her daughter to the Thénardiers, before Eponine sings of her love for Marius, which she knows will never be reciprocated. As opposed to assaulting spectators with an over-abundance of sound, *Les Misérables* reflects a deep understanding of the artistic effects that can be generated from the recurrence and repetition of musical structures.

The intricate musical framework of *Les Misérables* extends to the use of voice, and to the tension between excess and economy that underpins the lyrics for the production. Each of the roles in the show lends itself to a different vocal register. While the part of Valjean demands the high octave range of a tenor, that of Javert typically requires a classical baritone capable of adding dramatic weight to the policeman's intractable pursuit of his former prisoner. The part of Fantine, claims Kurt Gänzl, 'was composed in the equivalent feminine vein and colour, and the juvenile Eponine was for a plaintive country-rock voice'.[40] The chorus adds a further contrasting layer to these different registers, functioning as the collective voice of the poor, and building the intensity of the sound projected from the stage.[41] However, as the show exploits these multiple voices and vocal registers, so it also reduces lyrics to their most essential semantic components. As Kretzmer explains, in reference to the decision that saw him replace poet James Fenton as lyricist for the Barbican production, 'a musical must be accessible, must be instantly understood. There is no time for the audience to dwell on obscurities.'[42] Kretzmer's determination to produce lyrics that conveyed deep emotion while remaining free of what he considered poetic excess is particularly evident in the song 'Bring Him Home'. This number, in which Valjean pleads for God to spare Marius's life after the young man is wounded on the barricade, remained incomplete until seventeen days before the opening of the Barbican show, when co-director John Caird suggested that the song evoked the idea of a prayer. Caird's observation encouraged Kretzmer to penetrate to the heart of Valjean's concerns at this point in the narrative. Of the process of stripping down the piece to a single concept, Kretzmer explains that 'you ignore the sexual jealousy, you ignore the torment, you cut straight to Valjean the Christian altruist, who wants Marius saved for his beloved Cosette's sake'.[43] The result is a song in which the meaning of the individual lines is perfectly self-contained, with extended pauses in between each: 'He is young, / He's afraid. / Let him rest, / Heavens blessed.' Such verbal concision proves key to the powerful immediacy of 'Bring Him Home', and enables Kretzmer to remain faithful to the thoughts and feelings of the characters throughout the action. 'The story is the most important thing. What will always undermine and subvert the story', Kretzmer argues, 'are lyrics that are too smart, too attention-seeking.'[44] Indeed, *Les Misérables* departs from this template only when linguistic exuberance best serves the needs of plot and character. Thénardier's comic anthem 'Master of the House' represents one such moment in the show, as Kretzmer constructs a rhyme scheme that reflects the innkeeper's flamboyance and self-perceived cleverness. The repetition of 's' and 'z' sounds in this piece, connecting in particular to the word 'Jesus' ('Dirty bunch of geezers, / Jesus! What a sorry little lot!'), gives a playful flourish to the end of each verse, and underscores the extent to which Kretzmer's lyrics operate between the two poles of excess and restraint.

The stripping down of language practised by Kretzmer in *Les Misérables* assumes a more self-conscious dimension in *Le Complexe de Thénardier*. Like his counterparts in musical theatre, José Pliya reveals a fascination with the sonorous properties of speech: 'Mon travail sur la langue n'est pas un travail de grammairien ou de lexicologue, c'est un travail de musicien. A chaque fois que j'ai une pièce à écrire, j'essaie de trouver la juste voix, la juste musique des personnages.'[45] A telephone conversation with his mother, who speaks Fon, one of the indigenous languages of his native Benin, inspired Pliya to create the voice of La Mère in *Le Complexe de Thénardier*. Having been reminded of the distinctive rise and fall of his own mother's tonal vowels, 'tout mon travail', he revealed, 'a été alors de traduire la musicalité de la langue fon en français pour écrire ce personnage'.[46] The dramatist achieves this effect through short, precise sentences that give an aggressive rhythm to the dialogue between Vido and La Mère as each battles for control over the other. The impact of this language, which Sylvie Chalaye describes as a 'langue en miettes, dure et desséchée', is most evident when Vido announces her intention to leave.[47] In an exchange that echoes the linguistic iterations of Boublil's and Schönberg's musical, the servant declares: 'Je dois partir, Madame. Il le faut. Malgré le danger. Malgré les risques. Malgré la guerre qui continue' (*CT*, p. 43). Hearing Vido's desire to find her parents regardless of the war, La Mère responds in terms which repeat another set of speech elements, and whose precision is calculated to cause emotional damage to her interlocutor: 'Ils sont morts. On les a pris. On les a séparés. On les a déportés. On les a massacrés' (*CT*, p. 43). As this example illustrates, the language that Pliya deploys in *Le Complexe de Thénardier* is shorn of lexical variety, yet abundant in the potential to wound others.

As well as underscoring the musicality of *Les Misérables*, Pliya and Boublil and Schönberg reflect Hugo's own preoccupation with the theme of excess, and, in particular, the anxiety that characterises his representation of crime and poverty. While condemning the persistence of social deprivation, the novel portrays the figure of the outsider as a source of fear and hostility. As Jean Valjean enters Digne 'une heure environ avant le coucher du soleil' (p. 93), the impending darkness metaphorises the prejudice that he will encounter among the locals, who watch him with a mixture of contempt and suspicion. After the convicted thief has shown his papers at the town hall, a policeman 'sans répondre à son salut, . . . le suivit quelque temps des yeux' (p. 94). Outside the inn from which he is turned away, a crowd gathers 'parlant vivement et le désignant du doigt' (p. 95). In this provincial town where word spreads quickly, the anxiety sparked by the presence of a known thief reaches fever pitch when Valjean interrupts a couple and their small child having dinner: '[le mari] jeta un nouveau coup d'œil sur l'étranger, fit trois pas en arrière, posa la lampe sur la table et décrocha son fusil du mur' (p. 97). The successive instances of hatred and prejudice that greet Valjean's arrival are highlighted with particular skill by the West End and Broadway musical, which uses a revolving stage to depict the character's immediate experience of life outside of prison and the apparent endlessness of his journey towards redemption. Trevor Nunn recalls the background to this element of the set design for *Les Misérables*:

> We talked about a Berliner Ensemble production of *Coriolanus* that I'd seen many years before where they didn't just use a revolve simply for the mechanics of scene changing, they used it much more inventively, with the revolving stage going in different directions to create effects of travelling.[48]

The revolving stage transports Valjean through a series of quick, self-contained scenes which show him first working as a builder who receives only half the pay of his fellow workers, and then scaring a group of young women who see him waving his convict's yellow passport. A further revolution of the stage brings him to the inn where he is refused a meal and bed for the night, before Bishop Myriel finally welcomes him into his home. With each turn of the stage, Valjean provokes new anxiety in others, trapping him in a cycle of rejection that continues to repeat itself until Christian charity intervenes.

As the plot of *Les Misérables* denounces the prejudice suffered by the chronically poor and marginalised, so the novel also reflects a pervasive anxiety towards the eruption of violence and lawlessness that exceeds society's control. Indeed, in this fictional universe where evil, claims Kathryn Grossman, 'is all-consuming', the fear of violent acts is as widespread as their actual occurrence.[49] Hugo's portrait of the relationship between Cosette and the Thénardiers is especially notable for combining this anxiety with acute pathos. After returning from the woods on Christmas Eve, the child asks to take back the bucket that Jean Valjean has carried as far as the inn for fear of the punishment that she will face inside: 'si madame voit qu'on me l'a porté, elle me battra' (p. 317). So accustomed is the child to receiving physical blows that her whole posture seems to anticipate them: 'la crainte ramenait ses coudes contre ses hanches, retirait ses talons sous ses jupes, lui faisait tenir le moins de place possible' (p. 319). Hugo adds a further layer of authorial anxiety to this scene by having Cosette admit to cutting the heads off flies, a statement which appears to express the novelist's own fear that the savagery of one generation can quickly poison the next. While the Thénardiers delight in their cruel treatment of Cosette and the anguish that each of their renewed demands for money causes Fantine, La Mère in *Le Complexe de Thénardier* uses the threat of violence for similarly selfish ends. When Vido announces her wish to leave, the older woman details the violent excesses to which she predicts the servant will fall victim in the outside world: 'Vous serez arrêtée, emmenée, torturée' (*CT*, p. 25). In a further act of emotional blackmail, La Mère confronts Vido with the image of an interrogation in which she incriminates the entire household with false accusations of its involvement in terrorism:

> Hallucinée, vous décrirez avec minutie tous les détails de notre organisation: la fabrication des bombes dans la cave à la lueur d'une lampe-tempête, les attentats chirurgicaux sur des cibles stratégiques: ponts, garnisons, préfectures et combien d'officiers supérieurs nous avons liquidés. (*CT*, pp. 26–7)

Like its source text, *Le Complexe de Thénardier* is riddled with the fear of violence, and exposes the ease with which this can be manipulated in the service of greed and obsession.

The anxiety that Hugo associates with crime and social disorder is further linked to the life philosophies evoked in *Les Misérables*, which sometimes threaten to exceed the control of the characters that practice them. While Thénardier cherishes the mantra 'chacun pour soi' (p. 983), Javert professes his faith in an ordered universe in which God presides over the boundaries between good and evil.

As the novel demonstrates, however, the excessive adherence to, or rejection of, any one set of principles carries with it the risk of personal destruction. This is particularly true in the case of Javert, who, having seen his life spared by Valjean at the barricade, is confronted by the realisation that even a thief is capable of moral goodness: 'il [Javert] était réduit à confesser dans son for intérieur la sublimité de ce misérable. Cela était odieux' (p. 913). The challenge to Javert's notion of a world in which wrongdoers should always be caught and punished triggers an existential crisis in the policeman. As he wrestles with the implications of accepting Valjean's mercy, 'toute sa personne', writes Hugo, 'était empreinte d'anxiété' (p. 911). Images of fear and uncertainty pervade the subsequent description of Javert's final moments. As the character approaches the banks of the Seine, the site of his imminent death appears as a whirlpool that even sailors seek to avoid: 'l'eau se hâte formidablement sous les arches. Elle y roule de larges plis terribles; elle s'y accumule et s'y entasse' (p. 911). As Fiona Cox has argued, however, it is the notable absence of stars at this point in the text that signals the paroxysm of Javert's turmoil. The scene, she points out, 'evokes the hopelessness of Dante's *Inferno*. As Dante and Virgil emerge from hell they are greeted by a vision of the stars and realise that they are drawing closer to God'.[50] By having Javert commit suicide on a starless night, Hugo emphasises the character's anxiety that he has betrayed one of the core tenets of divine law, and that his rigid belief system is ultimately destined to collapse. It is especially fitting, then, that the most prominent number sung by Javert in the musical *Les Misérables* is entitled 'Stars'.[51] Performed at the heart of act 1, the song compels the audience to understand the religious motivation behind Javert's pursuit of Valjean: 'And so it has been and so it's written / On the doorway to paradise / That those who falter / And those who fall / Must pay / The price'. As Trevor Nunn explains, 'Stars' 'makes the audience aware of a man broken on the wheel of the intractability of his beliefs'.[52] The song gives a rationale to a life philosophy that otherwise might seem pointlessly excessive while echoing the anxiety with which Hugo represents the starless night of the source text.

In *Le Complexe de Thénardier*, José Pliya engages in his own exploration of obsessive anxiety and the desire to control markers of excess. Through Vido, La Mère seeks to reconnect with her own childhood. 'Je me sers de vous', she declares with brutal honesty, 'pour reconstruire les brèches de mon enfance' (*CT*, p. 43). However, while the presence of Vido awakens comforting memories of her past, such as the smell of her mother's cooking and the sound of her siblings' voices, La Mère's attachment to the girl develops into a monomania. As Vido asks repeatedly to be allowed to leave, the older woman responds with growing desperation: 'Je vous supplie de ne pas partir. J'ai besoin de vous. Je vous en prie' (*CT*, p. 45). Appropriately in a drama centred on the domestic relationship between mistress and servant, Pliya metaphorises La Mère's struggle to contain her anxiety using references to cleaning. The opening exchanges of the play announce this preoccupation with hygiene as La Mère accuses Vido of failing to remove stains from the furniture, and of ignoring the 'taches saumâtres' (*CT*, p. 13) in the bathroom. More disturbingly, she vents her anger about the rats that she believes have infested the house. 'On les entend dans les placards,' she cries, 'sous les fauteuils, derrière les portes. On les entend et ils ne meurent pas. C'est du laisser-aller' (*CT*, p. 14). La Mère's subsequent description of Vido as 'une rate de bas égout' (*CT*, p. 38), coupled with her claim that the property was free of vermin before the servant's arrival, underlines that Vido herself becomes a torment that cannot easily be eradicated. In simple terms, La Mère cannot bear to live with the genocide survivor on whom she has come to depend, but cannot live without her either. Thus, it is no accident that when her anxiety reaches its peak, La Mère turns to rat poison. In an ironic appropriation of the language of cooking, she describes a recipe with which she plans to rid herself of the rodents, and by extension, of her own obsession: 'prendre un raticide comme celui-ci. Un raticide foudroyant. Le verser dans une tasse. Une tasse à café . . . Bien mélanger le tout et boire à petits coups' (*CT*, pp. 46–7). In a conclusion that subtly recalls the death of Javert, La Mère chooses to drink the swirling liquid because she can no longer contain her mental anguish.

The musical *Les Misérables* further underlines the difficulty of containing dirt and unwanted residue that is a key theme in the source text. Hugo's own artistic preoccupation with human detritus is well known, and features most prominently in his digression on the Paris sewers. As the novel makes clear, the physical contents of the sewers symbolises the moral degeneracy of the city itself, and the ever-worsening poverty that passes unnoticed above ground: 'L'égout, c'est la conscience de la ville. Tout y converge et s'y confronte. Dans ce lieu livide, il y a des ténèbres, mais il n'y a plus de secrets' (p. 876). However, while this unseen accumulation of waste once again echoes his concern for the poor, Hugo also understands residue as a means of accessing the past. As Pierre Laforgue reminds us, the term 'residue' describes not only that which is no longer wanted, but that which continues to be. The residual, he explains, 'est ce qui s'obstine à être, ce qui refuse de cesser d'être. Il est le néant à son état presque zéro, et c'est précisément parce qu'il est *presque* rien qu'il contient en lui-même l'être dans toute sa pureté ontologique.'[53] In *Les Misérables*, Valjean's struggle to contain the residue of his former identity is central to his desire for redemption. During the 'tempête sous un crâne' that sees him battle with the moral dilemma of whether or not to reveal his true identity in order to save another man from prison, the narrative emphasises his turmoil as he attempts to reconcile himself with the transgressions of his early life. The episode is loaded with anxiety as Valjean paces from one side of his apartment to the other, fighting to control the thoughts that surge from his mind with such intensity that he puts his hand to his brow as if to stem their flow. 'Il lui semblait qu'il voyait lutter au-dedans de lui-même', observes the narrator, 'une déesse et une géante' (p. 207). This scene presented a particular difficulty for the West End musical given the need to convey the character's overwhelming anxiety in song without trivialising its dramatic importance. Boublil and Schönberg overcame this problem by amalgamating Valjean's mental thunderstorm with the trial of the fictional Champmathieu. Kretzmer, for his part, punctuated the lyrics for the song 'Who Am I?' with a series of exclamations and rhetorical questions to create a sense of feverish debate between Valjean and his own conscience: 'Can I condemn this man to slavery? / Pretend I do not see his agony? / This innocent who bears my face / Who goes to judgment in my place. / Who am I?' In contrast to the plot, where Valjean finds himself unable to deny the leftovers of his former identity without compromising his vow of honesty, Boublil and Schönberg thus succeed in accommodating the representation of his moral angst within the possibilities of their own medium.

While the plot of *Les Misérables* demonstrates Hugo's anxieties towards different forms of excess, the narrative itself reveals the confidence with which he strips down and refines the work of his artistic predecessors. As a textual construct, *Les Misérables* adapts a vast array of literary sources while simultaneously crossing the boundaries between them. Guy Rosa writes:

> Mêlant le roman feuilleton et le mélodrame à la tragédie, le roman social et psychologique au conte, la comédie au roman d'aventures, la prose à la poésie, le reportage à la prophétie, l'idylle à l'épopée, *Les Misérables* réalisent l'ambition romantique d'un 'livre unique'.[54]

However, for all the diversity of genres that the novel encompasses, Hugo does not restrict himself merely to piling up references to other texts, authors, or cultural media. Echoing the image of the writer as a sculptor that Hugo formulates in *William Shakespeare*, *Les Misérables* promotes creativity as an act of cropping and refining those materials already present in the artistic landscape and honing them into an entirely new creation. By focusing on a small cross-section of the intertexts referenced by the novel and its theatrical adaptations, it is possible to explore both the way in which Hugo reshapes these existing works of literature, and how the musical *Les Misérables* and *Le Complexe de Thénardier* continue his adaptive method in their own pursuit of originality.

Among the writers who help us to understand Hugo's paring down of his literary antecedents, Balzac has an especially prominent role. When *Les Misérables* appeared in 1862, critics greeted the novel with widespread hostility, with some reviewers claiming that it was a poor attempt at replicating the achievement of *La Comédie humaine*.[55] As more recent scholarship has shown, there are numerous similarities of character, situation and narrative technique between Balzac's work and *Les Misérables*.[56] One of the early titles of Hugo's novel, *Les Misères*, recalls *Splendeurs et misères des courtisanes* (1847), in which Balzac explored the subjects of criminality and slang language. However, if Balzac remains 'un des précurseurs des *Misérables*', it is clear that Hugo also trims elements of *La Comédie humaine* and resizes them to fit a new aesthetic purpose.[57] A comparison of two scenes from *Les Misérables* and *Le Père Goriot* offers a particularly revealing insight into Hugo's approach to adapting Balzac. In Balzac's 1835 novel, the eponymous father endures an anguished death crying out for the two daughters for whom he has ruined himself, but who at his final hour refuse to come to his bedside. As Jacques Seebacher has indicated, in terms which echo the central theme of this chapter, Balzac's description of Goriot's death 'abonde en exagérations; [elle] est, très volontairement, coulée de lave, passion, excès grotesque'.[58] His face contorted with pain, Goriot makes no effort to conceal his suffering from Rastignac and Bianchon, telling them: 'je souffre horriblement, et il faut que ce soit de la vraie douleur, vous m'avez rendu bien dur au mal'.[59] At the moment of his death, he reaches out to touch the heads of the two students, figures, in a final twist of bitter irony, he mistakes for his daughters.[60] In *Les Misérables,* Hugo clearly appropriates this scene, but evokes the death of Jean Valjean in much more understated terms. In contrast to his fictional predecessor Goriot, Valjean accepts his death with total serenity, declaring that 'ce n'est rien de mourir' (p. 994). As if to confirm the intertextual presence of *Le Père Goriot,* Hugo also has the dying man touch the heads of Marius and Cosette, who in a further reversal of Balzac's novel arrive in time to reassure Valjean of their love and forgiveness. However, in rejecting the hyperbole of Goriot's death, Hugo floods his own death scene with a sense of spiritual awe in keeping with his enthusiasm for the sublime. Emphasising that Jean Valjean has reached the final stage in his journey to redemption, the narrative describes the face of the former convict as illuminated by the light of the candlesticks he once stole, before suggesting that Myriel himself awaits to welcome him into heaven: 'Sans doute, dans l'ombre, quelque ange immense était debout, les ailes déployées, attendant l'âme' (p. 996). Having stripped away the satirical melodrama favoured by Balzac in *Le Père Goriot,* Hugo portrays Valjean's death with a mixture of subtlety and intense religiosity.

While the intertextual presence of Balzac is not discernible in the musical *Les Misérables,* Boublil and Schönberg can be seen to refine the artistic resources of English literature, in particular the work of Charles Dickens through its own adaptation for the theatre. Dickens occupies a key place in the history of the West End show, for it was after attending a performance of Lionel Bart's *Oliver!* in London in 1978 that Boublil conceived the idea for his reworking of *Les Misérables.* Boublil remembers of this experience:

> When the Artful Dodger came on singing 'Consider Yourself', the image of Gavroche came immediately into my mind. All of a sudden I could see how it would be on stage . . . – all the characters from *Les Misérables* up there singing and living through all the emotions, all the joys and sorrows that defined their lives.[61]

However, while *Oliver!* provided the creative spark for *Les Misérables,* it is another adaptation of Dickens, Trevor Nunn and John Caird's

The Life and Adventures of Nicholas Nickleby (1980), that best demonstrates how the musical develops and refines its own cultural inheritance. For *Nicholas Nickleby*, Nunn had requested a set that would give the actors greater physical proximity to the audience, and that conveyed a sense of the dirt and poverty that accompanied the rapid industrialisation of nineteenth-century Britain. After his initial frustration at trying to realise the director's vision, set designer John Napier created an elaborate network of platforms and wooden footbridges that extended into the theatre stalls, together with a runway supported by scaffolding around the front of the dress circle. While the set fulfilled Nunn's remit, assistant director Leon Rubin recalls that it terrified the actors themselves: 'with an unsteady bridge up high in the air, large wooden trucks on wheels and steps and stairs everywhere, there seemed to be hazards wherever we looked'.[62] Following the complexity, and instability, of his set for *Nicholas Nickleby*, Napier's work on *Les Misérables* involved a much simpler, uncluttered stage. With the notable exception of the hydraulic-powered barricade, the set reduced the wood, steel and sawdust that were so abundant in the earlier play, prompting Trevor Nunn to complain: 'I've always resented that John was criticised for doing another spectacular design dominated show. The show is unusual in the sense that most of its effects employ a bare stage with minimal scenery.'[63] To represent the poverty that surrounds the characters in Paris, Napier constructed a backdrop of tall grey houses adorned only by rotting shutters. With similar artistic restraint, he rendered the sewers using white light projected downwards onto the stage through a grill, a combination which evokes both the bars that once imprisoned Jean Valjean, but also the redemption that the character stands to gain as he trudges through the city's waste with Marius on his back. As both examples show, the musical *Les Misérables* pares down its Dickensian sources, but in so doing achieves new artistic effects of its own.

That theatrical adaptations of *Les Misérables* echo and reproduce the adaptive aura of Hugo himself is further illustrated by *Le Complexe de Thénardier* and Pliya's recreation of the well-known story of Cinderella. In Perrault's fairy tale of 1697, Cinderella is a young girl forced to live with her stepmother and two stepsisters. Like Vido, whose full name Vidomingon translates as 'girl placed [in domestic service]', Cinderella is saddled with an endless routine of domestic chores: 'c'était elle [Cendrillon] qui nettoyait la vaisselle et les montées, qui frottait la chambre de Madame, et celles de Mesdemoiselles ses filles'.[64] Moreover, Vido greets La Mère's cutting remarks with silence, just as Cinderella 'souffrait tout avec patience et n'osait s'en plaindre à son père' (pp. 157–8). The most inviting connection between the two works, however, is their common interest in the theme of refinement. Even when dressed in rags, Cinderella appears 'cent fois plus belle que ses sœurs' (p. 158). However, with a tap of her wand, the girl's fairy godmother accentuates her natural beauty to the point that she is no longer recognisable, turning her sullied clothes into a ball gown, and adorning her feet with glass slippers. The transformation of Cinderella anticipates Pliya's own refinement of the fairy tale. Whereas in Perrault's story the heroine forgives and secures happy marriages for the stepsisters who once abused her, Pliya cuts this happy ending, choosing instead to explore the suffering that Vido inflicts on La Mère once the balance of power in their relationship has shifted. In contrast to Cinderella, Vido uses the threat of her imminent departure to heap further anguish on La Mère, who informs the servant resentfully, 'vous avez pris pouvoir chez moi. Un pouvoir étonnant. Vous tenez le système. Vous possédez les clés' (*CT*, p. 45). In keeping with Julie Sanders's characterisation of fairy tales as stories which 'seem to transgress established social, cultural, geographical and temporal boundaries', Pliya strips away the contented resolution of Perrault's story, adapting this raw artistic material with such enthusiasm that, like the fictional Cinderella herself, the original is almost unrecognisable in the new work created from it.[65]

As *Les Misérables* approaches the 150th anniversary of its publication in 2012, it is clear that theatre has played a key role in sustaining popular and scholarly interest in Hugo's work. Dramatists have been attracted compulsively to the inbuilt theatricality of the novel while continuing to expose the strong ideological connections between their own medium and the source text. Among this corpus of stage adaptations, the musical *Les Misérables* and *Le Complexe de Thénardier* occupy an important place. While sharing Hugo's sensitivity to the plight of the chronically poor, Boublil's and Schönberg's musical provides a natural home for its canonical source. Appearing during a decade associated with greed and financial excess, the West End and Broadway show exemplifies the aesthetic and commercial principles of the 'megamusical', a genre that echoes the mass marketing of Hugo's novel while simultaneously paring down its vast narrative dimensions in order to fit the requirements of a three-hour show. Moreover, Pliya and Boublil and Schönberg throw into relief the musicality of *Les Misérables*. As songs and the sound of musical instruments feature in the novel, so Boublil and Schönberg create their own musical structures that spill over from one part of their show to the next, ensuring its cohesion. Pliya, for his part, experiments with the musicality of language itself, and the short, precise sentences that reflect the bitter tension between the protagonists in his own dystopian drama. However, it is in their treatment of the theme of excess that these adaptations truly demonstrate the proximity of their relationship to *Les Misérables*. At the level of plot, the Boublil and Schönberg musical and *Le Complexe de Thénardier* rearticulate Hugo's anxieties towards the social excesses – crime, poverty and violence – of his own time. More importantly, they attempt to resolve these anxieties by stripping down and refining the artistic resources of earlier texts. In so doing, Boublil and Schönberg and Pliya re-energise the adaptive aura of Hugo himself. Like the novelist who inspired them, they show that adaptation is not necessarily a reductive activity. As Benjamin grudgingly acknowledges, the reproduction of an original has the potential to 'meet the beholder or listener in his own particular situation' and 'reactivates the object reproduced'.[66] For Hugo, Boublil and Schönberg and Pliya, such reproduction is a powerful source of new artistic endeavour.

Notes

1 Kurt Gänzl, *The Musical: A Concise History* (Boston: Northeastern University Press, 1997), p. 396.

2 Jean Gaudon, 'Hugophobie et modernité', *Elseneur*, 10 (July 1995), 9–34 (11).

3 Walter Benjamin, 'The work of art in the age of mechanical reproduction', in Hannah Arendt and Harry Zohn (eds), *Illuminations: Essays and Reflections* (New York: Schocken, 2007), pp. 217–51 (pp. 220–1).

4 Edward Behr, *'Les Misérables': History in the Making* (London: Pavilion, 1996), p. 46.

5 For a short overview of these and other contexts in which songs from *Les Misérables* have been used, see Paul Prece and William A. Everett, 'The megamusical: the creation, internationalisation and impact of a genre', in William A. Everett and Paul R. Laird (eds), *The Cambridge Companion to the Musical* (2nd edn, Cambridge: Cambridge University Press, 2008), pp. 250–69 (p. 254).

6 Interview with José Pliya, *Le Complexe de Thénardier*, dir. by Jean-Michel Ribes (Arte, 2004 [on DVD]).
7 Benjamin, 'The work of art in the age of mechanical reproduction', p. 224.
8 Henri Scepi, *'Les Misérables' de Victor Hugo* (Paris: Gallimard, 2009), p. 291.
9 Victor Hugo, *William Shakespeare*, in *Œuvres complètes*, ed. Jean Massin, 18 vols (Paris: Le Club français du Livre, 1967–70), xii, p. 204.
10 Sheridan Morley, *Spread a Little Happiness: The First Hundred Years of the British Musical* (London: Thames and Hudson, 1987), p. 206.
11 For a bibliographic overview of adaptations of the novel in these media, see, for example, Arnaud Laster, *Pleins feux sur Victor Hugo* (Paris: Comédie-Française, 1981). A more recent discussion of film and television adaptations of Hugo's work including, but not restricted to, *Les Misérables*, is provided by Delphine Gleizes, *L'Œuvre de Victor Hugo à l'écran: des rayons et des ombres* (Paris and Saint-Nicolas, Canada: L'Harmattan and Presses de l'Université Laval, 2005).
12 Cited by Scepi, *'Les Misérables' de Victor Hugo*, p. 292.
13 Anne Ubersfeld, '*Les Misérables*, théâtre – roman', in Anne Ubersfeld and Guy Rosa (eds), *Lire 'Les Misérables'* (Paris: Corti, 1985), pp. 119–34 (p. 119).
14 Victor Hugo, *Les Misérables*, in *Œuvres complètes*, ed. Jean Massin, xi, p. 685. All subsequent references to *Les Misérables* are to this edition, and are parenthesised in the main text.
15 For further discussion of the use of aliases and disguises in the novel, see Kathryn M. Grossman, *'Les Misérables': Conversion, Revolution, Redemption* (New York: Twayne, 1996), pp. 91–2.
16 Ubersfeld, '*Les Misérables*, théâtre – roman', p. 124.
17 Grossman, *'Les Misérables'*, p. 90.
18 Aristotle, *Poetics*, trans. and ed. Malcolm Heath (Harmondsworth: Penguin, 1996), p. 20.
19 For further discussion of Thénardier as the 'duper duped', see Grossman, *'Les Misérables'*, pp. 99–100.
20 Peter Brooks, *The Melodramatic Imagination: Balzac, Henry James, Melodrama, and the Mode of Excess* (New Haven and London: Yale University Press, 1976), p. 91.
21 Myriam Roman and Marie-Christine Bellosta, *'Les Misérables': roman pensif* (Paris: Belin, 1995), p. 21.
22 Victor Hugo, 1832 preface to *Le Dernier Jour d'un condamné*, in *Œuvres complètes*, ed. Jean Massin, iv, p. 484.
23 Prece and Everett, 'The megamusical: the creation, internationalisation and impact of a genre', p. 251.
24 José Pliya, *Le Complexe de Thénardier* (Paris: Quatre-vents, 2001), p. 9. All subsequent references to *Le Complexe de Thénardier* are to this edition, and are parenthesised in the main text using the abbreviation *CT* followed by the relevant page number.
25 Philippa Wehle interviewed by Stéphanie Bérard, 'D'une langue à l'autre: le vrai défi, c'est trouver la voix de l'auteur, son rythme, sa

musique', *www.afribd.com/article.php?no=9354*, accessed 24 March 2012.

26 Graham Robb, *Victor Hugo* (London: Picador, 1997), p. 379.

27 Victor Hugo, *Les Misérables*, trans. Norman Denny (London: Penguin, 1982), p. 12.

28 Jessica Sternfeld, *The Megamusical* (Bloomington and Indianapolis: Indiana University Press, 2006), p. 3.

29 Ibid., p. 2.

30 Behr, *'Les Misérables'*, p. 21.

31 Ibid., p. 39.

32 Sternfeld, *The Megamusical*, p. 3.

33 Margaret Vermette, *The Musical World of Boublil and Schönberg* (New York: Applause Theatre and Cinema Books, 2006), p. 23.

34 For an overview of Hugo's musical tastes, see Arnaud Laster, 'Hugo et l'opéra', *L'Avant Scène Opéra*, 208 (May–June 2002).

35 Laster, *Pleins feux sur Victor Hugo*, p. 360.

36 Morley, *Spread a Little Happiness*, p. 205.

37 Sternfeld, *The Megamusical*, p. 190.

38 Ibid., pp. 194–5 and, for a full list of recurring music in *Les Misérables*, pp. 373–5.

39 Vermette, *The Musical World of Boublil and Schönberg*, p. 72.

40 Gänzl, *The Musical: A Concise History*, p. 395.

41 Mackintosh enhanced this effect for the 25th anniversary concert of *Les Misérables* in 2010 by adding a 170-strong choir to the ranks of the chorus.

42 Vermette, *The Musical World of Boublil and Schönberg*, p. 69.

43 Ibid., p. 75.

44 Ibid., p. 69.

45 Sylvie Chalaye, 'José Pliya: inventer sa langue', in *Afrique noire et dramaturgies contemporaines: le syndrome Frankenstein* (Paris: Éditions théâtrales, 2004), pp. 91–4 (p. 91).

46 Ibid., p. 92.

47 Sylvie Chalaye, '*Le Complexe de Thénardier*, de José Pliya: un théâtre d'hommes et de femmes ordinaires', *www.africultures.com/php/index.php?nav=article&no=2861*, accessed 12 March 2012.

48 Vermette, *The Musical World of Boublil and Schönberg*, p. 125.

49 Kathryn M. Grossman, *Figuring Transcendance in 'Les Misérables': Hugo's Romantic Sublime* (Carbondale and Edwardsville: Southern Illinois University Press, 1994), p. 17.

50 Fiona Cox, '"The dawn of a hope so horrible": Javert and the absurd', in J. A. Hiddleston (ed.), *Victor Hugo: romancier de l'abîme* (Oxford: Legenda, 2002), pp. 79–94 (p. 91).

51 While the intertextual parallels between novel and musical are inviting in this regard, lyricist Herbert Kretzmer's description of 'Stars' confirms that any such link is accidental: 'The theme and the title came to me at some ungodly hour of the night, when I was looking at the night sky and I chanced upon the idea of the heavenly stars as sentinels of the night and the symbols of unchanging order.' Vermette, *The Musical World of Boublil and Schönberg*, p. 74.

52 Cited by Behr, *'Les Misérables'*, p. 87.
53 Pierre Laforgue, *Gavroche: études sur 'Les Misérables'* (Paris: SEDES, 1994), p. 135.
54 Victor Hugo, *Les Misérables*, ed. Guy Rosa and Nicole Savy, 2 vols (Paris: Poche, 1998), i, p. 7.
55 On the negative critical reactions to both the novel and the musical *Les Misérables*, see Sternfeld, *The Megamusical*, p. 178, and Behr, *'Les Misérables'*, p. 39.
56 For a more extensive discussion of the parallels between *Les Misérables* and *La Comédie humaine*, see N. Banašević, 'Les échos balzaciens dans *Les Misérables* de Victor Hugo', in *Centenaire des Misérables (1862–1962): hommage à Victor Hugo, Bulletin de la Faculté des Lettres de Strasbourg* (January–March 1962), 117–25, and Renée de Smirnoff, 'Sur une Cosette balzacienne: Pierrette', in Pierre Brunel (ed.), *Hugo: 'Les Misérables'* (Mont-de-Marsan: Éditions InterUniversitaires, 1994), pp. 223–36.
57 Banašević, 'Les échos balzaciens dans *Les Misérables*', 118.
58 Jacques Seebacher, *Victor Hugo ou le calcul des profondeurs* (Paris: Presses Universitaires de France, 1993), p. 106.
59 Balzac, *La Comédie humaine*, iii, p. 272.
60 Ibid., iii, p. 284.
61 Vermette, *The Musical World of Boublil and Schönberg*, p. 33.
62 Leon Rubin, *The Nicholas Nickleby Story: The Making of the Historic Royal Shakespeare Company Production* (London: Heinemann, 1981), p. 155.
63 Vermette, *The Musical World of Boublil and Schönberg*, p. 126.
64 Charles Perrault, *Contes*, ed. Gilbert Rouger (Paris: Garnier, 1967), p. 157. All subsequent references to Perrault's fairy tale are to this edition and are parenthesised in the main text.
65 Julie Sanders, *Adaptation and Appropriation* (London and New York: Routledge, 2006), pp. 82–3.
66 Benjamin, 'The work of art in the age of mechanical reproduction', p. 221.

Chapter Five

Chez Maupassant: The (In)Visible Space of Television Adaptation

KATE GRIFFITHS

The space occupied by Guy de Maupassant in the cultural output of television is visible and shows no signs of declining. Jean-Marie Dizol's filmography for the period 1908 to 1993 details some forty-six adaptations of the author for television. The first dates from 1949 in the USA, S. Rubin's *Mademoiselle Fifi*, and the most recent, from 2011, is an eight-part anthology for France 2, the third in a highly successful series entitled *Chez Maupassant*.[1] Yet the place of these adaptations both in Maupassant criticism and in adaptation studies more generally is far less assured. In comparison to their counterparts in cinema, adaptations of Maupassant for television have remained largely invisible, triggering little critical comment.[2] This critical invisibility may be explained by the medium's frequently stripped-back, inconspicuous aesthetic and its habitual depiction as a collective commercial enterprise. Those who translate Maupassant into the language and imagery of television share the creative invisibility that Lawrence Venuti describes as the lot of translation more generally, as the translator mediates fictions in works whose artistry is not supposed to be discernible. However, if Venuti, flying in the face of discourses of transparency and fidelity in translation studies, urges the translation to make visible the space of its artistry and identity, series one and two of *Chez Maupassant*, the case studies for this chapter, answer his call, albeit in the sphere of adaptation studies.[3] The anthology's constituent works, which, like their source texts focus on space as a narrative theme, also contemplate their ability to find a place for their own adapted identities alongside that of Maupassant. Conceptualising authorship as an essentially cumulative and adaptive process, Maupassant and the adaptations of *Chez Maupassant* nevertheless make visible the space of their own artistry.[4]

The case for harnessing aspects of Venuti's work and translation theory more generally to the study of adaptation is a strong one for the places and spaces of both disciplines overlap. The boundary between the two art forms is by no means a concrete one. British and American law defines translation as an 'adaptation' or a 'derivative work' based on an 'original work of authorship'.[5] Likewise the Berne convention (1971) legislates for both art forms together: 'Translations, adaptations, arrangements of music and other alterations of a literary or artistic work shall be protected as original works without prejudice to the copyright in the original work.'[6] Translations of Maupassant such as that offered by H. C. Bunner in 1893 clearly adapt – *Made in France: French Tales by Maupassant Retold with a United States Twist* (New York: Kepler).[7] And heritage adaptations such as *Chez Maupassant* take seriously their claim to translate Maupassant to the small screen. Gérard Jourd'hui, *Chez Maupassant*'s originator, details not only the difficulty in translating the incomprehensible Norman 'patois cauchois' of Maupassant's rural tales into a 'faux patois crédible' for the twenty-first-century French ear, but also the broader difficulty of culturally translating the key themes of the author's texts for a modern context.[8] Adaptation and translation, moreover, are dominated by highly comparable fidelity and transparency discourses.[9] Such discourses, which require the translation or adaptation to make visible the source author at all costs, consign these re-creative art works, be they adaptations or translations, to a state of invisibility, allowing their artistry no place. Such discourses, moreover, unite translations and adaptations in a sense of their inevitable failure. Adaptations cannot be entirely faithful to an original for they change its form, translations cannot reflect an original transparently for they change its language.[10] Adaptation and translation studies are still further linked in aspects of their recent reactions to this prohibition. Venuti theorises an approach that urges the translation to make itself visible as an artistic space, suggesting that translators 'can work to revise the individualistic concept of authorship that has banished translation to the fringes . . . by developing innovative translation practices in which their work becomes visible to readers'.[11] His voice resonates with that of

Millicent Marcus, amongst others, an adaptation critic whose interest lies in self-reflexive adaptations which throw into relief in their images and dialogue what they have altered, assessing their adaptive act. Coining the term 'umbilical' moment, Marcus focuses on moments in adaptation 'in which the film reveals the traces of its derivation from the parent text and discloses its interpretative strategy'.[12] Both Venuti and Marcus value translations/adaptations that make visible the space of their own artistry. *Chez Maupassant* in many respects meets the terms of both theorists.

The cultural space occupied by *Chez Maupassant*, however, is not unique for it adapts, in structural terms, the form of earlier television adaptations of this nineteenth-century short story writer, illustrating the medium's continued love affair with his fiction. *Chez Maupassant*, a three-part collection of television anthologies of selected Maupassant adaptations aired on France 2 in 2007, 2008 and 2011 and was created by Gérard Jourd'hui and Gaëlle Girre, figures who oversaw the central unity of the series. Each series of *Chez Maupassant* has, to date, been made up of eight adaptations of either thirty- or sixty-minute length, and each of its individual adaptations created by a renowned director: Denis Malleval, Claude Chabrol, Laurent Heynemann, Gérard Jourd'hui, Olivier Schatzky, Marc Rivière, Jacques Rouffio, Jacques Santamaria, Philippe Monnier, Jean-Daniel Verhaege and Philippe Béranger, amongst others. There is, though, nothing new in the serial adaptation of Maupassant. Carlo Rim in 1963 adapted thirteen *contes* and *nouvelles* which, in the words of Dizol, 'constituent une série au sens feuilletonesque du terme, d'une durée uniforme d'une trentaine de minutes'.[13] Moreover, having made a variety of isolated Maupassant adaptations between 1973 and 1976, Santelli, ten years later, oversaw the creation of six films collectively entitled *L'Ami Maupassant* at the request of TF1, three of which he directed. The remaining three were undertaken by J. Treföel, A. Baslé and A. Dhénault respectively.[14] It is perhaps tempting to link the serial serialisation of Maupassant on television with the rhythms of the *feuilleton* form. Ellis writes: 'There is a passing resemblance between TV serials and series and the massive, often serialised, novels that are the high point of the nineteenth century.'[15] However, the logic behind television's recourse to Maupassant's texts more often than not proves to be commercial. Maupassant has long offered comparatively cheap subject matter that, in its brevity, affords adaptations the space to develop their own artistic ideas and identities. Writing on the early days of television as a medium and on the absence of writers working specifically for television in France, Dizol makes clear Maupassant's attraction to the new medium. He offers short scenarios to television directors, what Dizol deems a 'degré zéro du récit'.[16] Santelli writes:

> J'ai trouvé dans Maupassant un laboratoire pour recommencer quasiment à zéro . . . Personnage dépouillé. Scénario nu. Repartir à zéro au niveau de la construction d'un film, au niveau de la conception d'un personnage, au niveau dialogue, je dirai même au niveau de la direction des comédiens! . . . Donc Maupassant m'a proposé des sujets que je pouvais traiter d'une façon beaucoup plus personnelle, ne serait-ce parce que ce sont des sujets qui ont l'air plus brefs, plus restreints.[17]

Maupassant offers adaptations cost-effective inspiration and the space for their own creative identity.

This notion of Maupassant as a writer who is absent enough from his fictions to provide sufficient space for the artistic identity of an adaptation is reinforced by the multiple absences which characterise the space of the author's texts. Maupassant's texts repeatedly fracture themselves, offering a series of visible ellipses at the heart of their narrative structures. In 'Histoire d'une fille de ferme', the tale depicting the hidden pregnancy of an abandoned farm girl, Jacques, the seducing farmhand who will subsequently disappear, talks to Rose in a bid to weaken her defences. They talk about everything in a passage in which Maupassant allows them to say precisely nothing, offering as he does an abrupt elliptical summary of the scope and scale of their words:

> Ils parlèrent du temps qui était favorable aux moissons, de l'année qui s'annonçait bien, de leur maître, un brave homme, puis des voisins, du pays tout entier, d'eux-mêmes, de leur village, de leur jeunesse, de leurs souvenirs, des parents qu'ils avaient quittés pour longtemps. (i, p. 227)[18]

Such narrative ellipses spoken in words which paradoxically do not allow speech are far from rare in Maupassant's work and they fracture the space of the writer's works from within, serving as narrative holes. Fracture and fragmentation characterise the experiences of Maupassant's protagonists at key moments. Rose's experiences in 'Histoire d'une fille de ferme' leave her feeling empty, absent from herself, 'comme si quelqu'un l'eût déchiquetée avec un de ces instruments dont se servent les cardeurs pour effiloquer la laine des matelas' (i, p. 235). Maupassant's texts might be considered fragmentary on a second level, in terms of their own structure. They both exist and market themselves as fragments, short stories, fleeting moments of text. Daniel Grojnowski defines the reading of Maupassant's slivers of texts in the following terms:

> La nouvelle invite à une appréhension globale, on l'absorbe d'une traite. Dans la hâte ou dans la lenteur de la délectation, la lecture occupe un laps de temps mesuré. La limite est marquée au départ. Dès le premier mot j'anticipe le moment où j'aurai terminé. A peine entamé, le texte est perçu par rapport à son achèvement.[19]

Mariane Bury concurs: 'l'écriture de Maupassant donne au lecteur l'impression d'une parole brusquement prise et reprise, suspendue entre deux silences.'[20] The space of Maupassant's texts is often, even as it commences, already one of absence.

The fractured spaces of Maupassant's texts find expression in *Chez Maupassant.* Television is a medium of fragmentation. As Fiske points out, 'the movement of the television text is discontinuous, interrupted and segmented'.[21] The medium's content is fragmented by its separations into constituent programmes, often interrupted by adverts, news bulletins and the potentially fragmentary nature of the viewing experience. Cinema assigns us isolated seats and is screened in darkness, often inducing 'a concentration of psychic activity into a state of hyper-receptivity'.[22] However, according to Ellis, 'TV is not usually the only thing going on, sometimes it is not even the principal thing'. For Ellis the television viewer's interpellation is partial not total.[23] While Ellis overstates the case (we view television's output differently at different times and in different moods – a film or drama may engross us, a chat show may provide background noise to another household activity or vice versa), our experience of the television texts we watch can thus, often, be a fractured one. *Chez Maupassant* engages with the fractured space of its source author and that of its medium. While many of the fragmentary moments in Maupassant's plots are overwritten and explained as characters' speech is given in full rather than being summarised by an unseen narrator, elements of fragmentation persist. Only half of Sapeur's conversation as he chats to the painter protagonist of *Miss Harriet* is available to us, cropped as it is by the scene which starts in media res. Comparably Chabrol in *Le Petit Fût*, the tale of wily Maître Chicot and his attempt to drive a woman he claims to see as his mother to death, uses sound to underline the textual fragments he does not show. Mère Magloire drinks herself to death over a relatively extended period of time in drinking sessions whose length and nature Chabrol has no interest in showing. Instead he repeats the single violin note that was played when Chicot first poured Mère Magloire her first shot of free *fine*. This musical motif is repeated at an increasing tempo in the scene at Mère Magloire's graveside, symbolising the repeated acts of ingestion Chabrol's adaptation cuts. Such musical motifs while indicating narrative fracture in the form of events that are no longer there simultaneously function as a means to combat the frequently fragmentary experience of the television viewer. Ellis writes that 'sound is used to ensure a certain level of attention, to drag viewers back to looking at the set'.[24] *Chez Maupassant* thus not only contemplates the fractures and blank spaces in Maupassant's texts, it also considers those inherent in its own medium.

The natural affinity between Maupassant and television extends, moreover, to the apparent invisibility of technique with which they are both associated. If classic linear cinema such as that studied in chapter six is, as Ellis contends, dominated by elaborate photographic techniques, the television image, as a result of its largely lower budgets, 'tends to be simple and straightforward, stripped of details and excess of meanings'.[25] He continues:

> the rule is that the image must show whatever is before the camera with the minimum of fuss and conscious technique. The image is to be kept in its place . . . Being small, low definition, subject to attention that will not be sustained, the TV image becomes jealous of its meaning. It is unwilling to waste it on details or inessentials.[26]

This pared-down invisible technique, however, is highly suited to Maupassant's texts. The nineteenth-century author in many ways seeks to make himself invisible in his own texts. In his era opponents at times attacked his writing precisely for its lack of personality, a concept Mariane Bury interprets more positively a century later: 'Nous voici en présence d'un écrivain qui veut produire une écriture invisible, qui renonce aux effets faciles et se prive des délices narcissiques de la virtuosité stylistique pour faire disparaître de ses écrits toute trace de "littérarité".'[27] Sullivan concurs in words highly reminiscent of Ellis's definition of the pared-down technique of television: 'He [Maupassant] is inclined to strip off details rather than to accumulate them, to concentrate on the significant line rather than the diverting image.'[28] Maupassant's fictions leave space for the artistic actions of adaptations for the small screen.

While television screens have evolved and increased in size at home perhaps rendering problematic the use of the term 'the small screen' and requiring us instead to talk of the 'smaller screen', the spatial aesthetic of television is still, generally speaking, smaller and more claustrophobic than traditional, mainstream linear cinema.[29] Close-ups are far more frequently used in television than in cinema. Moreover, the smaller size of the screen, as opposed to the dominating, large image of cinema, pulls the viewer into a closer relationship, a smaller shared space with the television character. The greater equality of scale between the image and its viewer dramatically reduces the separation between image and viewer. Traditionally, television productions have been filmed using 4:3 boxy, interior shots in studio-produced pieces heavy with dialogue. Claustrophobia and spatial constriction, though, are central themes in Maupassant's plotlines, his conception of humanity more broadly and their adaptation in the series *Chez Maupassant*. Micheline Besnard-Coursodon identifies Maupassant's conceptualisation of the world as a 'piège', exploring how man in Maupassant's texts is hopelessly trapped at the hands of nature, woman, society and a maleficent God.[30] Space traps characters in Maupassant's fiction. Toine, the exuberant, enormous *bon viveur* ultimately paralysed and reduced to hatching eggs for his wife under the massive folds of his arms, offers a striking example in the *conte* bearing his name: 'Sa petite maison semblait dérisoirement trop étroite et trop basse pour le contenir, et quand on le voyait debout sur sa porte où il passait des journées entières, on se demandait comment il pourrait entrer dans sa demeure' (ii, p. 427). Even in stories like 'Histoire d'une fille de ferme', where space is plentiful, Maupassant uses its very expanse to mock the increasingly tiny lives of his protagonists. Living in the open space of the farm which will subsequently become her own as she marries the master, Rose feels 'enfoncée dans un trou . . . dont elle ne pourrait jamais sortir' (i, p. 239). Maupassant in any case depicts the space of the farm as a blocked, closed place, emphasising this blockage via the unusual, dissonant reflection of 'ferme' when he describes 'la cour de ferme, enfermée par les arbres' (i, p. 226). For

Maupassant, not only does space trap Rose, so too does time as she awaits the moment to give her master her refusal to his proposal: 'la grosse horloge de la cuisine battait lentement les heures, il lui venait des sueurs d'angoisse' (i, p. 235). The reader's spatial experience in Maupassant's texts more generally is hardly less claustrophobic than that of Rose. Numerous short stories, stories such as 'Ce Cochon de Morin', close before they have even begun. This tale of a bumbling would-be seducer of a young girl on a train, indicates its denouement, Morin's death, before his tale has fully started. Blocking our narrative journey, Maupassant gives the reader nowhere ultimately to go. Moreover, numerous of the short stories achieve a comparably closed feel by means of the process of prediction as the plot unfurls. Toine in the tale bearing his name mocks his wife with his fatness: '"Eh! la mé Poule, ma planche, tâche d'engraisser comme ça d'la volaille. Tâche pour voir." Et relevant sa manche sur son bras énorme: "En v'là un aileron, la mé, en v'là un' (ii, p. 428). While his words are spoken in jest, they pinpoint his fate as a paralysed mother-hen substitute. His words trap him in his fate just as they trap the reader in the *conte*'s inexorable narrative trajectory. The drunken humiliation of the *notaire* and would-be *artiste* of 'Une soirée', Maître Saval, at the hands of the artists who for him epitomise Paris, is likewise laid out at the *conte*'s opening. Foreshadowing his drunken fate, the character states at the outset: 'Dès que je débarque ici, il me semble, tout d'un coup, que je viens de boire une bouteille de champagne' (i, p. 988). Maupassant underlines the reader's lack of space for manoeuvre by means of reflective, repetitious phrasing in 'Le Petit Fût'. As Maître Chicot usurps Mère Magloire's property by driving her to drink and death, he predicts of his *fine* to his clients 'ça finira bien par lui jouer un mauvais tour' (ii, p. 82). In a closing reflective echo, the narrator states in the next line, cutting directly to the realisation of Chicot's prediction, 'ça lui joua un mauvais tour, en effet' (ii, p. 82). Claustrophobia, moreover, pervades many critical judgements of Maupassant's work. Ellen Glasgow states: 'His art is a little art.'[31] Marc Bernard details 'l'impression d'étouffement qu'elle nous donne'.[32] René Benjamin simultaneously hails and denigrates 'l'admirable et borné Maupassant'.[33] Space in Maupassant is a restricted property.

If spatial constriction is a visible feature of Maupassant's texts and television as a medium, then *Chez Maupassant* is perhaps a doubly claustrophobic work as it clearly plays with space and its lack as themes. While the stories adapted in the first two anthologies are diverse, all, in one sense or another, revolve around questions of space and its possession, be it personal or literal space. Though the space of Schatzky's *Aux Champs* is vast as the director details the landscapes from which the impoverished Norman families attempt to eke a living, the adaptation itself deals with the theft and diminishing space of the identity of its protagonist Charlot Tuvache as he discovers the wealth, riches and land he might have had had his mother sold him as a child to the sterile bourgeois couple. His discovery is triggered by the return of his childhood friend and double whose parents sold him in Charlot's place. As Charlot toils the vast lands that barely support his family, the camera depicts him in a low-angle shot that monumentalises him. The shot mockingly suggests his mastery over a land that in reality masters and enslaves him, swallowing his brother and mother. Schatzky, like Maupassant, traps the viewer in his fiction, affording him/her little narrative room for manoeuvre for his adaptation is as inexorable as its source text. Marie, Charlot's mother, refuses financial help for her sick son from the neighbour Madeleine (the characters' biblical names inscribe the betrayal dividing the two women in ineradicable lines), stating: 'Plutôt crever que prendre quelque chose de té [*sic*].' Schatzky immediately cuts to the death her words predict, to the funeral of her sick son. Rouffio's *Miss Harriet,* the story of a frustrated spinster's love for a rakish painter, likewise refuses to allow the viewer to contemplate an ending other than that towards which the adaptation moves so inexorably: Miss Harriet's death in the well. A gravedigger creates a space in the early stages of the programme, a space the like of which the English spinster will ultimately fill. The maid struggles early in the action to winch the bucket up. Miss Harriet crosses the shot as she does so. The same shot is repeated at the adaptation's close by which time Miss Harriet has become the blockage in question. The tyranny of time proves comparably claustrophobic elsewhere in the anthologies. *L'Héritage,* the adaptation in which the sterile couple try everything to fall pregnant and trigger an aunt's bequest before a set deadline, offers the viewer an initial shot of their father checking a watch. The adaptation's action is not only interrupted with repeated shots of Cachelin's hand scrubbing month after month off a calendar mockingly dedicated to 'La famille française', it is also punctuated with the repeated chimes of clock bells. They ring as the aunt urges the couple before her death to sexual action, 'sécouez-vous'. They ring as Lesable confesses the sterility of his marriage to his boss as his colleagues eavesdrop. Time, place and space are as claustrophobic in *Chez Maupassant* as they are in the anthologies' source author.

Maupassant's texts and their adaptations in *Chez Maupassant* consider not just space in their creative offerings, they also contemplate the space of their artistic offerings. Their works make visible, in highly intertextual ways, the space of their own artistry. Space in this latter context proves to be a far more capacious concept. Maupassant's artistry is not a defined, delimited narrow space of origin; rather, the substance of his texts is crafted using matter drawn from a broad range of textual places and spaces, other authors, art forms and realities. The first, and arguably the most prevalent, of Maupassant's sources is reality itself. While critics have long debated Maupassant's problematic relationship with the Naturalist school, that Maupassant's texts adapt reality in some form is clear.[34] Mariane Bury writes of Maupassant: 'il offre au lecteur des histoires simples, qui ne donnent pas l'impression d'être véritablement "écrites", mais qui semblent plutôt directement puisées dans la réalité et déposées sur le papier, comme par inadvertance'.[35] Maupassant seeks to offer fictions that cast light on and reveal slices of his contemporary reality. Critics have frequently attempted to unveil the origins or originals behind Maupassant's re-workings of reality. G. Thuillier in 'Maupassant fonctionnaire' and M. de Pradel de Lamase in *Le Commis Guy de Maupassant* propose and evaluate a series of real life models for the characters in Maupassant's 'L'Héritage'.[36] Louis Forrestier writes of 'Le Rosier de Madame Husson':

> On dirait volontiers que c'est une histoire vécue, et, précisément, les témoignages nous la donnent pour telle. Glissés dans le récit . . . les noms de Lapierre et de Brainne sont des cautions suffisantes: comme parents ou amis de Maupassant ils ont apporté leur contribution anecdotique à l'œuvre. Tout le monde en est d'accord.[37]

Maupassant's texts though do not conceive of themselves as facile panes of glass through which his contemporary reality and its personalities may be glimpsed and decoded. They conceive of themselves precisely as adaptations or translations. Maupassant writes of his contemporary realists:

> Les ancêtres des réalistes actuels s'efforçaient d'inventer en imitant la vie; les fils s'efforcent de reconstituer la vie même, avec des pièces authentiques qu'ils ramassent de tous les côtés . . . il en résulte que leurs romans sont souvent des mosaïques de faits arrivés en des milieux différents et dont les origines, de nature diverse, enlèvent au volume où ils sont réunis le caractère de vraisemblance et d'homogénéité que les auteurs devraient poursuivre avant tout.[38]

Fiction, for Maupassant, cannot render reality, it can only render its impression, its illusion, its adaptation, hence his famous assertion that 'les Réalistes de talent devraient s'appeler plutôt des Illusionnistes'. 'Faire vrai', he continues, 'consiste donc à donner l'illusion complète du vrai'.[39] Thus, while the short stories *Chez Maupassant* takes as its source texts are domestic and realistic to Maupassant's era in subject matter (none of the author's fantastic or exotic tales feature in the first two series), in very different ways Maupassant insists on their factiousness. 'Histoire d'une fille de ferme' offers a prime example. The tale turns to consider the landscape. Maupassant offers his readers not a naive belief in his prose's ability to offer reality, but a playful vision of the fictional, adaptive game that is realism. He inscribes this vision in the words of his text. The narrative contemplates 'des groupes de travailleurs lointains, tout petits comme des poupées, des chevaux blancs pareils à des jouets, traînant une charrue d'enfant poussée par un bonhomme haut comme le doigt' (i, p. 227). Maupassant's texts, *en filigrane*, playfully make clear their adaptive artistry.

Chez Maupassant, in its adaptive undertaking, revels in the spatial breadth of Maupassant's work as source, adapting, as he does, from reality, literature and art. Like the realists/naturalists, television's association with reality is an innately strong one. As a medium, television's association with the instantaneous dates from its earliest days when no form of video recording was possible and consequently all broadcasts were live. Though recording possibilities have evolved beyond recognition, the medium, perhaps as a result of its focus on chat shows, current affairs, news and adverts has never truly lost its effect of immediacy. It is, like reality, ever present, broadcast in some form all day every day of the year whenever the viewer turns on to watch it. If naturalism, as expressed by Zola, conceived of itself as a window or mirror on the world, Fiske defines television in highly comparable terms:

> [television] presents itself as an unmediated picture of external reality. This view of television realism is often expressed by the metaphors of transparency or reflection – television is seen either as a transparent window on the world or as a mirror reflecting our own reality back to us.[40]

Despite being an anthology of period dramas, *Chez Maupassant* cultivates a clear relationship with our reality as viewer. Ellis claims that 'TV produces its effect of immediacy even within dramas of historically remote periods by reproducing the audience's view of itself within its fictions'.[41] *Chez Maupassant* bears out Ellis's claim but in a variety of subsequent ways. Moments of direct address are frequent in television as newsreaders, adverts and announcers speak directly to us as audience to convey information, sell to us or simply keep us watching. Such moments of direct address, moments responsible for much of the immediacy attributed to the medium, infiltrate *Chez Maupassant*. Dramatic productions subsequent to the early silent film era have long shunned direct address shots following the powerful championing by figures such as André Antoine of the notion that actors should ignore their audience and play their role as if a fourth wall separated them from onlookers.[42] Specific adaptations within the collection *Chez Maupassant*, however, address us directly. In Claude Chabrol's *La Parure*, Mathilde's Emma-Bovary-like rapture at having cast off, albeit for a night, her mundane bourgeois existence in the exalted spheres of the ball is conveyed as she stares dreamily and directly at the audience before waltzing off in the arms of a dignitary. Chabrol later closes the direct connection he opens between the audience and Mathilde with a reflective direct address shot, this time of the heroine's madness at the programme's denouement.[43] Mathilde stares at the camera, unhinged by the realisation that she has spent ten years in financial penury to pay for a lost and, unbeknownst to her, false necklace. Chabrol's direct address shots implicate the viewer in the fiction, drawing him/her in to the space of these adaptations. Laurent Heynemann does something comparable in 'L'Héritage', the tale of a young, sterile couple who must have a child within a set time limit to trigger a generous bequest in an aunt's will, a clause they only fulfil following the wife's illicit affair with another man. Heynemann offers us a point of view shot from the perspective of César Cachelin as he walks around his office, the former military man who, with a military precision in keeping with his august first name, tactically plans his daughter's marriage to and child with the infertile Lesable. Cachelin is acknowledged by his office mates by gesture and the narrator's voice over introduces and explains Cachelin's colleagues to the viewer as he/she meets them for the first time. Heynemann's shot, however, subtly transitions to a direct address equivalent, implicating the viewer, making him/her present in the space of *Chez Maupassant*'s fictions. The final shot of Heynemann's *Ce Cochon de Morin*, the story of a middle-aged man who steals a kiss from an unwilling girl on a train and is saved from legal proceedings only by his friend who successfully seduces her in his place, also addresses the viewer in both visual and auditory ways. The seducing friend, Labarbe, speaks directly to us: 'Décidément, je dois beaucoup à ce cochon de Morin.' *Chez Maupassant*, though remote from the contemporary era, both acknowledges and seeks, playfully, to touch the space its viewer occupies.

However, the creative space of Maupassant's text reaches beyond its contemporary reality to touch upon literature, adapting a series of highly visible authors. The most well-established of Maupassant's intertexts in his short stories is the work of his mentor Gustave Flaubert. Pierre Cogny writes: 'Maupassant ne pouvait être ouvertement ni réaliste, ni naturaliste, ni décadent, ni symboliste, du fait qu'il était inconditionnellement . . . Flaubertiste.'[44] John Dos Passos views the textual relationship between the two authors in negative terms, as an implicit failing on Maupassant's part: 'I don't think that there is anything in him [Maupassant] that is not a fresh dishing up in short neat form of . . . Flaubert.'[45] Taine defines Flaubert's influence positively, in terms of creative succession: 'A beaucoup d'égards, c'est vous qui êtes le vrai et l'unique successeur de mon cher Flaubert.'[46] Maupassant's intertextual relations with Flaubert operate on different levels throughout the short stories as two works in particular make clear: 'La Parure' and 'Deux Amis'. Trevor Harris writes of 'La Parure':

> Mathilde Loisel is clearly indebted to Flaubert's great heroine, Emma Bovary. 'Bovarysme', or a desire to be other than we truly are, is what leads to Mathilde's downfall. Her inability, that is, to relate to what is authentic – in herself and in others – constitutes for her a fatal flaw. She goes in search of an illusion, a fake existence and has such faith in fakes that she is returned to a reality which is more unpleasant than the one she had aspired to leave.[47]

If 'La Parure' adapts Flaubert, 'Deux Amis', with its *Bouvard et Pécuchet*-like feel, is reminiscent of the earlier author in places.

Francis Marcoin writes: 'D'emblée le couple Sauvage et Morissot a quelque chose de flaubertien.'[48]

Reflecting on the multiplicity of adaptation as a creative process, the adaptations of 'La Parure' and 'Deux Amis' for *Chez Maupassant* adapt not just Maupassant but, in places, his Flaubertian intertext. In Gérard Jourd'hui's *Deux Amis*, the tale of two hapless friends who pass into enemy-occupied territory in the Franco-Prussian war simply to fish, the link to Flaubert appears tangential. In a scene that seems extraneous both to the action and the source text, one of the protagonists is unsettled by the wooden leg of a disabled man in the rooms above his home. The scene might be seen to send the viewer back to Charles and his horror of the sound of Hippolyte approaching on his prosthetic leg following the botched club-foot operation.[49] The resonance is made stronger when Jourd'hui's *Deux Amis* is watched in association with Chabrol's version of *La Parure*. A wooden-legged man who plays no part in the action stands watching Mathilde dance in a shot where the camera insists on his prosthesis. The scene's multiple mirrors and instances of reflection reference not only the adaptation's intertextual relationship with Maupassant but also that with Flaubert's *Madame Bovary* and Chabrol's famous cinema adaptation of it starring Isabelle Huppert (1991). If the wooden-legged man takes the viewer back to Flaubert's novel, Chabrol's filming of the dance scene he watches resonates with his own adaptation of Flaubert's text in cinema. Chabrol's big-screen *Madame Bovary* conveyed Emma's exhilaration in twirling, reeling camera shots that echo the movements of the waltz which sweeps Emma away. The director offers a comparably personified technique in *La Parure*. Following the direct address shot that allows the viewer to connect intimately with Mathilde's dreamy exultation to the exclusion of all else in the room, the scene's soundtrack is briefly filtered through the heroine's consciousness. The music drowns out the speech and experiences of the room to focus only on the rhythms that carry Mathilde away, the rhythms that subsequently provide the soundtrack to her life. *Chez Maupassant* thus adapts in passing aspects of the Flaubertian intertexts from which Maupassant wove his fictions as well as details of the adaptations which those intertexts triggered, proving, as Julie Sanders asserts, that adaptation is a cumulative rather than a singular process.[50]

Flaubert is, however, by no means the only intertext in Maupassant's work as a textual space. While ultimately the affinities between Maupassant's fiction and naturalism as a whole are uncertain, that something of an exchange takes place between the texts of Zola and those of Maupassant is clear. The overlaps between Maupassant's 'Le Père Amable', first published in *Gil Blas* between April and May 1886, and Zola's *La Terre*, first published in *Gil Blas* between May and September 1887, are visible. Both texts focus specifically on the question of place and property and the ratification the individual seeks in its possession. Both depict the rage of an old man as his lands pass literally and metaphorically beyond his grasp. In both the land is personified and the peasants who work on it animalised. Maupassant writes 'et les paysans, de nouveau, comme des fourmis laborieuses, passèrent leurs jours dans les champs . . . le long des sillons de terre brune qui enfantaient le pain des hommes' (ii, p. 744). Zola states:

> A perte de vue, des équipes manœuvraient du même train oblique . . . en trainées noires, ainsi que des fourmis, jusqu'au bord du ciel . . . La Beauce, lambeau à lambeau, au milieu de cette activité fourmilière, perdait son manteau de richesse, cette unique parure de son été, qui la laissait d'un coup désolée et nue.[51]

Both Amable and Fouan feel ejected from their own houses (Fouan is in literal terms while Amable chooses to go). Both wander like dogs, Amable 'avec des allures de vieux chien' and Fouan 'comme un chien battu', sleeping behind barns to avoid being seen.[52] The textual properties of Zola and Maupassant share common matter.

Zola, moreover, finds a place as an intertext in Maupassant's 'Au Bord du lit', the tale of a wife who, to tame her unfaithful husband, asks him to help her choose a lover, offering to be his mistress for a monthly fee, should he dislike the idea. Traces of *Nana*, Zola's infamous 1880 novel, are visible in Maupassant's 'Au Bord du lit', first published in *Gil Blas* of 23 October 1883. Maupassant's heroine admires herself Nana-like in the mirror. Moreover, in this tale about words changing mouths (the husband berates his wife for repeating another's words: 'ce qui peut paraître drôle dans la bouche de Mme de Gers devient inconvenant dans la vôtre', i, p. 1042), aspects of Zola's images and vocabulary resonate in Maupassant's prose. Echoing Zola's conceptualisation of love in the novel in alimentary terms, Maupassant has his heroine utter the following speech:[53]

> Quand on est à jeun, on a faim, et quand on a faim, on se décide à manger des choses qu'on n'aimerait point à un autre moment. Je

> suis le plat . . . négligé jadis que vous ne seriez pas fâché de vous mettre sous le dent . . . ce soir (i, p. 1043).

Moreover, if the heroine of 'Au Bord du lit' is a nascent Nana, Charlotte, the rich aunt of 'L'Héritage' might be read as her aged counterpart. Zola describes a former *fille de joie* whom Nana admires, a woman who, having made her fortune, has retired and turned to virtue and religion. Maupassant writes of Charlotte: 'La vieille fille, qui avait été galante, s'était retirée avec cinq cent mille francs, qu'elle avait plus que doublés en dix-huit ans' (ii, p. 8). Maupassant's textual property resonates with matter from the Zolian corpus.

Chez Maupassant picks up on and augments Zola's presence in its adaptive space. In scenes that have no equivalent in its source text, Philippe Monnier's *Une soirée* revolves around a visual Zolian joke. The Parisian innkeeper sells the gullible would-be *artiste* Saval a dish he detests by telling him it is M. Zola's favourite when he dines there. Subsequently, the Parisian artist who gulls and humiliates Saval at his soirée initially wins Saval's worshipful admiration by saluting 'Emile' at a table obscured from Saval's vision, a table that is comically empty. Zola may be absent in *Une soirée*, but his presence is clear elsewhere in the television anthology. Jean-Daniel Verhaege's *Au Bord du lit*, for example, amplifies Maupassant's adaptation of *Nana*. He has his female protagonist read *Nana* on screen as she seeks information on the *cocottes* who seduce her husband. In a deliberately confusing play of mirrors she states: 'il vous connaît bien ce M. Zola. C'est à croire que vous lui a servi de modèle', situating Maupassant's hero as the source for the Zolian novel that Maupassant's tale actually postdates. Verhaeghe's heroine, moreover, gluttonously consumes the pralines her Zolian predecessor so loves, the pralines that in both cases symbolise the ruthless devouring by these females of the men who surround them. As Verhaeghe has his heroine propose her husband pay for her favours while eating pralines and has her hapless husband place payment on them, Zola writes of Nana that she is 'une mangeuse d'hommes' who eats her lovers 'comme elle croquait . . . un sac de pralines'.[54]

Maupassant's text though, as an adaptive space, is informed by sources other than literature. His texts also adapt specific techniques and moments from the visual arts. As is well documented, Maupassant travelled briefly with painters Henri Gervex and Georges Legrand and was responsible for the *Salon de 1886*.[55] Bury makes a persuasive case for his interest in art extending to his own writing techniques, techniques that might be seen to adapt those of the Impressionists. She ascribes to his prose 'une sensibilité particulière aux couleurs et à la lumière'. And while, for Bury, Maupassant is not an Impressionist writer in the strictest sense, there are key links.[56] In 'Deux Amis', for example, the reader finds an equivalent of Monet's series paintings where the same space is painted in different moments, lights and seasons. The narrative depicts the same section of river:

> Au printemps, le matin, vers dix heures, quand le soleil rajeuni faisait flotter sur le fleuve tranquille cette petite buée qui coule avec l'eau . . . A l'automne, vers la fin du jour, quand le ciel ensanglanté par le soleil couchant, jetait dans l'eau des figures de nuages écarlates, empourprait le fleuve entier, enflammait l'horizon, faisait rouges comme du feu les deux amis, et dorait les arbres roussis déjà, frémissants d'un frisson d'hiver. (i, pp. 732–3)

Such a passage not only testifies to an interest in movement, light and its ability to alter the innate colours of things, it also points forward to the *conte*'s close when the executed bodies of Sauvage and Morissot merge with and stain the river which has given them so much pleasure (i, p. 738). Maupassant's work though arguably adapts more than just the landscapes of Impressionism. 'Deux Amis' offers a literary still life as 'un rayon de soleil faisait briller le tas de poissons qui s'agitaient encore' (i, p. 737). 'Le Père Amable', in prose and vocabulary, might be seen to reference Millet's 1858 *L'Angélus*. The sparseness of both Maupassant's prose and figures echoes the abbreviated style of Millet's painting depicting as it does an almost empty landscape with fragments of habitation only discernible in the far distance. Maupassant writes: 'Les paysans travaillaient encore, épars dans les champs, en attendant l'heure de l'Angélus qui les rappelerait aux fermes dont on apercevait, ça et là, les toits' (ii, p. 731). Moreover, the three women of Millet's famous *Les Glaneuses* become five in a parallel image in Maupassant's 'Le Père Amable'. Both Maupassant and Millet offer the viewer/reader visions of anonymous workers, focusing on the labour and hard graft they undertake to the exclusion of their identities. In both, the workers become symbolic and representative of the mass. They become, therefore, politicised thanks to their very anonymity. Maupassant writes: 'cinq femmes, courbées et la croupe en l'air, piquaient des brins de colza dans la plaine' (ii, p. 731). Millet's women turn their back on the viewer or crouch in their anonymity, their faces shrouded and their identity subservient to their labour, to their role in creating the sunlit harvest whose colours glow in the background in stark contrast to the muted dirty colours of the workers and their foreground. Maupassant's starkness stems largely from the cursoriness of his language. Like Millet, he monumentalises his gleaners' work by making them the sole focus of his sentence, but like the painter, he simultaneously reduces them by initially refusing them the possession of their own identity.

Chez Maupassant, like its source author, finds space for the methods and outputs of the visual arts. Teasingly the anthology twice focuses on empty art frames. In Jourd'hui's *L'Ami Joseph*, the eponymous protagonist removes the pope from his frame on his friends' wall, leaving them to contemplate the space where art once was. Likewise, in Monnier's *Une soirée*, having been humiliated by artists in Paris, Maître Saval's own artistic gathering in the closing scene takes place in a room marked by the paintings he has taken down, works visible in their absence as he declares painting to be a highly inferior art form. If *Chez Maupassant* details empty frames in its narratives, it is perhaps because the art works they contained pass into the body and flow of the adaptations themselves. Several of the constituent adaptations, in ekphrastic moments, frame scenes like paintings, asking the viewer to recognise them. Schatzky's *Aux Champs* is a case in point. As Charlot begins his confession of events the narrative passes back to his childhood offering a panning sequence of events which read as a gallery of visual adaptations of so many of Jean-François Millet's canvases. Schatzky shoots characters at close range in the foreground, monumentalising them against the vast expanses of the empty landscape as they undertake tasks which dispossess them of their own identity for none of the many faces of this tableaux is shown in full. Characters turn away from the viewer or look down on their labour. The dark, dun-like colours of the foreground in which these people toil, a darkness only emphasised by the glorious blue of the sky in the background in an effect comparable to the scene division in *Les Glaneuses*, is characteristic of many of the painter's rural scenes. Comparably Schatzky's *Le Père Amable* offers an ekphrastic moment that sends its viewer very clearly back to the woman and bath series of paintings by Degas in a scene which has no equivalent in Maupassant's source text. Céleste, in the darkness of the Amable house, washes herself awkwardly sitting in a small tub, her chemise soaked and the scene italicised by the yellow light streaming through the tiny window and the flickering of the fire. Like Degas's paintings, Schatzky's scene has no interest in the potential sensuality of the tableau, its focus is a purely functional one as it concentrates on the crouched strength of Céleste's body as it contorts itself for purely practical purposes. At no point does Schatzky show the viewer the sexual organs Céleste cleans, the organs at which Amable glares with such hate as he walks in on the scene. This act of obfuscation mirrors many of Degas's female bathing scenes which, like Schatzky's shot, blackout both the face and the sexuality of their model to focus on their muscles and intriguing postures as they carry out this most everyday of tasks. As Maupassant makes space for the techniques of the Impressionists in his fiction, so various instalments of the *Chez Maupassant* anthology give highly visible place to specific canonical artists and their art works.

Chez Maupassant's acts of adaptation across author, media and source are both multiple and highly visible. It is in this very visibility that the series answers, in the sphere of adaptation, the challenge Lawrence Venuti made to translators at the start of this chapter. The programmes force a clear space for their adaptive acts of authorship by italicising both their multiple acts of recreation in relation to other artists and their own artistry in television techniques. That *Chez Maupassant* turns away from the traditionally spartan techniques of television, eschewing the medium's generally unobtrusive aesthetic is perhaps made clear by the direct address shots this chapter has already discussed. Such shots not only implicate the viewer and increase the period piece's sense of immediacy to the viewing public, they also italicise the machinery of television. *Chez Maupassant*, taken as a collective entity, is highly aware of its own televisual techniques and puts them to telling use. While television often favours straight cuts from one scene to another, in *Chez Maupassant* even such cuts speak volumes. In Chabrol's *La Parure*, the rapacious moneylender offering a loan at exorbitant cost, urges the hapless Loisels to speak their decision. Chabrol cuts from the husband's shocked open mouth to his handing over the money to pay his debt to the jeweller elsewhere, Chabrol's cut speaking both his silence and the financial violence enacted on him by the money lender. *Chez Maupassant*, though, indulges in a series of very visible and telling scene transitions which foreground the medium's aesthetic artistry while still contributing to the adaptations' plots. In

La Parure Chabrol uses a symmetrical series of five screen wipes as Mathilde walks back and forth along the same passage, a little older, poorer and more lamentable after each wipe. The scene transitions reflect on the cuts Chabrol makes to Maupassant's source text, to the fragments of text Chabrol does not show: Mathilde's prolonged descent into misery. However, these wipes also metaphorise the erasure and wiping out of Mathilde's life first by the crushing debt she bears and subsequently by the onset of madness. Schatzky's *Aux Champs* offers an instance of comparably visible televisual technique in a moment where the director offers his medium and its artistry for our consideration. Midway through his confession, the camera pulls in for a close-up of Charlot's eyes before dissolving into the flashback from Charlot's consciousness that forms the basis of the adaptation. Highly visible in terms of its technique, the shot takes us into the stifling confines of the consciousness of a character in the process of being erased. Charlot disappears into the night at the close of Maupassant's short story, unable to bear the usurpation of his dream identity as the rich bourgeois he would have been had his mother sold him. *Chez Maupassant*, in its direct address shots and arresting scene transitions, makes visible its technique and the artistry of the adapted televisual artefact.

It also makes apparent its own adaptive artistry, assessing its success and limitations with a clear self-reflexivity. In what is a prolonged and playful undermining of the notion of origin and originals, *Chez Maupassant* alludes to its status as a reproduction. Heynemann's *L'Héritage* is key in this respect. César Cachelin, in his victorious conquest of son-in-law, lover and fortune for his daughter, fabricates new and prestigious origins for the foodstuffs he buys locally for the gala dinner first to woo his son-in-law-to-be and subsequently the dinner to do likewise for his daughter's would-be lover. They are, he claims, sent in from across Europe or gifts from relatives in the French regions renowned for these products. Cachelin's treatment of a bottle of Bordeaux is indicative. He covers it in coal dust from the grate, proudly proclaiming of the bottle he will present as coming from his cellars, 'voilà deux bouteilles qui ont pris quinze ans en moins d'une minute'. While such obfuscations of origin are comic, they become more probing when considered against the adaptation's obfuscation of personal origins. Lesable welcomes a daughter who is not, at point of origin, his. She is the daughter of Maze who purloins Lesable's wife only to have the resulting daughter stolen back by Lesable himself to trigger the bequest. Property and its possession is, in *L'Héritage*, in many senses an impossible concept. It proves even more thorny an issue in Maupassant's source text of the same name in which Lesable knows his wife's child is not his own, and yet, conquered by the wealth the child brings, proudly displays his wife's bump as proof of a masculine identity which ultimately is not his. Jourd'hui's *Deux Amis* takes up this notion of problematic, impossible origins. Morisot and Sauvage, in a scene which has no equivalent in Maupassant's text, eat sparingly of the *civet* in the country restaurant, its taste and their besieged mentality leading them to believe that it is the dog or cat that so many of their compatriots have turned to for sustenance. They drink copiously, however, of the wine their apparently patriotic innkeeper claims is made locally, the wine at the origin of their downfall as, drunk, they fail to hear the approach of the Prussians who kill them. Chancing upon the rabbit hutch outside the restaurant in question, they humorously exclaim: 'mais alors le civet, c'était vraiment du lapin. Si j'avais su j'aurais mangé un peu plus!' The wine, by contrast, sold to them as local, closes the adaptation with its origin still shifting. In the final scene the wily innkeeper marks and sells it to their Prussian executioner as a beverage imported from the winemaking regions of the Franco-Prussian border. Origins are of little import in *Deux Amis* and *L'Héritage*. They shift and mutate in what are always fundamentally successful commercial transactions.

Chez Maupassant, too, is visibly playful in relation to the serial nature of its adaptive act. In Maupassant's work themes return not just between stories but within them. In 'Aux Champs', the same series of words and events return seemingly endlessly as one mother berates another for selling her son: 'Et, pendant des années et encore des années, ce fut ainsi chaque jour; chaque jour des allusions grossières qui étaient vociférées devant la porte' (i, p. 611). Comparably in 'L'Héritage', the same set of words appears with serial regularity in the administrative office: 'On recommençait sans fin des discussions soutenues la veille et qui devaient revenir invariablement le lendemain avec les mêmes raisons, les mêmes arguments et les mêmes mots' (ii, p. 5). However, if repetition is a fleeting theme in Maupassant's stories, in *Chez Maupassant*, a work which itself repeats in altered form the fictions of Maupassant, it is core to the anthology's existence. *Chez Maupassant* establishes a chain of associations or echoes in the mind of its viewer between its constituent parts, despite those parts being made by very different directors. It is not for nothing that the would-be *artiste* protagonist of *Une soirée* repeats his rendition of his song 'Quand reviendrez-vous?', for in *Chez Maupassant* almost everything seems to come back. The overlap between adaptations is at times thematic. In series two, Schatzky's *Aux Champs* is aired in the slot before Claude Chabrol's *Le Petit Fût.* Side by side, these pieces by Schatzky and Chabrol both depict the death of a mother figure at the hands of her son by drowning – Marie in *Aux Champs* drowns herself having been reproached by her son for not selling him into a better life, Mère Magloire is drowned in the brandy her pseudo son, every bit as avaricious as she, feeds her. *Chez Maupassant*'s seriality is further conveyed by means of specific imagery and props. Marc Rivière's *Hautôt Père et fils,* the tale of a dying father who entrusts the care of his mistress and illegitimate son to his son and cipher, a mistress and arrangement the son will implicitly take on as his own is screened in the slot immediately before Jacques Rouffio's *Miss Harriet. Miss Harriet,* the story of an English religious spinster consumed by love for a young painter, a love which drives her to take her own life, has little visibly to do with Rivière's plot. Rouffio, though, has his artist hero pronounce the following words: 'Nous ne sommes pas les animaux en cage Miss Harriet. Nous avons le droit de choisir notre destin.' His words send us back to the adaptation we have just seen, to *Hautôt Père et fils,* to the son who, like Miss Harriet, shows the lie of the painter's words as he offers his illegitimate brother a mechanical bird in a cage, a bird which embodies his actions as he accepts the destiny of his father, sitting in his place, eating his bread and potentially taking his mistress on as his own. Comparably, Denis Malleval's *Le Rosier de Madame Husson,* a narrative depicting a shy boy given a financial reward in honour of his virtue only for it to corrupt him with a taste for wine, women and song, was aired in the slot immediately before Gérard Jourd'hui's *L'Ami Joseph.* Jourd'hui's piece, the depiction of a would-be radical who comes to stay with and ultimately usurps his aristocratic hosts in their own home, driving them away with his despotism, sends the viewer back to the adaptation which preceded it, *Le Rosier de Madame Husson.* Jourd'hui's eponymous hero Joseph claims: 'les curés veulent qu'on les traite comme les rosières'. While Maupassant's source text had Joseph ban the curé from his friend's house, Jourd'hui has Joseph push the curé, a man whose virtue is as supposedly unimpeachable as 'le rosier' of Malleval's piece, to drink and dissipation. Repetition is underlined in and by the adapted spaces of *Chez Maupassant.*

The anthology reflects, via such repetitions, not only on what it does – adapt – but also how well it does it. *Chez Maupassant,* in specific instances, reflects on its ability to reflect Maupassant's text. Olivier Schatzky's *Le Père Amable,* the tale of a father so unwilling to accept his new daughter-in-law as a result of her illegitimate son that he drives his own son to his death through overwork, triggering the dispossession of his family he so feared in the first place, is key in this respect. Schatzky twice has recourse to a filming technique reminiscent of the shadow plays so popular in nineteenth-century France most notably in the form of the 1880 *ombres chinoises* at *Le Chat noir.* He films both the return of the newly-weds with their son and father from the inn and that father's subsequent return from the same inn following his son's death in dark silhouette outline only. The most striking in a series of shots which underline Schatzky's fascination in this adaptation with reflections and mirror images, these shadow pictures simultaneously draw attention to the borrowed nature of Schatzky's fictions by pointing to the insertion of a foreign art form. This art form, perhaps consciously, perhaps not, can also be seen to reflect on the terms according to which television adaptations are so often received. Writing in *Fields of Vision: Essays on Literature, Language and Television,* D. J. Enright claims, 'The best dramatisations are shadows of the novels they derive from'.[57]

Maupassant's texts, like Schatzky's adaptation, proclaim their status as adaptations, as textual spaces borrowed from other narratives. The reproduced nature of Maupassant's reality is perhaps clearest in relation to his borrowing from fairy tales. In 'Deux Amis', the Prussians appear like a magical force barring the entrance to the enchanted fishing forest to the two friends: 'ils n'en avaient jamais aperçu, mais ils les sentaient là depuis des mois, autour de Paris . . . invisibles et tout-puissants' (i, p. 734). Mont Valérien, as it belches smoke from the cannon fire, is personified in ogre-like terms. The narrative depicts 'la grande silhouette du Mont-Valérien, qui portait au front une aigrette blanche, une buée de poudre qu'il venait de cracher' (i, p. 735). Trevor Harris, in a comparable manner, reads 'La Parure' as a parody of Cinderella, working not from rags to riches but the inverse as the ball, instead of realising

Mathilde's wildest dreams, annihilates them and her ability to dream.[58] The age-old visibility of such fictions adds weight to Richard Bolster's assertions that '[Maupassant] had a marked preference for plots which almost proclaim their fictionality'.[59] However, Maupassant's adaptation of fairy tales is perhaps doubly resonant in a work on adaptation for these stories told and retold across era, context, media and nation, stories with no true origin or text, metaphorise the adaptive process itself. Julie Sanders writes:

> There are particular bodies of texts and source material such as myth, fairy tale and folklore which by their very nature depend on a communality of understanding. These forms and genres have cross-cultural, often cross-historical, readerships; they are stories and tales which appear across the boundaries of cultural difference and which are handed on, albeit in transmuted and translated forms, through the generations. In this sense they participate in a very active way in a shared community of knowledge.[60]

The space of the Maupassantian text is one visibly constructed by adaptation.

In harnessing fairy tales to his adapted borrowings from other writers, visual artists and from reality itself, Maupassant inscribes the movement and motion of adaptation at the heart of his texts. He fashions a clear textual space for himself by italicising the matter he borrows from elsewhere. *Chez Maupassant* achieves something comparable in the medium of television. It not only adapts Maupassant's authorship in a very real sense, affording the nineteenth-century writer a discernible presence in television, it also answers, in the sphere of adaptation, Venuti's call to translations to make themselves visible. The directors of *Chez Maupassant* make not themselves visible but, rather, the weave and weft of their medium and their adaptive act. They question the very terminology of the critics who would dismiss them as facile copies of a superior original by echoing and amplifying Maupassant's critique of the very possibility of origin. As adaptations they allow us to see the artistry of their own medium.

Notes

1 'A peine la television est-elle née', writes Dizol, 'que c'est vers [Maupassant] qu'elle se tourne pour nourrir sa création dramatique'. Jean- Marie Dizol, 'Maupassant de l'écrit à l'écran', in Y. Reboul (ed.),

Maupassant multiple (Toulouse: Presses Universitaires du Mirail, 1995), p. 87.

2 I am indebted to Jean-Marie Dizol's analysis of Maupassant's suitability for the screen in general, 'Maupassant de l'écrit à l'écran', and Etienne Ithurria's interview with renowned television director Claude Santelli who directed ten Maupassant adaptations between 1973 and 1992, Etienne Ithurria, 'Claude Santelli et Maupassant', in Y. Reboul (ed.), *Maupassant multiple* (Toulouse: Presses Universitaires du Mirail, 1995), pp. 107–19. Writing on the adaptation of Maupassant for cinema is more prevalent. For specific analysis, see, *inter alia*, Floriane Place-Verghnes, '"Il fallait brûler Maupassant". Du danger d'adapter *Bel-Ami*', *Bulletin Flaubert-Maupassant*, 12 (2003), 61–84, and Nancy C. Mellerski and Richard B. Kline, 'Liberating Maupassant: Christian-Jaque's *Boule de suif*, *French Review*, 72 (1999), 867–76. This comparative disjunction in terms of critical attention devoted to both media can be explained either on the grounds of quality, as television is at times treated as an inferior cultural medium, or as a result of an erroneous belief that television, cinema's heir, adapts in the same way as its larger screen colleague. Critics such as Colin McCabe, for example, are keen to underline the continuity of narrative devices between the nineteenth-century novel, cinema and subsequently television, McCabe cited in John Ellis, *Visible Fictions: Cinema, Television, Video* (London: Routledge, 1992), p. 61. Cinema and television, though, are distinct aesthetic artefacts and, necessarily, they adapt differently. See Ellis, *Visible Fictions*, p. 1.

3 Lawrence Venuti, *The Translator's Invisibility: A History of Translation* (London: Routledge, 1999), p. 311.

4 Series one of *Chez Maupassant* comprises: *Histoire d'une fille de ferme* (Denis Malleval), *La Parure* (Claude Chabrol), *L'Héritage* (Laurent Heynemann), *Deux amis* (Gérard Jourd'hui), *Le Père Amable* (Olivier Schatzky), *Hautot Père et fils* (Marc Rivière), *Miss Harriet* (Jacques Rouffio), *Toine* (Jacques Santamaria). Series two comprises: *Le Rosier de Madame Husson* (Denis Malleval), *L'Ami Joseph* (Gérard Jourd'hui), *Aux champs* (Olivier Schatzky), *Le Petit Fût* (Claude Chabrol), *Ce Cochon de Morin* (Laurent Heynemann), *Une soirée* (Philippe Monnier), *La Chambre 11* (Jacques Santamaria), *Au Bord du lit* (Jean-Daniel Verhaeghe).

5 For further details, see Venuti, *The Translator's Invisibility*, p. 8.

6 The Berne convention cited in Venuti, *The Translator's Invisibility*, p. 9.

7 For further details of this translation, see David Coward, 'Traduire Maupassant', in C. Lloyd and R. Lethbridge (eds), *Maupassant conteur et romancier* (Durham: University of Durham, 1994), pp. 1–11 (p. 1).

8 See the following interview with Jourd'hui, Pascal Muscarnera, 'Les dessous de Maupassant, révélés par Gérard Jourd'hui', *www.allocine.fr/article/fichearticle_gen_carticle=18483535.html*, accessed 21 October 2011.

9 While the predominant fidelity discourses that have long informed the study of adaptation have already been discussed in this volume,

Lawrence Venuti sums up the historical dominance of the comparable transparency discourses that have been prevalent in the assessment of translations since the seventeenth century: 'A translated text . . . is judged acceptable by most publishers, reviewers and readers when it reads fluently, when the absence of any linguistic or stylistic peculiarities makes it seem transparent, giving the appearance that it reflects the foreign writer's personality or intention or the essential meaning of the foreign text – the appearance, in other words, that the translation is not in fact a translation, but the "original".' Venuti, *The Translator's Invisibility*, p. 1. This notion of a desired transparency resonates in a chapter based on Maupassant, a writer who sought to translate and adapt reality in his fiction using a medium, the French language, which he deemed an 'eau pure', a writer affiliated, however loosely, with Zola's naturalist thought and its conceptualisation of literature as 'un simple verre à vitre'. Cited in Trevor Harris, *Maupassant: Quinze Contes* (London: Grant and Cutler, 2005), p. 44.

10 The impossibility of translation is, as George Steiner makes clear, inscribed in the Bible: 'He who has been in Christ and has heard unspeakable words – '*arcana verba*' – shall not utter them in a mortal idiom.' George Steiner, *After Babel: Aspects of Language and Translation* (Oxford: Oxford University Press, 1992), p. 251. Judaism is, Steiner continues, even more absolute on the topic. The *Megillath Ta'anith* claimed in the first century that three days of utter darkness fell on the world when the Law was translated into Greek. Steiner, *After Babel*, p. 252. Modern depictions of the ultimate impossibility of transparent translation, though secular in nature, are in many respects equally decided. Noam Chomsky writes: 'The possibility of a reasonable procedure for translation between arbitrary languages depends on the sufficiency of substantive universals. In fact, although there is much reason to believe that languages are to a significant extent cast in the same mould, there is little reason to suppose that reasonable procedures of translation are in general possible.' Noam Chomsky, *Aspects of the Theory of Syntax* (Cambridge, MA: MIT Press, 1965), p. 30.

11 Venuti, *The Translator's Invisibility*, p. 311.

12 Millicent Marcus, *Filmmaking by the Book: Italian Cinema and Literary Adaptation* (Baltimore: Johns Hopkins University Press, 1993), p. 140.

13 Dizol, 'Maupassant de l'écrit à l'écran', p. 94. Rim adapted *Le Petit Professeur* (Maupassant's 'La Question du latin'), *Les Deux Amis, La Parure, Les Tombales, En famille, Toine, Les Dimanches d'un bourgeois à Paris, Le Premier Rendez-Vous* (from Maupassant's 'Le Verrou'), *La Confession de Théodule Sabot, Le Condamné à mort, Les Bijoux, L'Ami Joseph* and *Les Regrets de M. Saval*.

14 For further details, see Dizol, 'Maupassant de l'écrit à l'écran', p. 96.

15 Ellis, *Visible Fictions*, p. 64.

16 Dizol, 'Maupassant de l'écrit à l'écran', p. 87.

17 Santelli in Ithurria, 'Claude Santelli et Maupassant', p. 113.

18 Guy de Maupassant, *Contes et nouvelles*, ed. L. Forestier, 2 vols (Paris: Gallimard, 1974–9). All subsequent references to Maupassant's short

stories are to this edition and are parenthesised in the main text using the relevant volume and page number(s).

19 Daniel Grojnowski, 'L'amateur de nouvelles', in J. Lecarme and B. Vercier (eds), *Maupassant miroir de la nouvelle* (Saint-Denis: Presses Universitaires de Vincennes, 1988) pp. 10–20 (p. 10).

20 Mariane Bury, *La Poétique de Maupassant* (Paris: SEDES, 1994), p. 227.

21 John Fiske, *Television Culture* (London: Routledge, 1989), p. 105.

22 Ellis, *Visible Fictions*, p. 40.

23 Ibid., p. 128.

24 Ibid.

25 Ibid., p. 129.

26 Ibid., pp. 129–30.

27 Bury, *La Poétique de Maupassant*, p. 5.

28 Edward D. Sullivan, *Maupassant: The Short Stories* (London: Edward Arnold, 1962), p. 11.

29 There are, of course, exceptions. See, for example, *Mad Men* (Matthew Weiner).

30 Micheline Besnard-Coursodon, *Etude thématique et structurale de l'œuvre de Maupassant* (Paris: Nizet, 1973).

31 Cited in Artine Artinian, *Pour et contre Maupassant: enquête internationale. 147 témoignages inédits* (Paris: Nizet, 1955), p. 74.

32 Cited in ibid., p. 39.

33 Cited in ibid., p. 38.

34 Halina Suwala claims: 'Jamais Maupassant ne se définit lui-même comme naturaliste, jamais il ne se situe à l'intérieur du mouvement, gardant une position d'out-sider'. Halina Suwala, 'Zola et Maupassant, lecteurs de Flaubert', *Cahiers naturalistes*, 65 (1991), 57–77 (77). Bernard Joly concurs that Maupassant 'n'est réductible à aucune formule, à aucune école', citing Maupassant's own statement to Catulle Mendès in support of this argument: 'Je veux n'être jamais lié à . . . aucune secte, à aucune école; ne jamais entrer dans aucune association professant certaines doctrines, ne m'incliner devant aucun dogme.' Bernard Joly, 'Maupassant et Zola', *Cahiers naturalistes*, 46 (1973), 205–26 (210 and 222). Similarly, J. H. Matthews states: 'Maupassant a cru devoir se séparer de Zola . . . D'ailleurs, sa défection – si on peut dire – date d'avant même la publication des *Soirées*: on connaît la lettre où il avoue à Flaubert: "la bande de Zola me lâche".' J. H. Matthews, 'Maupassant écrivain naturaliste', *Cahiers naturalistes*, 16 (1960), 655–61 (660).

35 Bury, *La Poétique de Maupassant*, p. 5.

36 On this point, see Louis Forestier in Guy de Maupassant, *Contes et nouvelles*, ed. L. Forestier, 2 vols (Paris: Gallimard, 1974–9), II, p. 1303.

37 Ibid., p. 1643.

38 Maupassant cited in Bury, *La Poétique de Maupassant*, p. 35.

39 Maupassant cited in ibid., p. 34.

40 Fiske, *Television Culture*, p. 21.

41 Ellis, *Visible Fictions*, p. 135.

42 See André Antoine, *Mes Souvenirs sur le Théâtre Libre* (Paris: Arthème Fayard, 1921).

43 Such direct address shots might also be seen as the direct legacy of Chabrol's affiliation with the French New Wave/Nouvelle Vague, the movement that made comparatively frequent use of direct address in its output (see, for example, Godard's *A Bout de souffle*, 1960) and advocated the breaking of the Fourth Wall.

44 Pierre Cogny, 'Maupassant, écrivain de la décadence?', in J.-M. Bailbé and J. Pierrot (eds), *Flaubert et Maupassant: écrivains normands* (Paris: Presses Universitaires de France, 1981), pp. 204–5.

45 Cited in Artinian, *Pour et contre Maupassant*, p. 59.

46 Taine cited in Mary L. Poteau-Tralie, *Voices of Authority: The Criminal Obsession in Guy de Maupassant's Short Works* (Oxford: Peter Lang, 1994), p. 5.

47 Harris, *Maupassant: Quinze Contes*, p. 33.

48 Francis Marcoin, 'Mutisme de Maupassant', in J. Lecarme and B. Vercier (eds), *Maupassant miroir de la nouvelle* (Saint-Denis: Presses Universitaires de Vincennes, 1988), pp. 61–9 (p. 69).

49 Gustave Flaubert, *Madame Bovary*, ed. Claudine Gothot-Mersch (Paris: Garnier, 1971), pp. 191–2.

50 Julie Sanders, *Adaptation and Appropriation* (London and New York: Routledge, 2006), p. 24.

51 Emile Zola, *La Terre*, in *Les Rougon-Macquart: histoire naturelle et sociale d'une famille sous le Second Empire*, ed. Henri Mitterand, 5 vols (Paris: Gallimard, Bibliothèque de la Pléiade, 1960–7), iv, p. 566.

52 Maupassant, ii, p. 750 and p. 746. Zola, *La Terre*, p. 725. These canine descriptions lead both texts back to Shakespeare's *King Lear*, another tale about territorial possession and filial love. Having wandered homeless in a manner comparable to Fouan and Amable, Lear hears the following words from Cordelia:

> Mine enemy's dog,
> Though he had bit me, should have stood that night
> Against my fire. And wast thou fain, poor father,
> To hovel thee with swine and rogues forlorn
> In short and misty straw?

(William Shakespeare, *King Lear*, ed. Elspeth Bain, Jonathan Morris and Rob Smith (Cambridge: Cambridge University Press, 1996), iv.6, p. 169)

Zola made explicit his text's adaptation of *King Lear* in his preparatory notes, writing 'Et à la fin, le pain jeté comme à un chien, le roi Lear'. Zola cited in Guy Robert, *'La Terre' d'Emile Zola: étude historique et critique* (Paris: Les Belles Lettres, 1952), p. 226. Claude Santelli, following his adaptation of Maupassant, interprets 'Le Père Amable' as a modern allegory of Shakespeare's tale: '"Le Père Amable", c'est le Roi Lear', Santelli in Ithurria, 'Claude Santelli et Maupassant', p. 114.

53 The descriptions of the women at Nana's dinner party are interspersed with details of the dishes and the men present ultimately consume

both. Emile Zola, *Nana*, in *Les Rougon-Macquart: histoire naturelle et sociale d'une famille sous le Second Empire*, ed. Henri Mitterand, ii, p. 1176.

54 Zola, *Nana*, pp. 1118 and 1455–6.

55 For further details, see Mariane Bury, *Maupassant* (Paris: Éditions Nathan, 1992), p. 14.

56 Bury, *La Poétique de Maupassant*, p. 98.

57 D. J. Enright, *Fields of Vision: Essays on Literature, Language and Television* (Oxford: Oxford University Press, 1988), p. 8.

58 Harris, *Maupassant: Quinze Contes*, p. 33.

59 Richard Bolster, 'Mademoiselle Fifi': an unexpected literary source', in C. Lloyd and R. Lethbridge (eds), *Maupassant conteur et romancier* (Durham: Durham University Press, 1994), pp. 29–39 (p. 36).

60 Sanders, *Adaptation and Appropriation*, p. 45.

Chapter Six
Le Tour du monde en quatre-vingts jours: Verne, Todd, Coraci and the Spectropoetics of Adaptation

KATE GRIFFITHS

Adaptations are arguably the most haunted of all art forms. In a new medium, they simultaneously reincarnate and dispossess an earlier art form. Derrida writes of the haunted nature of any canonical work's recreation at the hands of its would-be artistic heirs: 'L'œuvre animée . . . *s'ingénie* à habiter sans proprement habiter, soit à hanter, tel un insaisissable spectre, et la mémoire et la traduction. Un chef-d'œuvre toujours se meut, par définition, à la manière d'un fantôme.'[1] The bond between this chapter's three case studies, Jules Verne's *Le Tour du monde en quatre-vingts jours*, the 1956 Academy Award-winning large screen version of it produced by Michael Todd, *Around the World in Eighty Days*, and the 2004 film of the same name directed by Frank Coraci, is precisely one of ghosts. As Verne explores the multitude of earlier texts whose disembodied voices he has adapted into his own novels, contemplating the ghost of his own text, so Todd's adaptation engages with the hidden ghostly voices that inform any act of adaptation for cinema. While adaptations in this medium are habitually assessed in works which focus on the original source in relation to the creative vision of a film's director, Todd's film makes visible important identities whose influence tends all too often to go untraced: the film's producer and its stars. While Todd's film explores the spectral interaction of Verne, Todd's own identity and those of its glittering cast, Coraci's film engages with ghosts on a different level. Alongside Verne's text, it adapts the mythical persona cumulatively fabricated for Verne as an individual and, more importantly, it adapts Todd's film. Verne, Todd and Coraci, in what are very different works, revel in the spectral intertextual possibilities of the act of adaptation.

Verne's status in the modern cultural consciousness has something of the spectral to it as a result of its simultaneous presence and absence. Verne's cultural presence is ensured by the ever-growing number of translations and adaptations of his work in fiction, television, cartoons, theatre, radio and, above all, film. Cinema's love affair with the fictional adventures of Jules Verne is an abiding one. Claude Faber notes that 'Au temps du cinéma muet, pas moins d'une quarantaine d'adaptations ont été réalisées'.[2] If anything, sound film's passion for Verne is even more pronounced. As early as 1929 Maurice Tournier, Benjamin Christensen and Lucien Hibbard created a silent adaptation revolving around Verne's Nemo character that featured specific sound sequences.[3] Some 148 adaptations of a variety of Verne's texts have appeared on the large and smaller screen in works whose flow shows no signs of abating. Verne clearly makes cinematic sense. Crowd pleasing in Verne's lifetime, the thrills and spills innate to much of the novelist's prose have much to offer film and its abiding love of special effects.[4] Moreover, Verne, in the public persona that has cumulatively been crafted for him, is something of a worldwide brand. Faber writes of the mythical nature of this identity:

> on ne peut s'empêcher d'évoquer tous les événements, les projets, les lieux et machines en tout genre baptisés '*Jules Verne*' comme pour mieux affirmer une filiation spirituelle. Qu'il s'agisse de ponts, de viaducs, d'une université . . ., d'un bâtiment de la Marine française . . ., du restaurant au deuxième étage de la tour Eiffel, d'une bourse réservée aux ouvrages de vulgarisation scientifique ou encore d'une soufflerie climatique destinée aux architectes et à recréer les climats les plus extrêmes.[5]

We have, according to Timothy Unwin, fallen for the seductive and misleading image of Verne as 'the great Jules Verne, honorary world citizen and dreamer of scientific tomorrows, the writer translated into dozens of languages and adapted into every existing medium, still astonishing us with his "uncanny" insights into the future'.[6] Cinema turns to Verne both for his dramatic plots and for his strong cultural presence and the guaranteed market it brings.

However, as well as enjoying a very real cultural presence, Verne is also culturally absent in key respects. Verne's public image as a scientific prophet and avatar of progress, has, to an extent, eclipsed his oeuvre, an oeuvre which for Daniel Compère 'est marquée à la fois par une grande popularité et – paradoxalement – une marginalisation'.[7] Cultural suspicion all too often greeted Verne's very popular books upon their publication. Alluding to the educational context in which Verne was published and marketed for children, Zola writes damningly: 'si les *Voyages extraordinaires* se vendent bien, les alphabets et les paroissiens se vendent bien aussi à des chiffres considérables . . . [Ils sont] sans aucune importance dans le mouvement littéraire contemporain'.[8] This cultural suspicion, felt all too keenly by Verne himself, remains, to an extent, today. According to Unwin:

> The dismissive attitude has persisted right through to modern times and, despite the revival of Jules Verne studies in France and his reinstatement alongside the great figures of French literature, a current of scepticism surfaces regularly on both sides of the Channel about whether such fiction is genuinely artistic, or whether it was simply a canny money-making venture.[9]

Writing both of critics and general readers, Compère claims: 'L'œuvre de Jules Verne est un continent encore à découvrir: combien de lecteurs peuvent se vanter de connaître les 64 titres des *Voyages extraordinaires* dont certains sont aujourd'hui introuvables?'[10] Moreover, critics have repeatedly underlined the ways in which the majority of cinema adaptations deform Verne to such an extent that they absent him from works which ostensibly bear his name. Faber writes damningly of film adaptations of Verne: 'Dans l'ensemble, les grandes réussites sont plutôt rares.'[11] Daniel Compère concurs: 'Il faut préciser . . . que la plupart de ces films ne sont pas à l'hauteur du roman dont ils s'inspirent. Les réalisateurs se permettent souvent de grandes libertés.'[12] Overshadowed by the public image popular culture has fashioned for him, by frequently unfaithful adaptations, by the insistent questions as to his literary value, Jules Verne is at times as culturally absent as he is present, a present absence or an absent presence which finds perfect expression in the metaphor of the ghost.

Questions of ghostwriting haunt discussions of the ontology of Verne's own authorship in three key respects: the role of Verne's publisher, his collaborative and allegedly plagiaristic activities as an author and the completion of his work posthumously at the hands of his son. Verne's relationship with his publisher, Pierre-Jules Hetzel, was a close and interactive one. Hetzel was integral to the genesis and completion of Verne's texts. A study of the manuscripts that appeared in the twenty-five-year collaboration between publisher and author reveals the extent of Hetzel's modifications to Verne's texts. He not only modified the detail of specific texts, he also controlled their interaction as a corpus as a whole, grouping them under a general title, *Les Voyages extraordinaires*, and guiding their intent through publicity which came to serve as a manifesto for Verne's literary endeavour. Specific critics cast Hetzel's authorial impact on Verne in a largely beneficial light.[13] Others see it as an innate and ultimately minor part of Verne's literary environment. Simone Vierne writes:

> Il ne faudrait pas cependant exagérer la part d'Hetzel dans la création de l'œuvre, comme on le fait trop souvent depuis qu'on a accès à certaines des premières versions soumises à l'éditeur. Dans la mesure où Hetzel incarne l'idéologie du temps, il ne fait que rendre visible l'influence qui s'exerce sur tout créateur.[14]

Others, however, cast Hetzel as a ghostwriter, and an inferior one at that, in Verne's fiction, as a figure who undermined his originality and authenticity. Jean-Pierre Picot maintains that only Verne's initial manuscripts should be studied, 'tant le moralisme calamiteux, l'opportunisme commercial, l'absence de génie poétique, l'esprit de punaise de sacristie laïque du sieur Hetzel ont, quoi qu'en pensent certains, gravement parasité la créativité vernienne'.[15] If Hetzel may be seen, to whatever extent, to ghostwrite Verne, so too he enabled Verne to ghostwrite other authors. Inspired by Verne's success, other authors in the Hetzel stable published novels along similar lines. Hetzel arranged for Verne to rewrite two of the manuscripts of one such would-be Verne, André Laurie, creating a work entitled *Les Cinq Cents Millions de la Bégum* (1879), *L'Etoile du sud* (1884) and a work which appeared in 1885 under the names of both writers, *L'Epave du 'Cynthia'*.[16] Such legitimate acts of ghostwriting must be paralleled to the number of lawsuits Verne had to fight in his career from writers and figures claiming, rightly or wrongly, that Verne had plagiarised their life or their work. If Verne himself ghostwrote others, so too was he posthumously ghostwritten by his son. Following Verne's death, his son, Michel, in the words of Dumas, 'se passionne pour l'entière réécriture des œuvres posthumes de son père'.[17] Such acts of rewriting were discovered only by Pierro della Riva in 1977. For some they absent Verne from himself and must be ignored, for others Michel's rewritings 'are well attuned to the corpus and must be treated as integral to it'.[18] Verne's corpus and authorial voice remain spectral in the midst of their very materiality and scope.

Ghosts, in many respects, appear antithetical to the materiality and revelatory intent of the Vernian project as formulated by Hetzel in 1866: 'Son but est, en effet, de résumer toutes les connaissances *géographiques, géologiques, physiques, astronomiques,* amassées par la science moderne, et de refaire, sous la forme attrayante et pittoresque qui lui est propre, l'histoire de l'univers.'[19] Verne attempts in his fiction to capture in print the ontology of the universe and his novels are very much, Unwin argues, descendants of the realist impulse.[20] And yet, ghosts, the bodies simultaneously absent and present in a manner that challenges the dictates of ontology, are, in metaphorical forms at least, prevalent in Verne's *Le Tour du monde.* The narrative is driven by, in Unwin's words, 'a phantom character', the perpetrator of the bank robbery for which Fogg is initially blamed.[21] For all his visible influence on the narrative, this character remains spectrally absent, his only materiality afforded in the following, partial, elliptical, stuttered description by the apologetic Fix: 'Pardon . . . une ressemblance déplorable . . . voleur arrêté depuis trois jours . . . vous . . . libre!'[22] The arrest of Fogg for the crime committed by this phantom character leads to a phantom ending, to a misleading and universally believed pre-denouement which suggests, in the final lines of chapter thirty-four, that Fogg has lost the bet: 'Phileas Fogg, après avoir accompli ce voyage autour du monde, arrivait avec un retard de cinq minutes! . . . Il avait perdu' (p. 241). Fogg, however, is saved from this phantom criminal and this phantom ending by the 'phantom day' they have gained on their travels by always travelling eastwards in a world in which the international date line does not yet exist:

> En effet, en marchant vers l'est, Phileas Fogg allait au-devant du soleil, et, par conséquent, les jours diminuaient pour lui d'autant de fois quatre minutes qu'il franchissait de degrés dans cette direction. Or, on compte trois cent soixante degrés sur la circonférence

> terrestre, et ces trois cent soixante degrés, multipliés par quatre minutes, donnent précisément vingt-quatre heures, – c'est-à-dire ce jour inconsciemment gagné. (p. 253)

This day is, arguably, rendered still more phantomatic since it is the literary ghost of a writer much admired by Verne, Edgar Allan Poe, and his story 'Three Sundays in a Week'. Unwin writes:

> The story which was to give *Le Tour du monde* one of its central devices, that of the 'phantom day', demonstrated that the apparent impossibility of three Sundays occurring in the same week can come about in the case of three different individuals. If one of them leaves London on a westwards journey around the globe, another remains on the spot, and the third departs on an eastwards journey, then each will be living a different time-scale by the time they meet up again. The first will have lost a day; the second will neither have lost nor gained; the third will have gained a day. For the first, then, tomorrow is Sunday; for the second, today is Sunday; for the third, yesterday was Sunday. In both the Poe story and Verne's novel, the gaining of a day relates to a decision to get married.[23]

Moreover, it is not for nothing that Passepartout dresses up as and reincarnates the dead rajah to rescue Aouda, 'comme un fantôme . . . au milieu des tourbillons de vapeurs qui lui donnaient une apparence spectrale' (p. 85). Metaphorical ghosts drive Verne's *Le Tour du monde.*

While the spectral afterlives of Verne's *Le Tour du monde* in sound film constitute the focus of this chapter, adaptations of Verne are far from the preserve of the twentieth and twenty-first centuries. They were, in a variety of forms, very much a feature of the cultural landscape in Verne's era and specific adaptations took place at his behest. In theatre, Verne, with D'Ennery, wrote the theatrical version of *Le Tour du monde* that premiered in 1874 at the Théâtre de la Porte Saint-Martin.[24] Verne's adaptation of his own work was anything but faithful. According to Unwin, 'the emphasis was on grand, stagey effects and greater complexity of plot, and in one production of *Le Tour du monde* (whose stage version contains many more characters and sub-plots than the novel), a live elephant was used'.[25] Such adaptations were, though, a key part of Verne's cultural presence and his financial security. Compère writes: 'Ces adaptations théâtrales, surtout *Le Tour du monde en 80 jours* et *Michel Strogoff*, maintes fois reprises, ont apporté à Jules Verne une célébrité encore plus grande que ses romans, ainsi qu'une aisance financière.'[26] It is through adaptation that Verne thrived in his lifetime. Verne, though, adapted himself not just into theatre, but also into fiction. Specific critics have commented incisively on Verne's tendency to self-cite in his fiction, to reprise previous texts in later form. Compère writes: 'Dans l'ensemble des *Voyages extraordinaires* se tissent de multiples liens intertextuels (retour de personnages, autoréférences, allusions, variations, etc.) qui soulignent le souci et le plaisir de Verne de créer une œuvre cohérente.'[27] *Le Tour du monde* appeared in adapted, comically altered form, Unwin notes, as *Claudius Bombarnac* in 1893:

> The miserably corpulent (and improbably named) Baron Weissschnitzerdörfer is attempting to complete a circuit of the world in 39 days, vying with the much more modest record set by the American journalist Nellie Bly two years before the novel was published. The reference to *Le Tour du monde en quatre-vingts jours* is clear, the more so since Verne's novel had been the acknowledged inspiration for so many real attempts at reducing the time of a global circuit, including those of Nellie Bly herself. However, the theme here becomes open self-parody. A hopeless and hapless caricature of Fogg, the constantly out-of-breath baron is always running out of time and running after trains. He misses every opportunity to get ahead, yet finds no means of compensating for his setbacks. At the end of the story we learn that, having missed two ships across the Pacific, and after getting shipwrecked on a third, he finally completes his circuit in no less than 187 days.[28]

Le Tour, though, not only found a series of spectral afterlives at the pen of Verne himself, so too was it worked and reworked by others in fiction. Commenting on the first of many would-be Verne imitators, Hetzel wrote: 'C'est une imitation. C'est la première. Mais vous en aurez vingt, si votre succès continue et j'espère bien qu'il continuera. Vous ne pouvez pas espérer de ne pas faire école.'[29] The publisher was proved right as his competitors, spurred on by Hetzel's success, set up outlets comparable to his and nurtured would-be Vernes. An article published by Yves Oliver-Martin in 1974 and an edited volume which takes up both the mantle and title of that article, 'Dans le sillage de Jules Verne', both trace the intriguing webs of influence Verne enjoyed in his lifetime, detailing the workings and reworkings of his fiction in contemporary literature.[30] Those of *Le Tour du monde* are particularly visible. Louis Boussenard penned *Le Tour du monde d'un gamin de Paris*, which appeared in *feuilleton* form in *Le Journal des Voyages*. More outrageously, and with a breadth and textual scope which characterises many adaptations of Verne, Albert Robida in 1879, published *Les Voyages très-extraordinaires de Saturnin Farandoul dans les cinq ou six parties du monde et dans tous les pays connus et inconnus de M. Jules Verne*, a work involving Nemo, Michel Strogoff, Phileas Fogg, Hector Servadac and others.[31] Verne's *Le Tour du Monde* was adapted during and beyond its creation into spectral texts that, to varying degrees, make present the ghost of Verne's corpus.

Verne's *Le Tour du monde*, though, is in some respects itself made up of the ghosts of previous texts since, in a highly spectral sense, adaptation is a feature of both its plot and textual practice. While, as this book has pointed out, Balzac, Hugo, Flaubert, Zola and Maupassant engaged intertextually with specific sources and authors in a comparatively sustained fashion, Verne's adaptation of other sources is in many ways as vast as the textual endeavour he himself undertakes. Balzac, Hugo, Flaubert, Zola and Maupassant interact with specific authors, artists and moments, encouraging their reader to identify them, but Verne, more often than not, delights in making visible the act of citation without affording his reader the means to attribute it. Much has been made of the meticulous research Verne undertook before each novel, research he recorded on note cards before integrating it, with varying degrees of visibility, into his novels. Unwin writes: 'the sources often remain openly on display, either because he [Verne] refers explicitly to them, or indeed because he conspicuously writes in different modes and assumes the voices associated with different forms of text (scientific, journalistic, pedagogical and so on)'.[32] Such sources and voices are clearly visible in *Le Tour du monde*. The novel's introduction to India is a case in point. Chapter ten's opening paragraph offers the reader an introduction to the political system of the country, paragraph two, an overview of its population, paragraph three, an assessment of its history, paragraph four, an analysis of its ethnographic life, paragraph five, a description of its transportation system, shortly before returning to the narrative's plot. Verne's insertions of different voices and forms are not always, however, so straightforward. Borrowing from the discourse of meteorology, Verne writes teasingly: 'A une époque moins avancée de l'année, le typhon, suivant l'expression d'un célèbre météorologiste, se fût écoulé comme une cascade lumineuse de flammes électriques, mais en équinoxe d'hiver, il était à craindre qu'il ne se déchaînât avec violence' (p. 141). That Verne cites is clear. What he cites, in this instance, is less so. The novelist accords a tangible presence to a source which he ultimately absents by refusing it identification, forcing his reader to contemplate the voices, named and unnamed, which people his narrative with varying degrees of spectrality. Even when Verne does identify the source of his creative borrowing, the act of citation remains fundamentally problematic. In the oft-analysed introduction to the character of Aouda he writes the following:

> Lorsque le roi-poète Uçaf Uddaul, célèbre les charmes de la reine d'Ahméhnagara, il s'exprime ainsi: 'Sa luisante chevelure, réguilèrement divisée en deux parts, encadre les contours harmonieux de ses joues délicates et blanches, brillantes de poli et de fraîcheur. Ses sourcils d'ébène ont la forme et la puissance de l'arc de Kāma, dieu d'amour, et sous ses longs cils soyeux, dans la pupille noire de ses grands yeux limpides, nagent comme dans les lacs sacrés de l'Himalaya les reflets les plus purs de la lumière céleste. Fines, égales et blanches, ses dents resplendissent entre ses lèvres souriantes, comme des gouttes de rosée dans le sein mi-clos d'une fleur de grenadier. Ses oreilles mignonnes aux courbes symétriques, ses mains vermeilles, ses petits pieds bombés et tendres comme les bourgeons du lotus, brillent de l'éclat des plus belles perles de Ceylan, des plus beaux diamants de Golconde. Sa mince et souple ceinture, qu'une main suffit à enserrer, rehausse l'élegante cambrure de ses reins arrondis et la richesse de son buste où la jeunesse en fleur étale ses plus parfaits trésors, et, sous les plis soyeux de sa tunique, elle semble avoir été modelée en argent pur de la main divine de Vicvacarma, l'éternel statuaire.' Mais, sans toute cette amplification, il suffit de dire que Mrs Aouda . . . était une charmante femme dans toute l'acceptation européenne du mot. (pp. 88–9)

Verne revels in the cumulative admiration of the citation, in the crescendo of textual love for the woman in question, textual love the reader expects to be able to transfer to Aouda, only for Verne to undercut it in the most deflating of terms. Verne both allows and disallows the quotation in relation to Aouda, drawing attention, in Unwin's words,

> to the fact that this is a textual strategy, a grafting of the story onto another text – or the grafting of another text into the story – by way of showing up its status as a textual artefact. The borrowing of

> another text thus has precisely the effect of reinforcing the notion that texts circulate at all times and that every narrative, every journey, uses them as a way to move forward.[33]

That Verne adapts and cites previous texts is clear, making them simultaneously present and absent in various ways in his fiction. Whilst critics remain divided as to the effect of Verne's narrative citational strategy (for Compère it results in a harmonious textual depth, for Unwin it can result in moments of fracture as a result of the occasional flaws in Verne's writing), their incisive readings of the prevalence and intricacy of this process make clear its importance to Verne's literature.[34] Verne's fiction is perforated by the spectral voices of hosts of textual ghosts.

Verne thus perforates specific citations in his novel, as is the case with his borrowed introduction to Aouda, but so too does he perforate some of this own character constructions, most notably his hero Phileas Fogg. While Fogg is the focus of the novel's drama, beats the enemy (time and Fix) and ultimately gets the girl (Aouda), critics have written persuasively on the nothingness of his being. Fogg is famously introduced via a plethora of negative formulations that, though they make clear what he is not, offer no sense of what he truly is:

> On ne l'avait jamais vu ni à la Bourse, ni à la Banque, ni dans aucun des comptoirs de la Cité. Ni les bassins ni les docks de Londres n'avaient jamais reçu un navire ayant pour armateur Phileas Fogg. Ce gentleman ne figurait dans aucun comité d'administration. Son nom n'avait jamais retenti dans un collège d'avocats, ni au Temple, ni à Lincoln's-inn, ni à Gray's-inn. Jamais il ne plaida ni à la Cour du chancelier, ni au Banc de la Reine, ni à l'Echiquier, ni en Cour ecclésiastique. Il n'était ni industriel, ni négociant, ni marchand, ni agriculteur. (p. 8)

Unwin concludes: 'the enumeration of Fogg's non-credentials degenerates into a discussion of trivia. Fogg emerges as a negative image, a space to be filled in, a series of gaps.'[35] In keeping with the findings of such critics, it is significant that Fogg's speech, more frequently than being given, is reported through and absented from itself by the narrator's voice: 'Phileas Fogg répondit qu'il tiendrait compte de ces observations et qu'il aviserait' (p. 87). To perforate his character still further, Verne offers definitions of his character that he then goes on to contradict. Fogg is presented as quintessentially English and, according to Verne, 'pour tout Anglais, la loi est sacrée' (p. 94). Such a statement is given shortly before Fogg breaks the law and skips bail, making a mockery of his progenitor's statement. Having later stolen a ship, Fogg affirms to the man piloting it: 'C'est votre métier, et non le mien, pilote, et je me fie à vous' (p. 137). This assertion that Fogg is not a sailor is then undercut no less than three times. The narrator asserts: 'Phileas Fogg, le corps droit, les jambes écartées, d'aplomb comme un marin, regardait sans broncher la mer houleuse' (p. 137). The narrator later repeats, 'Mais Phileas Fogg était un marin hardi, qui savait tenir tête à la mer' (p. 230), stating: 'Seulement, il était très clair, à voir manœuvrer Mr Fogg, que Mr Fogg avait été marin' (p. 228). A man doubled in the text (in inverse form by the garrulous and dissipated Sheridan whose house he now occupies and more straightforwardly by the whist-playing Fix who dogs his every step, driven, like Fogg, by what he sees as his 'devoir', p. 7 and p. 237), Fogg's doubles beyond the text he inhabits are multiple in the Vernian corpus. Unwin points to Colonel Everest in *Aventures de trois Russes et de trois Anglais* as a 'Fogg lookalike, a man whose existence is entirely regulated, measured and mathematical', and the English army officers in *Hector Servadac* who do nothing other than play chess.[36] However, Verne seeks not to reinforce Fogg by doubling him elsewhere in his oeuvre for these reference points are, all too often, as lacking in origin as Fogg himself. Robur-le-conquérant, in the novel bearing his name, a man who circles the globe by air as Fogg does on land and sea, is as inscrutable as Fogg himself. The narrative offers no narrative closure as to his identity or origin: 'Et maintenant, toujours cette question: Qu'est-ce que ce Robur? Le saura-t-on jamais?'[37] What Verne doubles is the nothingness of Fogg, dramatising his space as a ghostly hole perforating the fictions in which he abides. Ever present in *Le Tour du monde*, Fogg is simultaneously always multiply absent.

Verne not only perforates Fogg as a narrative construct, he might also be seen to perforate the very narrative body that Fogg inhabits, both allowing and disallowing its fictions. The narrative frequently alludes to what characters do not see. Night falls on the train as it passes through the Indian landscape and Verne offers us a negative construction that echoes that used to introduce his protagonist:

> on n'aperçut plus rien des merveilles du Bengale, ni Golgonde, ni Gour en ruine, ni Mourshedabad, qui fut autrefois capitale, ni

> Burdwan, ni Hougly, ni Chandernagor, ce point français du territoire indien sur lequel Passepartout eût été fier de voir flotter le drapeau de sa patrie. (p. 93)

As the narrator does not step in to fill in the blanks as the characters sleep, these places are present and absent in the fictions he narrates. The narrator's principal incapacities relate to Fogg himself, a man seemingly impervious to the narrator's scrutiny: 'Ce que pensa l'honorable gentleman en apprenant que son domestique n'était rentré à l'hôtel, nul n'aurait pu le dire' (p. 129). However, the novel's narrative holes expand far beyond Fogg. The narrator indicates to us what he will not do: 'Inutile de décrire ici les prodigieux exercices des acrobates et gymnastes de la troupe' (p. 159). He also underlines what he cannot do: 'Il faut renoncer à peindre l'anxiété dans laquelle, pendant trois jours, vécut tout ce monde de la société anglaise' (p. 248). And of Passepartout's trip on the Carnatic, the narrator writes: 's'il mangea et but pendant cette traversée, cela ne saurait se décrire' (p. 149). The narrator makes clear the very incapacity of his words and images:

> Rien qu'avec son petit morceau de toile, la Tankadère fut enlevée comme une plume par ce vent dont on ne saurait donner une idée exacte, quand il souffle en tempête. Comparer sa vitesse à la quadruple vitesse d'une locomotive lancée à toute vapeur, ce serait rester au-dessous de la vérité. (pp. 141–2)

Comparably, the narrator might also, through his repeated use of the word 'invraisemblable', be seen to make clear the incapacity of his work as a reflection of the real, underlining its status as fiction. The 'happy ever after' afforded to Aouda and the ever-impassive Fogg is described precisely in terms of the implausible: 'Qu'avait-il rapporté de ce voyage? Rien dira-t-on? Rien, soit, si ce n'est une charmante femme, qui – quelque invraisemblable que cela puisse paraître – le rendit le plus heureux des hommes' (p. 255). Passepartout cannot believe he is travelling through India on the Great Peninsular Railway: 'Cela lui paraissait invraisemblable. Et cependent rien de plus réel' (p. 63). Passepartout plies his trade as an acrobat in the Japanese circus, 'exécutant les tours les plus invraisemblables' to try to make some money, before miraculously being found by Fogg as he passes (p. 159). At times Verne's narrative underlines the factitious nature of the very fictions it spins. Far from seeming real, in *Le Tour du monde*, China Town in San Francisco 'semblait avoir été importée du Céleste Empire dans une boîte à joujoux' (p. 169). Verne repeatedly punctures his narrative, underlining what it cannot and will not do, both allowing and disallowing its fictional existence in the same spectral breath.

The problematic ghostly space of Verne's *Le Tour du monde* is echoed by the no-place of the territories it describes. The narrative ostensibly works to fix the nations and countries it traverses. Fogg notes them meticulously in his notebook and Verne's narrator inducts his audience into their history, culture and society. And, yet, in a narrative where borders and boundaries of all kinds prove labile and porous, the spaces and places of the novel, even in their very specificity, merge and mix to become nowhere. Much has been made of the stasis of Fogg's travel, of his unchanging, unmoving identity, somehow still even while traversing the globe. Unwin, for example, writes of 'the oddly motionless and emotionless Fogg'.[38] As Fogg makes no personal progress in his journey ('le Fogg du retour était exactement le Fogg du départ', p. 244), so too his physical progress through nations seems illusory as these nations collapse, merge and become one homogenous mass. The narrator may insist, in his travel-guide-like introduction to the country on the specificity of India, but that specificity unravels as the narrative gazes at one of the last visible cities on their Indian stage, 'ville plus qu'européenne, anglaise comme Manchester ou Birmingham, renommée pour ses fonderies de fer, ses fabriques de taillanderie et d'armes blanches' (p. 93). The language of the novel is comparable when it considers another English colony, this time Hong Kong:

> Des docks, des hôpitaux, des wharfs, des entrepôts, une cathédrale gothique, un 'government house', des rues macadamisées, tout ferait croire qu'une des cités commerçantes des comtés de Kent ou de Surrey, traversant le sphéroïde terrestre, est venue ressortir en ce point de la Chine, presque à ses antipodes. (p. 120)

Verne concludes, 'à peu de choses près, c'était encore Bombay, Calcutta ou Singapore, que le digne garçon [Passepartout] retrouvait sur son parcours. Il y a ainsi comme une traînée de villes anglaises tout autour du monde' (pp. 120–1). Interestingly, though, this homogeneity extends even beyond the English colonial reach. In San Francisco Passepartout's experience, despite the world they have almost circled, is one of cultural sameness: 'Lorsque Passepartout arriva à International-Hôtel, il ne lui semblait pas qu'il eût quitté l'Angleterre' (p. 169). The cultural specificities of each nation in *Le Tour du monde* collapse into a spectral no-place.

Verne's novel thus contemplates the ghosts of the textual voices from which it writes itself and those of its own authorial identity. The 1956 adaptation produced by Michael Todd, a similarly spectral piece, engages with ghosts of a different kind. Most notably it makes visible, in an extremely heightened way, the ghost of the producer's influence on any given adaptation and that of the star personalities of its cast. Film criticism tends, by and large, to attribute films to their director, situating him/her as the guiding authorial presence in the work's creation. Todd's film, however, lists a huge number of people under direction, and his *Around the World*, like all his previous shows, clearly bears witness to the showman's life, personality and artistic signature. Todd's son writes in his father's biography, 'everything he produced was dominated by his personality. No matter who wrote, directed or appeared in one of his productions, it was treated – critically and publicly – as the "new Mike Todd show".'[39] Todd was, in many respects, the perfect man to drive through a Verne adaptation. Despite lucrative offers from Hollywood studios, Todd, a Broadway impressario, was a cinema novice when he created his *Around the World in Eighty Days*, the only film he was ever to make and which would win him Academy recognition and huge financial success. Todd conceived of himself first and foremost as a showman and, as his son points out in his biography, conceived of *Around the World* in comparably theatrical terms:

> Many years later, when he [Todd] finally did get around to making motion pictures . . . he produced them as though they were legitimate stage shows: *Cinerama* as a revue, and *80 Days* as if it were a stage musical with a thin book, freely manipulating the material to produce the most effective running order.[40]

Todd's film screened with a theatrical musical intermission and featured some of the greatest stage actors of the era. Todd's theatrical interests intersect with those of Verne, the novelist who composed some forty plays for the stage and recognised, in 1893, that 'j'adorais la scène et tout ce qui la touchait . . . le travail que j'aime le plus est d'avoir écrit pour la scène'.[41] Commenting on the 'abondance de dialogues, fréquence des coups de théâtre, intervention d'un *deus ex machina*, plantation de décors comme sur une scène, présentation de personnages comme on le fait dans les livrets de pièces, terminologie théâtrale qui ne cesse d'être employée, citations innombrables et privilégiées d'ouvrages dramatiques', characteristics which may all be found in *Le Tour du monde*, R. Pourvoyeur claims that in writing his novels Verne never really left the realm of the theatre.[42] Todd was no stranger to adaptation in the theatre and his past form in this area leads the viewer, correctly, to expect a very free reworking of Verne. In 1939 he produced a spiced-up version of a Gilbert and Sullivan classic with attractively clad female dancers, *The Hot Mikado*, and in 1945 he offered a liberally adapted version of Shakespeare's *Hamlet* for a GI audience. His *Around the World in Eighty Days* was arguably no less free in its adaptive act. Verne's trajectory alters to encompass different countries and different means of transport (most famously, a balloon over the Alps). However, critics have been keen to see the ghost of Phileas Fogg and his herculean endeavour in Mike Todd's quest to produce this film as an independent producer financing the piece on a wing and prayer. Jeffrey M. Pilcher writes:

> Hollywood insiders found the filming of *Around the World* remarkably similar to the original novel and considered the producer, Michael Todd, to be an incarnation of the gambler Phileas Fogg. Where Jules Verne kept the Englishman one step ahead of . . . Mr Fix, Todd filmed the movie completely on credit and was constantly in search of his next payroll. But through ingenuity and improvisation both Fogg and Todd won their bets and married beautiful princesses.[43]

Herbert Kupferberg in the *New York Herald Tribune* wrote:

> Phileas Fogg, Michael Todd – the names seem somehow to go together . . . Michael Todd may be neither proper nor English, but he shows Phileas's intrepidity and purposefulness. He has made a movie version of *Around the World in 80 Days* which in its fantasy, freshness and fun leaves poor old Jules far behind . . . Mr Todd's mighty spectacle is far-ranging, imaginative, fanciful entertainment.[44]

While the impassive Fogg and the impetuous, charismatic Todd are hard to cast as even spectral incarnations of each other, Todd did, thanks to this film, (re)attain great wealth (he made and lost several fortunes in his lifetime), academy recognition and make a well-publicised marriage with Elizabeth Taylor upon the film's completion.

Verne, the author Todd professed to admire, is clearly present in the film but, while keeping the nineteenth-century setting, Todd affords him something of a spectral presence as he clearly adapts for his contemporary era. Thus, while the colonial vision of the world remains, it is subtly mocked in Todd's film. Sir Francis Cromarty, the British soldier who accompanies Fogg on the train in India, is key in this respect. He mouths offensive platitudes about the natives and Passepartout as 'foreigner' (Passepartout is played by the Mexican actor Cantinflas – aka Mario Moreno). Yet, his words and judgements are rubbished when, as he ponderously plots an impossible rescue for the imperilled Aouda, wasting valuable time, Passepartout, the 'foreigner' slips away and efficiently rescues the princess single-handedly. Comparably, the decolonisation underway in Todd's era features in ghostlike form at the film's close. Fogg appears in the Reform Club to win his bet, to the mild surprise of the members. Mild surprise becomes utter shock and stupefaction as Aouda, an Indian woman, and Passepartout, a Mexican servant, join him, breaching and polluting the sanctity of this all-male, all-white club. Robert Morley, playing a governor of the Bank of England, utters the final words of the film, 'this is the end', words which enjoy a threefold polyphony. They refer to the end of the club's sanctity, the end of the colonial hold on the world and ultimately the end of the film as, in a moment of visual/aural reflection, the word 'end' appears superimposed on the screen immediately after Morley utters his shocked words. The era depicted in Todd's adaptation is spectral, at once the nineteenth century of Verne and the twentieth century of Todd.

Verne may be present in Todd's film, but his identity clearly negotiates its presence alongside the personality of its flamboyant producer. The trace of Todd's identity is everywhere apparent in the film. Ghosts of Todd's autobiography may be gleaned in scenes such as the picturesque footage of the Thai royal barge. Todd had used, but never paid for, songs written by the prince of Thailand in one of his shows, and the prince offered his barge as a thank you. However, it is in the camera work of Todd's *Around the World* that the producer's identity is most visible. Frustrated with the limitations of Cinerama, the new cinema camera which allowed for a widescreen cinema experience, albeit one requiring multiple lenses and with some technical problems (most notably distortions), Todd, in collaboration with American Optical, pioneered the Todd-AO which allowed *Around the World* to be printed on 70mm film using an improved single camera version of Cinerama, minus the seams on screen. Todd had filmed a demo tape to showcase the cinematic process he asked be named after him using iconic tourist sites and cultural monuments in widescreen.[45] And much of *Around the World* reads as a demonstration of the process and the man who helped push it through.[46] Interspersed in the film at regular intervals appear wide-screen scenic shots, picture postcards of exotic land and seascapes which dissolve into each other. Such shots revel in the breadth of their focus and in the documentary authenticity of their subject matter, an authenticity sharply counteracted by the Hollywood studio sets Todd used to film India, for example, peopling it with spray painted actors. As Pilcher puts it:

> This wide-screen technology simulated a three-dimensional effect for viewers without having to wear colored glasses, and Todd made the most of it by filming everything possible on location, from Fogg's balloon rising past the gargoyles of Notre Dame and over the Loire Valley châteaux to the magnificent landscapes of the Rocky Mountains and the Far East.[47]

That Todd intended the film as an advert for the process is clear. The film opens with a dialogue on the mythical Jules Verne in the habitual 35mm shot of the era. The camera cuts ever closer to the presenter, a respected journalist, Edward R. Murrow, chosen to add cultural authenticity to the film. The cut takes place specifically, and playfully, immediately after the word 'shrink', as Murrow discusses how modern travel has made the world smaller. Todd's film, in an interfilmic moment, showcases, again in 35mm film, George Méliès's silent adaptation depicting a rocket to the moon. Having allowed the audience to enjoy Méliès's film, a film at once miraculous and restricted in its technology, in what would have been a breathtakingly dramatic moment, the film opens out at the end of a space shuttle countdown into a 70mm contemporary image of a space rocket at the moment of blastoff. Todd showcases the spectacular nature of Todd-AO, metaphorically signing the film's opening images with his own identity. The Todd-AO process not only offers a powerful means to express the vast spaces of Verne's text, it also simultaneously testifies to the ever-present trace of Todd in the cinematic gamble he pushed through against the financial odds.

Todd's spectral identity as a showman is imprinted on his *Around the World* in another key respect: the film's exploration of the power of the media. The veteran showman Todd was only too aware of the power of publicity to transform a show's fate, regardless of its quality. According to Michael Todd Jr, 'no promotional stunt or publicity scheme was too bold for either Todd or Doll [his publicity agent] to attempt'.[48] No stone was left unturned in the media in relation to Todd's *Around the World.* Michael Todd Jr writes: 'The London opening was on the front page of practically every newspaper and was the best publicised picture opening in English film history.'[49] With a lavishness characteristic of Todd, the London after-party 'was the grandest party in London since the days of the Vauxhall Gardens', as Todd took over a fun fair and set up fourteen different restaurants serving all the different foods from the countries his film visited.[50] In this era, when films were a year old, they had practically completed their theatrical distribution. Todd harnessed the power of publicity to prevent this happening to his film. He hosted a first-anniversary party that attracted national attention. His son writes: 'Todd was paid $175,000 by CBS for the rights to televise the party . . . Walter Cronkite narrated the event backed up by a team of assistants that made it seem like a national political convention.'[51] Business shot up 15 to 25 per cent in the smaller cities so that practically all the engagements were selling out again. The power of the media is dramatised as a theme in Todd's film. The adaptation's opening image of its protagonist, Fogg, is introduced by a newspaperman carrying a billboard announcing the robbery of the Bank of England. Not only does the press track Fogg's progress, but the speed at which its organs can pass information is underlined by the scene transition in which a telegraph office, cabling news of Fogg's arrest, cuts directly to the members of the Reform Club reading the journalistic rewritings of that cable in at least five different papers. If travel has made the world smaller, so too, the film intimates, has the press. Indeed, newspapers form the narrative thread leading the viewer through seemingly disparate scenes in the adaptation. At the opening of the film's second act, a *Daily Telegraph* billboard, perambulating on one of its papersellers, announces Fogg's arrival in America. The silent words of the paper immediately pass to the lips of two guards in busbies outside Buckingham Palace before permeating the castle walls. They become a newspaper passed between the anonymous hands of no less than four servants before being delivered to the bedside and equally anonymous hands of a clearly royal personage. The media thread passes even to the subsequent scene where the two potential ladies of the night (comically played by stage greats Hermione Gingold and Hermione Baddeley) discuss Fogg's character in a dialogue that takes place with a torn *Morning Telegraph* poster about Fogg on the wall. The film's message is clear. From the highest monarch, to the commonest *fille de joie*, the press permeates all. It is not for nothing that in Todd's film it is the seemingly ever-present newspaperman's billboard, this time announcing the Saturday results, which alerts Passepartout to the fact that they have arrived a day earlier than they think. The power of the press is undeniably a theme in Verne's novel as a range of papers debate Fogg's cause: 'Le *Times*, le *Standard*, l'*Evening Star*, le *Morning Chronicle* et vingt autres journaux de grande publicité, se déclarèrent contre Mr Fogg. Seul le *Daily Telegraph* le soutint dans une certaine mesure' (p. 30). Newspapers regulate Mr Fogg's life before the bet (he timetables his day around their reading, p. 18), trigger the bet (he undertakes it having read about the completion of the Indian railway in the paper) and whip London and the world into a frenzied debate about Fogg's life and journey. However, in Todd's film, such a theme takes on an extra resonance, reflecting as it does the modus operandi of this showman for whose productions publicity was the lifeblood.

Sharing more than Verne's interest in communication and the press, Todd's film, like Verne's novel, at times perforates its fictions, contemplating the ghost of its own endeavour, the ultimate impossibility of adapting Verne as a whole. As Verne's narrative underlined what it could not or would not say, so Todd's film might be seen to do something comparable. Specific scenes underline, in dialogue, their inability to recount. In a comic cameo which draws on his typecasting as a Gallic womaniser, Charles Boyer, plays a travel agent in the Paris office of Thomas Cook. He mentions the women of Bali in a scene whose subject matter is barred in no less than three ways. In the first instance, the women of Bali are barred to the curious Passepartout because his route around the globe will not take him there. They are subsequently barred not only by the fact that Boyer refuses to describe them ('But no, women of Bali cannot be described . . . words would fail me') but because he reiterates this refusal in French, a language which the vast majority of the film's audience would not have spoken: 'si seulement je pouvais vous les décrire'. Comparably, Fix, in the Hong Kong bar where he will administer the drink that will deprive Passepartout of his senses, refuses to describe the beverage he offers: 'It's indescribable. Liquid music.' In another moment of comically barred origin, Philip Ahn, playing the Chinese passerby whom Fogg addresses in insulting pigeon English to ascertain the whereabouts of Aouda's relative, responds with deliberate, fluent eloquence: 'He [Aouda's relative] amassed a considerable fortune by means I shall not attempt to describe and has retired to Amsterdam to raise tulips.' Ahn, an American-born Korean, had his ethnic origin repeatedly barred in his long film career, playing nationalities of a whole host of nations, if rarely his own.

Todd's film takes its blockages and bars still further, extending them to its relationship with Verne's text. The film makes considerable changes to Verne's novel but intriguingly finds ways to signal what it has omitted, giving a ghostly material presence to the aspects of Verne which are no longer there. Todd, as has already been mentioned, famously cuts Fogg's journey by train across France, replacing it with a balloon trip. Having listed the route Fogg took as their intended route in the travel agents, Fogg cancels their tickets for it. He metaphorically signals this blocked story line by describing the literal blockage of the train line in question which forces them to adapt their route: 'An avalanche has sealed the Montfort tunnels and nothing can get through for a week.' Moments of playful reversal abound. Fix, in Verne's novel, alleges 'mal de mer' as an excuse for having kept below deck while trying to hide his presence. Todd, meting out cinematic revenge for crimes against Fogg in his previous incarnations, gives the character the malady for real on the hired boat Fogg and Fix share in place of the missed Carnatic. Such scenes as the blocked tunnel can be deemed, to use the vocabulary of Millicent Marcus discussed in the chapter on Maupassant, umbilical scenes, as the artistic descendant of the text negotiates in its images its own deviations from the source it has supplanted. Such moments are plentiful in Todd's film. Todd has the helmsman of the steamboat Henrietta, the steamboat Fogg has paid to deviate from its course, argue with the engineer in the following terms when he questions an action: 'have you assumed command of this ship?' Such words appear innocuous, but they refer us to Fogg's more dastardly approach in Verne's novel where the protagonist does, by means foul, assume command of the ship against the captain's will. Verne's Fogg allows the captain to believe he is taking them to Bordeaux. He then bribes the ship's crew to take him to Liverpool, locking the captain in his cabin and assuming command in his place (p. 228). Todd gives a spectral presence to the original Verne scene that he has omitted/altered in a moment which is in a sense doubly spectral. The helmsman and the engineer are played by Victor McLaglen and Edmund Lowe, character actors who had bickered together in comparable ways in a series of films in their long careers. Todd's film sends the viewer back not just to the Verne novel which is no longer fully there in this scene, but also to a selection of films which are equally spectral in their presence.

Through such ghostly references, Todd's film playfully questions its position as a point of artistic origin, pointing back to the textual and cinematic spectres that haunt its dialogue and images. However, as Todd's film adapts Verne, so too will its images be adapted, a process incarnated by Todd's use of the balloon as a means of locomotion for Fogg. While this image plays no part in Verne's novel, it came to represent, in Pilcher's words, 'the defining symbol of the movie', and the key publicity image used by Todd.[52] It subsequently graced editions of the novel in which it does not feature, either as a means to exploit the film's popularity or because the editors had not read the work, and was adapted by several subsequent cinema adaptations of the same novel, including the Coraci piece shortly to be discussed. Such moments of interadaptive congress which underline the cumulative nature of adaptation are, theorist Julie Sanders suggests, frequent in this art form: 'adaptations perform in dialogue with other adaptations as well as their informing source. Perhaps it serves us better to think in terms of complex processes of filtration, and in terms of intertextual webs or signifying fields, rather than simplistic one-way lines of influence from source to adaptation.'[53] The mobility of Todd's film, adapted post-release into other images and films, is echoed by the theme of mobility in the film. If the novel emphasised, as this chapter has suggested, the essential stasis of Fogg even in the midst of his travels, Todd's Fogg, as played by Niven, is an entirely different beast. Todd does emphasise the stasis of Fogg's origin – the space of the Reform Club. Characters sit or stand dressed in costumes of a habitually dark palette in carbon-copy poses in shots where the only motion is usually provided by servants. While Niven's Fogg begins as static and as dark as his contemporaries in the club, not only does the motion and the commotion of shots including him increase as he travels, but his costumes lighten to whites and neutrals, incorporating colours as he opens himself to the beauties of travel as his novelistic predecessor never did. While Verne's hero looks at nothing on his journey, save timetables and transport, Niven's Fogg taps his cane to the flamenco routine in Spain, pauses to smile at a beautiful sunset while taking his tea on ship and enthusiastically converses with the beautiful Aouda. Todd's more personable Fogg, like his balloon ride, has become grist for the mill of subsequent adaptations that adapt his version of Fogg rather than Verne's mechanical original. Inhabited by the spectres of Verne's novel as art form, Todd's film itself becomes a textual spectre in the adaptations of others.

Ghosts, though, are key to Todd's film in another key respect. The producer peopled his film with a plethora of glittering cameos, a term he himself coined in his successful attempt to persuade some of the greatest stars of stage and screen to feature in short or silent parts in his cinematic extravaganza. The sheer number of cameos in the film is staggering. David Niven writes in his biography of the galaxy of stars who played opposite him in short vignettes often at very short notice:

> In London . . . cameo parts were played by Noël Coward, Beatrice Lillie, Hermione Gingold, Hermione Baddeley and Glynis Johns, and back finally in California for the major portion of the work, I became inoculated against surprise when I found myself playing scenes almost daily with different distinguished visitors – among them Ronald Colman, Charles Boyer, Marlene Dietrich, Frank Sinatra, George Raft, Red Skelton, Victor McLaglen, Andy Devine, Joe E. Brown, Cedric Hardwicke and Buster Keaton.[54]

Todd arranged such cameos in different ways. Noël Coward claimed to have been 'bullied' into the part 'over an inferior lunch'.[55] Sir John Gielgud followed, driven he claimed by a curiosity to see the great Coward, playing a bit part as a supplier of servants.[56] Subsequently it became, in the words of Todd Jr, the 'vogue' to be in the film and Todd amassed, for very little financial outlay, a sparkling array of cameo gems. That such cameos function as a savvy marketing technique is clear. They added cinematic standing to the film of this novice in the seventh art and they were also tailored to the many nations in which this film was released. The stars of the British and North American stage and screen may prevail in this work, but in the Spanish sequences some of the most legendary bullfighters of the era star, most notably Luis Miguel Dominguín. In France, Fernandel and Martine Carol feature in passing vignettes. These cameos, however, also have an intriguing intertextual function. They perforate the flow of the film, even while they add to its allure, sending the viewer elsewhere, to the ghosts of the actors' previous roles, to the memory of their public persona. That such cameos are used to playful effect is clear. Frank Sinatra's cameo is a case in point. Having entered, with Passepartout, a San Francisco bar, the camera teasingly rests four times on the back of the piano player's head, before finally revealing a silent Sinatra. In Saul Bass's animated credits, Sinatra's animation is an empty piano stool, testifying to the fact that, at one of his career peaks, this piano player needed no introduction. Many of the cameos used play to the typecasting of the actors in question, to the spectres of their previous roles. Charles Boyer, for example, is cast as an avid admirer of the female form around the world. César Romero plays a henchman of uncertain origin in Spain, the indistinctness of his nationality a suitable part for the actor who made his living either as a Latin lover of some description or as a villain of varying ethnicities. Such cameos ask the viewer to find pleasure in his/her recognition of the similarity between these cameo roles and the spectre of the actor's previous films. However, other cameos comically work in contrast to the actor's past roles as Todd's film asks us to find humour precisely in discrepancy. Sir John Gielgud, an actor made legendary by his repeated incarnation of Hamlet, prince of Denmark, plays seemingly his polar opposite, a browbeaten gentleman's gentleman, the former valet of Fogg dismissed for not being precise enough. And yet, in their dialogue, Gielgud and Coward (playing the employment broker) find means to allude, via the trope of madness, to Gielgud's star persona, to the spectres both of Hamlet and Gielgud's Hamlet. Coward states dismissively: 'you are allowing your natural imperturbability to be swept away by a spate of mounting hysteria'. If some of Todd's gems shine brightly for us, others are less than spectres in our contemporary cultural consciousness. A silent and taciturn man sits in the Reform Club refusing to rise to any questions about his life or his identity. He answers no to each question before leaving the scene, its occupants none the wiser as to his identity. Such attempts at identification would, though, have been greeted with laughter by the contemporary British audience who would have recognised the unforthcoming Reform Club member as A. E. Matthews, the so-called dean of the London stage, whose sixty plays and fifty films meant no introduction was necessary. Todd's film plays not only with the spectral memories of its actors' past roles, but also with the viewer's ability to recognise such actors in cameo parts which simultaneously perforate the narrative flow and enable it by giving it cultural legitimacy. As Fix seeks to solve the bank robbery, we too are asked to play detective but our hunt is not for stolen money, but instead to recognise the gems, hidden and ostentatious, Todd's film carves in celluloid.

Amongst the stars whose previous roles haunt and bring their trace to the words and images of Todd's film, Cantinflas looms large. Flying in the face of the Frenchness of Verne's character, Todd settled upon Cantinflas, born Mario Moreno, the undisputed star of Hispanic cinema of the era, a man whose films were so successful he had the freedom to film what he wanted. Todd Jr writes:

> Mario got the highest salary of anyone in the film, plus a hefty percentage of the gross film rental for all the Spanish-speaking territories – and he was worth it, if for no other reason than record-breaking grosses in the so-called Cantinflas territories.[57]

Todd's decision may have been a financial one, but in fact Todd's showmanship had much in common with the theatrical path via which Cantinflas came to celebrity. He began his life working in the *carpas* in Mexico. Pilcher explains:

> These improvised tent theatres flourished during the 1920s and 1930s in working-class *barrios* of the nation's capital and in many provincial cities. For just a nickel, spectators could enjoy a *tanda* (show) or two, of four acts each, including comic monologues, lewd songs and dances, acrobatic stunts and romantic skits . . . The artists brought their stock characters to life through their own unique personalities.[58]

Relating the *carpa* to Todd's *Around the World*, Pilcher continues:

> the *carpa* aesthetic that Moreno retained throughout his career proved ideal for a film that resembled a theatrical spectacle, a series of episodes unified loosely by a few central characters and the concept of traveling around the world to win a bet.[59]

Cantinflas certainly played Passepartout as himself and his role in Todd's film adapts not just Verne's text but also the accumulated traces of the Cantinflas persona. The film's plot was reshaped to showcase Cantinflas's specialisms. His comic bullfighting demonstrations, usually in aid of charity, regularly filled the greatest arenas in Mexico.[60] Consequently, a comic bullfight scene appears in Todd's film in a country not visited by Verne's novel. Cantinflas's artistic signature permeates this scene. The ongoing joke throughout his films as his trousers droop, threatening at every moment to reveal his behind, one of the most offensive gestures in Mexican popular culture, features in the bullring as the authentic nineteenth-century outfits Dominguín provided sag on Cantinflas, much to the amusement of the audience. Film legend had it that Cantinflas, famed for his acrobatic skills, could ride anything. Consequently, Todd depicts Passepartout in his opening scene on a penny-farthing, has him ride an ostrich in Hong Kong and engage in a bareback horse rescue in the Wild West when under attack by Indians. Verne's valet character, in the novel, scales the bottom of the runaway train. Yet Todd, in a characteristically spectral moment, has Cantinflas scale the length of the train's roof, dodging bullets and jumping flat in the face of an oncoming tunnel in reference to a host of cinematic precursors. Most notable among them are Georges Méliès's (1898) *Panorama from the Top of a Train*, which shot its action from the roof of a moving train, and Buster Keaton's *The General* (1926), in which the silent film actor who plays a cameo role for Todd precisely as the train conductor runs along a train's roof. This stock silent-film gag has enjoyed a series of spectral reincarnations in sound film, enacted as it is, in varied forms, by Keanu Reeves in *Speed* (1994) and Denzel Washington in *Unstoppable* (2010). Such a scene in Todd's *Around the World* not only allows Cantinflas to showcase his acrobatic abilities and star persona, it also taps into the phantomatic borrowing of the film more broadly. Passepartout is at once himself and Cantinflas in the film, in scenes that are at once Todd's and Verne's.

Like Todd, Frank Coraci's 2004 *Around the World in 80 Days* engages with cinematic ghosts, but it does so specifically in relation to Todd. As Todd adapted Verne, Coraci adapts the prevalent myth of Verne in the contemporary cultural consciousness but he also, more importantly, adapts Todd's adaptation as one of his sources. Coraci's film is a very loose adaptation of Verne's novel: Jackie Chan, playing Lau Xing, masquerades as a French valet named Passepartout to avoid capture for having stolen a Jade Buddha from the Bank of

England, a Buddha he returns to safeguard his village as his master traverses the world in a bet undertaken not for money but to take over as head of the Royal Academy of Science. Despite its deformations of Verne's text though, Coraci's film clearly seeks to afford its nineteenth-century source author a tangible presence. What Coraci adapts though, is not so much Verne's novel, as the mythical persona of Verne himself, the prophet of the future. Coraci states: 'part of the idea we talked about when retelling the story was to put a new spin on it. The idea was to make Phileas Fogg sort of in the spirit of Jules Verne, make Phileas Fogg an inventor so he's a man ahead of his time like Jules Verne and have this sort of vision of the future.'[61] Coraci's film has none of the doubts as to the value of progress that, however quietly, surface in Verne's novel. At Coraci's hands, Verne's impassive, mysterious Fogg, becomes a clumsy kind-hearted, emotionally vulnerable childlike character played by comedian Steve Coogan, driven, above all, by progress, by a need to lead humanity into the future. Coraci's Fogg is cerebrally powerful but, an otherworldly dreamer, impotent in terms of every day practicality. The scene transitions in Todd's film were designed to show Fogg's all-powerful nature as he overcomes enemies and elements: the scene on the incomplete Indian railtrack closes with the rail official doubting that Fogg will be able to purchase the local elephant to convey him to the new section of track since it is a dearly beloved pet, before cutting to Fogg and his companions on the aforementioned pet. Those in Coraci's film are designed to show his character's powerlessness and haplessness. Fogg (Coogan) orders Monique Laroche (the Aouda figure who far from being rescued by Fogg, imposes herself on him and his world tour) to leave them when they land the balloon. The next scene opens with a point of view shot from Monique's perspective as she gazes out of the train window, her will clearly having been accomplished in the face of Fogg's sulking opposition.

Not only does Coraci seek to give voice to the myth of Verne himself, but it might also be argued that he shares, in part, in Verne's artistic mission both to entertain and to instruct his youthful audience. Coraci's film, unlike Todd's theatrical extravaganza, is clearly aimed at children. The film not only opens using animation as the camera swoops down to earth in a scene which anticipates the flying machine which will bring about the bet's successful close, but animations, created by Micha Klein, form the scene transitions between continents and countries. Animation too seeps into the non-animated sequences that still borrow from this art form. Ewen Bremner, playing a far more slapstick version of Fix than is present in either Verne or Todd, is hit by people, vehicles and objects with such vehemence and regularity that such instances inevitably recall Disney's Wile. E. Coyote. Moreover, while Jackie Chan as Passepartout wracks his brain in Paris for a way to remove his master from the square in which they currently stand, a square filled with kung fu villains, his moment of revelation comically comes before a poster of a lightbulb and is accompanied by the sound effect of a bicycle bell. The comic intertextuality of the moment is threefold. The poster clearly underlines Coraci's borrowing from the visual gags of classic animation. Yet it also allows Passepartout to tap into the scientific discourse Fogg brings to the film. Passepartout claims the poster is an advert for electricity and an exhibition given by Thomas Edison of his new invention in Paris. In truth the poster is an advert for corsets, a metaphorical representation of Monique (she will wear a corset in the hot tub scene), the character whom Fogg will in fact meet at the exhibition in place of Edison. Far from being scientific, as Passepartout promises, the exhibition proves to be an Impressionist showing. Coraci, like Verne, uses his subject matter to instruct his audience, even while amusing them. Coraci intersperses Passepartout's kung fu fight in the gallery with an admittedly partial and problematic definition of Impressionism for his young viewers as well as summarising the principal criticisms of the movement in the mouth of Fogg. In a scene with key Impressionist works laid out for the viewer to identify as well as some of their creators (a one-eared Van Gogh), Fogg claims: 'that painting is highly inaccurate'. Monique replies: 'It is not supposed to be accurate, the artist views reality through imagination, rather than simply recording it. It's called Impressionism.' Fogg, summarising some of the critical reactions to Impressionism retorts: 'Trees are not violet. Grass is not charcoal.' The film instructs its youthful viewers in the rudiments of electricity, flight (via interaction with the Wright brothers, characters who would have been only infants at the time of Verne's novel) and the artistry of Impressionism. It does so in a filmic vehicle clearly intended to entertain. Humour is a clear part of Verne's novel: Cromarty responds to Fogg's suggestion that they rescue Aouda, 'mais vous êtes un homme de cœur', to which Fogg riposts, 'quand j'ai le temps' (p. 78). The verbal witticisms of Verne's Fogg, however, translate into a far more visual slapstick humour at Coraci's hands. The kung fu fight which takes place in the Impressionist gallery not only has something of the three stooges about it as Chan's three attackers are prodded, painted and spattered with colour, it also produces a pseudo-Impressionist painting as the various assailants impress parts of their anatomy on the canvas as they fight. From Coraci's merger of art history, kung fu and slapstick humour, art, albeit of questionable quality, is produced. The ghost of Verne's intention to entertain and instruct lingers in Coraci's film.

However widespread the changes Coraci makes to Verne's text, traces, however faint, of the nineteenth-century novelist remain in spectral form. Throughout the film Chan's Passepartout comically and somewhat inexplicably insists on his ability to sing in French, a skill he demonstrates while he, Fogg and Monique are locked in the stocks in China. His insistence refers the viewer to Verne's character and his musical skills. Lost and penniless, the character plans to give a concert to earn money and answers in the affirmative when asked by the circus boss subsequently if he can sing: 'Oui, répondit Passepartout, qui avait autrefois fait sa partie dans quelques concerts de rue' (p. 157). Coraci, like Todd, alters Fogg's means of locomotion (instead of pulling down the exterior of the steamship *Henrietta* to burn for fuel as Verne and Todd do, Coraci's work dismantles the renamed ship, the *Carmen*, named after the director's mother, to build a flying machine). As Todd's balloon insertion into the text might be seen to have a clear antecedent in Verne (Verne's first novel in the *Voyages extraordinaires* was *Cinq semaines en ballon* and his novel *L'Ile mystérieuse* has prisoners use a balloon as a means of escape), so too might Coraci's flying machine. Verne's *Robur-le-conquérant* makes clear the novelist's interest in flight in a narrative with many parallels with the author's *Le Tour du Monde.* Fogg, a mysterious, unreadable character, traverses the globe by sea and land in eighty days. Robur, an equally obscure and inexplicable individual, circles the globe in a flying machine which he claims can make the trip in just eight days.[62] While his flying machine bears little resemblance to that in Coraci's film ('*L'Albatros,* semblable à un gigantesque scarabée, allait doucement au-dessus de la grande ville'), Robur provides a Vernian trace for Coraci's adaptation.[63] And Coraci does make clear, *en filigrane*, his spectral debt to Verne. Before Fogg builds his flying machine on the steamer that has run out of fuel, its captain canvases the crew and, desperate for Fogg to win the bet, they offer to burn their shoes as fuel. This moment, comic precisely as a result of the futility of the action (the steamship is a great distance from port), also teasingly refers back to Verne's text where all is burned to propel the *Henrietta* and to the Todd adaptation where Fogg, in frustration at having seemingly failed and lost his status, burns his cane and top hat, objects which inexplicably seem to propel the boat the remaining distance for land is sighted just as they burn. While umbilical moments are not as prevalent in Coraci's film as in that of Todd, they do nevertheless exist. Jim Broadbent, playing the head of the Royal Academy of Science, harangues Coogan's Fogg, claiming, 'your contempt for tradition is appalling'. His words might just as easily be applied to Coraci's deformation of Verne's text in cinematic form. Comparably, Passepartout's words as he steals a police car in which to begin their world tour might also be seen to assume something of a meta-cinematic function: 'It's not stealing, it's borrowing.' Coraci's film in any case inscribes itself under the sign of impossibility, casting Fogg as a member of and driven by the Royal Academy of Science, an institution to which Coraci's source novel categorically states Fogg did not belong (p. 8).

Coraci's film though is as much the spectral, textual ancestor of Todd's film as it is of Verne's novel. Its adaptive act is always a double one. Coraci's film acknowledges Todd's film as the 'original' from which he works when discussing Fogg's balloon ascent.[64] And, enacting his spectral debt to Todd, Coraci, on a far smaller scale, adapts Todd's use of cameos, casting actors in vignettes which not only refer the viewer to their past roles and media lives but simultaneously to Todd's film. As Fogg, Passepartout and Monique scramble into the balloon to make their escape from yet more marauding kung fu assailants, the balloon operator protests their madness at choosing this means of travel to cross the globe. He is well placed to comment on their endeavour for the part is played by Richard Branson, a man famous for his failure to fly around the world by balloon. John Cleese features as a London bobby with one line, Kathy Bates as Queen Victoria and a whole host of Hong Kong action stars have cameo fight scenes. Coraci himself features in a cameo as a crass and flashy passerby who hits his protagonist as he begs for alms in San Francisco. While some of Coraci's cameos are inexplicable (singer Macy Gray plays a French mother whom, with her child, Passepartout saves from a house fire), others take the viewer to the heart of the thematic of repetition and alteration that characterises this adaptation. Arnold Schwarzenegger plays the frizzy-haired narcissist Prince Hapi who orders the travellers to interrupt their journey for drinks in his hot tub, before proposing that Monique be his seventh wife. His lavish apartments contain a version of Rodin's *Le Penseur* modelled on Hapi by the great French sculptor as a birthday gift: it is inscribed 'Hapi Birthday'. While the visitors ultimately destroy this bad adaptation of Rodin's work as they make their escape, the scene's emphasis on mutation and alteration resonates throughout the film. Hapi, in a schoolboy bid to get the girl, competes with Fogg and insistently gets his name wrong. Fogg's is just one of the names which will be mangled by the film's progress. The Indian children address Fogg as 'Feelsidious Frog' on the train. Fogg himself misnames the valet leaving his employ in the film's opening scenes. Passepartout's variations on the name he clearly cannot grasp, Thomas Edison, are multiple: Edy Thomason, Mr Eddie, Mr Edimon. Identities in Coraci's film shift and mutate, in their content but also in their appellations, a little like the play of Chinese whispers in which Passepartout engages in the Royal Academy. The valets pass whispered gossip as to the identity of the bank thief, gossip that could identify Passepartout. As the gossip reaches him in the line, he delights in altering it, watching the power of his whispers as, under his ministrations, a new rumour circulates that redheaded Norwegians with very small feet robbed the Bank of England. Identities do not remain the same in Coraci's film, they shift and adapt in the course of this adaptation which is always itself double, shifting and adapting both the work of Verne and Todd.

Moreover, in its casting of Passepartout, Coraci's film again makes clear the cinematic spectre of Todd in its images. Verne's Passepartout, a man who moves between trades in his novelistic incarnation, becomes a man who moves between nations in his cinematic afterlife. A Mexican acrobat and comic in Todd's film, Passepartout becomes a Chinese action star in Coraci's version. Drawn, like Todd, by the worldwide brand of his choice of actor, Coraci nevertheless has Chan's Passepartout pay homage to his Vernian ancestor. Coraci's Fogg claims only to accept French valets (Fogg's previous valet was English in Verne's novel) and thus the Chinese Lau-Xing pretends to be a Frenchman, his doubleness of identity in one role replicating that of the very recognisable Cantinflas as he played Passepartout as Cantinflas. If Todd's film was shaped and in part authored by Cantinflas's star persona, Coraci's offering is very much conceived as a Chan vehicle. Chan, as Cantinflas did, enjoys a great deal of authorial control over the films he makes. He choreographed the ingredients and form of the fight scenes. His dominance is such that the scenes in which he features frequently take on the very aesthetic of his Hong Kong action films, works for which he is so famed. Only when Chan appears do the film's narrative conventions move to include the fast edits and whip cuts so characteristic of a Chan film in which multiple camera angles magnify the speed of the action as well as ensuring stunts need not be repeated. Coraci's recasting of Fogg's travel as hijacked by a need to return the Jade Buddha to land enemies want for its riches owes more to previous Jackie Chan films than it does to Verne. In *Drunken Master II* (1995), directed by Lau Kar Lueng and Jackie Chan, Chan's character faces conflict on a train when his father's ginseng gets swapped for a rare piece of jade. His father is approached to sell his land to a local mining company. Likewise, in *Rush Hour* (1998), directed by Brett Ratner, we first meet Chan recovering ancient Chinese artefacts from unscrupulous villains.[65] Chan, like Cantinflas, brings his cinematic personality to the character of Passepartout, playing a part as spectrally informed by Chan's previous roles as it is by Verne himself.

As the bet of Verne's Fogg is both spectrally won and lost as the character circumnavigates the globe by the correct date, but not in the allotted number of days, both Todd's film and that of Coraci might be seen to enjoy a comparable spectral success or phantomatic failure. Neither fully succeeds in adapting the detail of Verne's text, detail often reduced, at best, to a mere textual trace in the abundant changes both filmmakers effect. However, to an extent, neither Todd nor Coraci position their own artistry in the recreation of Verne's details. Rather, both conceptualise their own cinematic acts in far more phantomatic terms as they adapt the broad lines of Verne's novel along with hosts of other spectral textual voices. Todd's film adapts the showman identity of its producer, his relationships with its stars and his reverence for the power of publicity. Coraci's film, engaging with the spectral afterlives of Verne's text which precede his film, adapts both Verne and Todd as points of spectral origin, reworking them alongside the traces of Coraci's actors' previous roles and incarnations. Todd and Coraci, though very different in their narrative approaches to Verne's novel, nevertheless share in part his concept of authorship, not as a space of fixed origin and presence but, rather, as a mutating, ever-changing voice, shot through with the ghostly whispers of authors, moments, realities and texts gone by.

Notes

1 Jacques Derrida, *Spectres de Marx: l'état de la dette, le travail du deuil, et la nouvelle Internationale* (Paris: Galilée, 1993), p. 42.
2 Claude Faber, *Jules Verne: le roman de la terre* (Milan: Éditions Milan, 2005), p. 50.
3 See ibid.,
4 *Le Tour du monde* sold strongly upon its release and, as Timothy Unwin points out, its theatrical adaptation ran to '415 performances in 1874–5 . . . and later featured regularly right up until the Second World War'. Timothy Unwin, *Jules Verne: Journeys in Writing* (Liverpool: Liverpool University Press, 2005), p. 97.
5 Faber, *Jules Verne: le roman de la terre*, p. 53.
6 Unwin, *Jules Verne*, p. 1.
7 Daniel Compère, *Jules Verne: parcours d'une œuvre* (Amiens: Encrage, 2005), p. 8.
8 Emile Zola, 'Jules Verne', *Le Figaro Littéraire*, 22 December 1878, also cited in Unwin, *Jules Verne*, p. 14.
9 Unwin, *Jules Verne*, p. 14.
10 Daniel Compère, *Jules Verne*, p. 9.
11 Faber, *Jules Verne: le roman de la terre*, p. 50.
12 Compère, *Jules Verne*, p. 104.
13 Ibid., p. 20.
14 Simone Vierne, *Jules Verne: mythe et modernité* (Paris: Presses Universitaires de France, 1989), pp. 24–5.
15 Picot cited in Olivier Dumas, *Voyage à travers Jules Verne* (Quebec: Stanké, 2000), p. 164.
16 For further details see Compère, 'Dans le sillage de Jules Verne', *Le Rocambole*, 30 (2005), 13.
17 Dumas, *Voyage à travers Jules Verne*, p. 228.
18 Unwin, *Jules Verne*, p. 42.
19 Hetzel cited in Unwin, *Jules Verne*, p. 26.
20 Unwin, *Jules Verne*, p. 3.
21 Timothy Unwin, *Le Tour du monde en quatre-vingts jours* (Glasgow: Glasgow Introductory Guides to French, 1992), p. 36.
22 Jules Verne, *Le Tour du monde en 80 jours* (Paris: Gallimard, 2004), pp. 239–40. All subsequent references to the novel will be from this edition and will be indicated in parentheses in the text.
23 Unwin, *Le Tour du monde en quatre-vingts jours*, p. 5.

24 For further details see Compère, *Jules Verne*, p. 101.
25 Unwin, *Jules Verne*, p. 97.
26 Compère, *Jules Verne*, p. 103.
27 Ibid., p. 84.
28 Unwin, *Jules Verne*, pp. 145–6.
29 Hetzel cited in Compère, 'Dans le sillage de Jules Verne', 17.
30 See *Le Rocambole: Bulletin des amis du roman populaire*, 30 (2005).
31 See on this point, Compère, 'Dans le sillage de Jules Verne', 15. This multiple adaptation is not unique in fictional reworkings of Verne's novels. Compère points out that in 1973 American writer Philip José Farmer produced *Chacun son tour* in which 'il imagine que Phileas Fogg et Nemo sont des extraterrestres appartenant à des races ennemies; ils se livrent sur terre à un combat acharné et l'histoire racontée dans *Le Tour du monde en quatre-vingts jours* n'est que la partie visible de l'iceberg qui constitue leur lutte'. Compère, *Jules Verne*, p. 107.
32 Unwin, *Jules Verne*, p. 53.
33 Ibid., p. 71.
34 For further discussion of this point, see ibid., p. 182.
35 Ibid., p. 157.
36 Ibid., p. 173.
37 Jules Verne, *Robur-le-conquérant* (Paris: Librairie générale française, 2004), p. 247.
38 Unwin, *Jules Verne*, p. 124.
39 Michael Todd, Jr and Susan McCarthy Todd, *A Valuable Property: The Life Story of Michael Todd* (New York: Arbor House, 1983), p. 80.
40 Ibid., p. 147.
41 Verne cited in Dumas, *Voyage à travers Jules Verne*, p. 55.
42 R. Pourvoyeur cited in Dumas, *Voyage à travers Jules Verne*, p. 59.
43 Jeffrey M. Pilcher, *Cantinflas and the Chaos of Mexican Modernity* (Wilmington: Scholarly Resources, 2001), p. 165.
44 Kupferberg cited in Todd, *A Valuable Property*, p. 321.
45 Todd's son writes: 'they filmed in the canals of Venice, and in the beautiful opera house where they shot the New York City Ballet Company. In Spain they shot a bullfight, this time with the camera in the ring.' Todd, *A Valuable Property*, p. 257.
46 The process was named after Todd while the initials of his collaborator, American Optical, were abbreviated and appended to the producer's name to produce Todd-AO.
47 Pilcher, *Cantinflas and the Chaos of Mexican Modernity*, p. 166.
48 Todd, *A Valuable Property*, p. 57.
49 Ibid., pp. 312–13.
50 Ibid., p. 338.
51 Ibid., p. 342.
52 Pilcher, *Cantinflas and the Chaos of Mexican Modernity*, p. 163.
53 Julie Sanders, *Adaptation and Appropriation* (London and New York: Routledge, 2006), p. 24.
54 David Niven, *The Moon's a Balloon* (London: Penguin, 1994), p. 299.
55 Todd, *A Valuable Property*, p. 283.

56 Ibid., p. 283.
57 Ibid., p. 276.
58 Pilcher, *Cantinflas and the Chaos of Mexican Modernity*, pp. 23–4.
59 Ibid., p. 165.
60 Ibid., p. 157.
61 Director's commentary, Coraci, *Around the World in 80 Days.*
62 Verne, *Robur-le-conquérant*, p. 35.
63 Ibid., p. 140.
64 Director's commentary, Coraci, *Around the World in 80 Days.*
65 For further details, see Michelle Le Blanc and Colin Odell, *Jackie Chan: The Pocket Essential* (Harpenden: Pocket Essentials, 2000).

Conclusion

ANDREW WATTS

Balzac, Flaubert, Hugo, Maupassant, Verne and Zola show no signs of disappearing from the adaptive landscape. Their work continues to be adapted and re-adapted across time, media and nation. However, this book has sought not merely to illustrate the artistic potency of nineteenth-century French prose fiction, but also to highlight the sometimes unexpected affinities between certain authors and specific media. Zola, the novelist famed for his claim to translate the Impressionists into fiction, for his attention to colour, light and detail, finds a natural home in the reputedly blind, black medium of radio. While radio cannot show us the spaces, colours and panoramas of Zola's fiction, its capacity for allowing the listener to enter the inner recesses of a character's mind functions as a powerful vehicle for translating Zola's aim to dissect the consciousness of his characters and offer an inner vision of their life. Comparably, while pre-sound film silences much of Balzac's text, it alerts us both to the predominance and importance of silence as a theme in the very profusion of this novelist's words. Television, with its at times stripped-back, spatially constrained aesthetic, may strip Maupassant's texts of some of their geographical scope, confining the author in spatial terms, but in so doing this medium underlines the importance of spatial constraint as a key theme in the writer's works. Collectively, the adaptations assessed in this work show that different media adapt differently and while one may talk of adaptive loss between such media, just as one may talk of translation loss, so too can one talk usefully of adaptive gain. Adaptive affinities exist between specific authors and specific media. Adaptations, moreover, at their best, reflect on the key themes of their source text, helping us better to read that text.

Specific adaptations, as the case studies explored in this book have sought to demonstrate, reflect not just on the themes of their source text, but on their own existence as adapted artefacts. The 'umbilical' scenes Millicent Marcus explores in the field of film studies as certain adaptations integrate elements that underline their alterations of their source text, can usefully be extended to adaptations in each of the media discussed in this work. The adaptations selected for this project stand out from many of their counterparts because they reflect on their own adaptive acts, on their borrowed status, incorporating such reflections in the form and content of their creative offering. In cropping the dialogue at the end of scenes in places, Diana Griffiths, in her radio adaptation of *Germinal*, not only replicates a technique of the Impressionist school so influential on her source author, she also indicates the matter of the Zolian text which inevitably escapes her adaptation, spilling beyond its confines. Olivier Schatzky in his television reworking of 'Le Père Amable' integrates other media, most notably the shadow plays so popular at the time of his source text's publication, into his adaptation. He references his work's status as a shadow of its canonical source, drawing attention to the borrowed and perhaps partial nature of his adaptive act. Whether such umbilical scenes are born of a textual anxiety à la Bloom in relation to the textual ancestor, or of a more joyous intertextual approach, is open to debate. What is clear though is that specific adaptations of nineteenth-century French texts of the type illustrated in this book both reflect on and dramatise their own status as adaptations.

In so doing, such adaptations lead us back to the authorial stance of the canonical writers they adapt. Balzac, Flaubert, Hugo, Maupassant, Verne and Zola all reflect, in very different ways, on their own acts of authorship. They position their texts, not as integral moments of absolute origin but, rather, as textual composites influenced by and authored from a whole host of earlier sources: reality, myth, history, folklore, literature, art and theatre. Balzac, Flaubert, Hugo, Maupassant, Verne and Zola reflect on their own art in adaptive terms. In their relations with other texts these authors vary widely and this book has no wish to homogenise them. Balzac, as chapter two underlined, engages with specific texts and moments in quite direct terms: the Bible and the tenets and trends of Gothic fiction as a whole. Zola, like the maze of his mine in *Germinal*, borrows in a more labyrinthine manner. He mixes and merges material from multiple myths, elements of reality and earlier fiction to offer his reader multiple textual threads with which to navigate his novel. Verne, as chapter six argued, borrows in still more elusive a fashion. Adapting the vocabulary and tones of the very different scientific, sociological and geographical treatises which informed his research for *Le Tour du monde*, Verne does not seek to unify them into a single textual voice. He cites yet playfully obfuscates his sources, both allowing and disallowing them a textual presence as he delights in the polyphonies of his own textual moment. Such self-reflexivity in relation to the influence of other texts and sources is not the preserve of nineteenth-century France – far from it. But it is key to the century and perhaps accounts for some of its appeal to the adaptations studied in this book. Such adaptations stand out for they assess their own adaptive act and contemplate the sources they rework to find their own artistic originality. They both echo and engage with the authorial stance of the canonical 'original' that lies behind their fictions.

The self-reflexivity of our chosen adaptations and art forms finds intriguing echoes in a variety of media whose scope falls beyond the confines of this book. As film, television, radio, theatre and fiction as adaptive media continue to find grist in nineteenth-century French sources, so too do other key fields of cultural endeavour. The emergence of new media, together with the ongoing development of existing technologies, provides seemingly endless scope for fresh adaptive possibilities and their study. Although they have featured only fleetingly in this work, the relationship between graphic novels and nineteenth-century French prose fiction is a fertile and strong one. Each of the novelists studied in this volume has been adapted into graphic novel form in recent years in works that resonate with many of the key concerns of this study. In 2010, cartoon versions of *Les Misérables* and *Germinal* both featured in the series 'Les Incontournables de la littérature en BD', which aimed to bring canonical works of French literature to a wider audience, and to encourage reading and re-reading of the source texts themselves. Since 2007, *Madame Bovary, Notre-Dame de Paris, Le Tour du monde, Le Père Goriot* and a collection of Maupassant's short stories have also appeared in France in this format, reflecting the enthusiasm of graphic novelists for reinterpreting nineteenth-century texts using their own narrative practices and illustrative techniques.

In their formal characteristics, graphic novels stand apart from the other media discussed in this book. As Douglas Wolk explains:

> Comics are not prose. Comics are not movies. They are not a text-driven medium with added pictures; they're not the visual equivalent of prose narrative or a static version of a film. They are their own thing: a medium with its own devices, its own innovators, its own clichés, its own genres and traps and liberties.[1]

The graphic novel, like each of the media discussed in this work, adapts differently, creating, by necessity, a very different art work in formal terms. A graphic novel makes specific demands of the reader's interpretative ability, combining text and illustrations with traditional comic-strip panels, and requiring its reader to follow how the action unfolds both within the panels and in the blank spaces between them. The format, moreover, enables the graphic novelist to exploit the artistic advantages of other media without replicating any of these entirely. As characterised by Scott McCloud, comics offer 'range and versatility with all the potential imagery of film and painting plus the intimacy of the written word'.[2] Thus, in Daniel Bardet's recreation of *Les Misérables,* the illustrations depicting the death of Gavroche proceed through a series of panels which show the street urchin triumphant at collecting ammunition for the students at the barricade, before a soldier hits him with two rifle shots. In the final sequence of panels at the base of the page, three illustrations pan outwards from a close-up of the boy's face to a full-length image of his body lying in the street. The three panels, each one smaller than the last, function as a visual metaphor for the text, which describes the character's soul as taking flight: 'Cette fois il s'abbatit la face contre le pavé, et ne remua plus. Cette petite grande âme venait de s'envoler.'[3] Through the use of such narrative techniques, the graphic novel asserts its status as a unique medium that delights in creating its own artistic effects by borrowing from other media.

Like each of the artists studied in this project, specific graphic novelists showcase the possibilities of their medium, reflecting on the adaptive process and the place of their work within it. In their 2008 version of *Madame Bovary,* Daniel Bardet and Michel Janvier underscore their ability to capture the social satire of Flaubert's text, as evidenced by their drawing of a farmer standing next to his cow with the same expression of bovine stupidity on his face as the animal.[4] At other junctures in their work, however, Bardet and Janvier draw attention to the adaptive palimpsest that is their work. This tendency is evident in their reuse of certain illustrations to reflect the progressive disillusionment of Emma and Charles. As the *officier de santé* draws closer to the Bertault farm on the opening page of this graphic novel, a panel shows the rear of his carriage with Emma waiting on the doorstep in the distance. The same panel recurs later in the text, but with Emma seated next to Charles as they arrive to attend the ball at La Vaubyessard. While both episodes feature prominently in the source text, the graphic novel makes the link between them explicit to a far greater degree than Flaubert, as Bardet and Janvier portray Charles and Emma as being carried towards events that will ultimately blight the lives of both characters. However, this adaptation of *Madame Bovary* does not merely demonstrate that it has reinterpreted the source text. Underscoring the cumulative nature of the adaptive process, the notion that an adaptation is often not a straight transfer of a single text into a subsequent work, these artists gesture to the multiplicity of their sources. Most notably, in their rendering of the 'comices agricoles', Bardet and Janvier replicate shots and camera angles previously employed by Claude Chabrol in his 1991 film adaptation of the novel. As in the film, Rodolphe and Emma are shown from a low angle as they climb the stairs of the town hall, while in a further reference to Chabrol as intertext, Rodolphe stands to one side of Emma in a gesture of demonic temptation as he whispers romantic platitudes in her ear. Within this sequence, however, Bardet and Janvier also place the two characters in silhouette in an elongated panel that makes them appear as if standing in front of a cinema screen. In so doing, their graphic novel playfully acknowledges the borrowed sources of its own existence while presenting itself as a new creation.

While engaging with the adaptations that have preceded them, graphic novels echo the acts of borrowing which underpin their source texts. In his 2009 redrawing of *Le Père Goriot*, Bruno Duhamel can be seen to adapt an array of visual references.[5] Among the artistic resources that he exploits, the illustrator cites Sergio Leone's film *Once Upon a Time in the West* (1968) as having shaped his approach to Balzac's text. In his epic spaghetti western, Leone emphasised the wickedness of his villains by making them appear physically attractive, a technique that Duhamel reapplies to his portrait of Goriot's daughters Anastasie and Delphine, whom he represents as wearing the finest clothes and latest Parisian fashions while continuing to bleed their father of his money. By contrast, his illustrations of the young nobleman Rastignac recall the image of Prince Charming in Disney's *Sleeping Beauty* and *Snow White.* As Duhamel explains, 'Rastignac était conçu pour ne pouvoir vieillir sans que cela ne brise l'harmonie de son visage de "prince charmant", sur lequel une simple calvitie deviendrait alors une véritable catastrophe'.[6] In borrowing from a wide spectrum of often visual sources, Duhamel returns us to the source text, in which Balzac draws, in an equally eclectic manner, upon the visual arts. While the novelist's description of the Vauquer boarding house, with its yellowing furniture and greasy tablecloth, reflects his intensely visual sensibility, he also borrows from highly specific and sometimes unusual material. The images from Fénelon's *Télémaque* that adorn the walls of Madame Vauquer's dining room featured in a nineteenth-century wallpaper catalogue, while Balzac's descriptions of the guests themselves owe much to caricature.[7] The fictional Poiret, with his 'face bulbeuse' (iii, p. 58), recalls Honoré Daumier's famous depiction of King Louis-Philippe as a pear, a link which Balzac exploits as he seeks to convey the dullness of Poiret's character. Viewed through this lens, *Le Père Goriot* and its graphic novel counterpart expose Balzac and Duhamel's shared understanding of authorship as an adaptive activity that brings both of them into dialogue with their artistic predecessors.

The cultural landscape of nineteenth-century France was dominated by the working and reworking of the era's artistic artefacts and it is perhaps thus fitting that such artefacts continue to be reinvented with such regularity across time, media and nation. While both the intentions of such reinventions and their artistic currency continue, rightly, to be debated, the adaptations studied in this book underline that specific reworkings engage their source author in a highly intertextual debate on artistry and the originality to be found in the act of adaptation. While motivated by very different artistic concerns, Balzac, Flaubert, Hugo, Maupassant, Verne and Zola, in very different ways, place adaptation at the heart of their literary endeavours. At the level of their plots, adaptation functions as a key theme. In *Madame Bovary*, Emma's demise can be traced to her status as a bad adaptor, as someone who attempts in vain to use the dreams and fantasies of sentimental fiction as a framework for her life in the provinces. In *Les Misérables,* Jean

Valjean adapts the conventions of the theatre, with its abundance of masks and disguises, to ensure his survival in the face of poverty and prejudice. At a textual level, the writers featured in this book recognise adaptation as an integral element of their own creativity. Whether tracing the threads of myth in the case of Zola, or piecing together the fragments of fairy tales in that of Flaubert and Maupassant, each of these figures remembers and reworks the resources of the past in their pursuit of originality. The urge thus to adapt these authors not only makes commercial sense, it might also be argued to make artistic sense. Their fascination with the limitless possibilities of adaptation offers artists in other media the space and place to develop their adaptive intentions. In the canonical authors of this period, film, television, radio, theatre, fiction and, more recently, the graphic novel, find a template for creating their own artistic artefacts.

Notes

1 Douglas Wolk, *Reading Comics: How Graphic Novels Work and What They Mean* (Philadelphia: Da Capo, 2007), p. 14.

2 Scott McCloud, *Understanding Comics: The Invisible Art* (New York: HarperPerennial, 1994), p. 212.

3 Victor Hugo, *Les Misérables*, adapted and illus. Daniel Bardet, Bernard Capo and Arnaud Boutle, 2 vols (Luçon: Glénat, 2010), ii, p. 31.

4 Gustave Flaubert, *Madame Bovary*, adapted and illus. Daniel Bardet and Michel Janvier (Creteil: Adonis, 2008), p. 15.

5 Thierry Lamy, Philippe Thirault and Bruno Duhamel, *'Le Père Goriot' d'Honoré de Balzac*, 2 vols (Paris: Delcourt, 2009).

6 Bruno Duhamel, 'Balzac en bande dessinée: l'image en mémoire', *L'Année balzacienne* (2011), 365–81 (369).

7 On the possible sources of the wallpaper of the Pension Vauquer, see Honoré de Balzac, *La Comédie humaine*, ed. Pierre-Georges Castex, 12 vols (Paris: Gallimard, Bibliothèque de la Pléiade, 1976–81), iii, pp. 1225–6. All subsequent references to this edition are parenthesised in the main text using the relevant volume and page number(s).

Bibliography

Printed works

Abel, Richard, *French Cinema: The First Wave, 1915–1929* (Princeton, NJ: Princeton University Press, 1984).

Adeney, Martin and John Lloyd, *The Miners' Strike 1984–5: Loss Without Limit* (London: Routledge, 1987).

Allen, Woody, 'The Kugelmass Episode', in *Side Effects* (New York: Ballantine, 1991; first published 1975).

Altman, Rick, 'Dickens, Griffith, and film theory today', in R. Abel (ed.), *Silent Film* (London: Athlone, 1996).

Antoine, André, *Mes Souvenirs sur le Théâtre Libre* (Paris: Arthème Fayard, 1921).

Archer, Lionel, 'Réécritures et suites de *Madame Bovary*', *http://flaubert.univ-rouen.fr/derives/artic.php*, accessed 9 January 2010.

Aristotle, *Poetics*, trans. and ed. Malcolm Heath (Harmondsworth: Penguin, 1996).

Artinian, Artine, *Pour et contre Maupassant: enquête internationale. 147 témoignages inédits* (Paris: Nizet, 1955).

Aumont, Jacques (ed.), *Jean Epstein: cinéaste, poète, philosophe* (Paris: Cinémathèque française, 1998).

Baguley, David, '*Germinal*: the gathering storm', in B. Nelson (ed.), *The Cambridge Companion to Emile Zola* (Cambridge: Cambridge University Press, 2007).

Balzac, Honoré de, *La Comédie humaine*, ed. Pierre-Georges Castex, 12 vols (Paris: Gallimard, Bibliothèque de la Pléiade, 1976–81).

Banaŝević, N., 'Les échos balzaciens dans *Les Misérables* de Victor Hugo', *Centenaire des Misérables (1862–1962): Hommage à Victor Hugo, Bulletin de la Faculté des Lettres de Strasbourg* (January–March 1962), 117–25.

Barnard, Stephen, *Studying Radio* (London: Arnold, 2000).

Baron, Anne-Marie, *Balzac cinéaste* (Paris: Klincksieck, 1990).

——, *Balzac et la Bible: une herméneutique du romanesque* (Paris: Champion, 2007).

——, *Romans français du dix-neuvième siècle à l'écran: problèmes de l'adaptation* (Clermont-Ferrand: Presses Universitaires Blaise-Pascal, 2008).

Becker, Colette, *Emile Zola: 'Germinal'* (Paris: Presses Universitaires de France, 1984).

Béguin, Albert, *Balzac lu et relu* (Paris: Seuil, 1965).

Behr, Edward, *'Les Misérables': History in the Making* (London: Pavilion, 1996).

Bellalou, Gaël, '*Nadia Coupeau, dite Nana*: a modern adaptation of Zola's eponymous work', *Bulletin of the Emile Zola Society*, 30 (2004), 16–22.
Benjamin, Saint-Amant and Paulyanthe, *L'Auberge des Adrets* (Paris: Pollet, 1823).
Benjamin, Walter, 'The work of art in the age of mechanical reproduction', in Hannah Arendt and Harry Zohn (eds), *Illuminations: Essays and Reflections* (New York: Schocken, 2007).
Bertrand, Denis, '*Germinal*' *d'Emile Zola* (Paris: Pédagogique moderne, 1980).
Besnard-Coursodon, Micheline, *Etude thématique et structurale de l'œuvre de Maupassant* (Paris: Nizet, 1973).
Best, Janice, *Expérimentation et adaptation: essai sur la méthode naturaliste d'Emile Zola* (Paris: José Corti, 1986).
Bloom, Harold, *The Anxiety of Influence: A Theory of Poetry* (London, Oxford and New York: Oxford University Press, 1973).
Bolster, Richard, '"Mademoiselle Fifi": an unexpected literary source', in C. Lloyd and R. Lethbridge (eds), *Maupassant conteur et romancier* (Durham: University of Durham, 1994), pp. 29–39.
Botham, Noel, *Valentino: The First Superstar* (London: Metro, 2002).
Bourgeois, Jean, 'De *Thérèse Raquin* à *Germinal*: une structure obsédante d'Emile Zola', *Cahiers naturalistes*, 74 (2000), 43–59.
Brewster, Ben and Lea Jacobs, *Theatre to Cinema: Stage Pictorialism and Early Film* (Oxford: Oxford University Press, 1997).
Brooks, Peter, *The Melodramatic Imagination: Balzac, Henry James, Melodrama, and the Mode of Excess* (New Haven and London: Yale University Press, 1976).
——, *Reading for the Plot: Design and Intention in Narrative* (New York: Knopf, 1984).
Buisine, Alain, 'Emma, c'est l'autre', in Alain Buisine (ed.), *Emma Bovary: figures mythiques* (Paris: Autrement, 1997), pp. 26–51.
Bury, Mariane, *Maupassant* (Paris: Éditions Nathan, 1992).
——, *La Poétique de Maupassant* (Paris: SEDES, 1994).
Carter, Lawson A., *Zola and the Theater* (New Haven, CT: Yale University Press; Paris: Presses Universitaires de France, 1963).
Cartmell, Deborah and I. Whelehan (eds), *Adaptations: From Text to Screen, Screen to Text* (London: Routledge, 1999).
Cervantes, Miguel de, *Don Quijote de la Mancha*, ed. Martín de Riquer (2nd edn, London: Harrap, 1950).
Chalaye, Sylvie, '*Le Complexe de Thénardier*' de José Pliya: un théâtre d'hommes et de femmes ordinaires', *www.africultures.com/php/index.php?nav=article&no=2861*, accessed 12 March 2012.
——, *Afrique noire et dramaturgies contemporaines: le syndrome Frankenstein* (Paris: Éditions théâtrales, 2004).
Chomsky, Noam, *Aspects of the Theory of Syntax* (Cambridge, MA: MIT Press, 1965).
Clark, Roger, *Zola: 'Nana'* (London: Grant and Cutler, 2004).
Cogny, Pierre, 'Maupassant, écrivain de la décadence?', in J.-M. Bailbé and J. Pierrot (eds) *Flaubert et Maupassant: écrivains normands* (Paris: Presses Universitaires de France, 1981), pp. 204–5.

'Comment Léon Mathot fut fusillé', *Mon Ciné*, 73 (12 July 1923), 19.

Compagnon, Antoine, *Les Cinq Paradoxes de la modernité* (Paris: Seuil, 1990).

Compère, Daniel, 'Dans le sillage de Jules Verne', *Le Rocambole*, 30 (2005), 11–16.

——, *Jules Verne: parcours d'une œuvre* (Amiens: Encrage, 2005).

Constable, Liz, 'Consuming realities: the engendering of invisible violences in Posy Simmonds's *Gemma Bovery*', *South Central Review*, 19, 4 (2002–3), 63–84.

Cousins, Russell, 'Adapting Zola for TV: the example of Jacques Rouffio's *L'Argent*', *Excavatio*, 12 (1999), 153–61.

Coward, David, 'Traduire Maupassant', in C. Lloyd and R. Lethbridge (eds), *Maupassant conteur et romancier* (Durham: University of Durham, 1994), 1–11.

——, 'Popular fiction in the nineteenth century', in Timothy Unwin (ed.), *The Cambridge Companion to the French Novel: From 1800 to the Present* (Cambridge: Cambridge University Press, 1997), pp. 73–92.

Cox, Fiona, '"The dawn of a hope so horrible": Javert and the absurd', in J. A. Hiddleston (ed.), *Victor Hugo: romancier de l'abîme* (Oxford: Legenda, 2002), pp. 79–94.

Crisell, Andrew, *Understanding Radio* (London: Routledge, 1994).

Delattre, Geneviève, *Les Opinions littéraires de Balzac* (Paris: Presses Universitaires de France, 1961).

Derrida, Jacques, *Spectres de Marx: l'état de la dette, le travail du deuil, et la nouvelle internationale* (Paris: Galilée, 1993).

Dickinson, Linzy Erika, *Theatre in Balzac's 'La Comédie humaine'* (Amsterdam: Rodopi, 2000).

Dizol, Jean-Marie, 'Maupassant de l'écrit à l'écran', in Y. Reboul (ed.), *Maupassant multiple* (Toulouse: Presses Universitaires du Mirail, 1995), pp. 87–105.

Dolar, Mladen, *A Voice and Nothing More* (Cambridge, MA: MIT Press, 2006).

Donaldson-Evans, Mary, *'Madame Bovary' at the Movies: Adaptation, Ideology, Context* (Amsterdam and New York: Rodopi, 2009).

Doumenc, Philippe, *Contre-enquête sur la mort d'Emma Bovary* (Arles: Actes Sud, 2007).

Doumens, Laure, 'Répertoire des adaptations cinématographiques et télévisuelles des œuvres de Balzac' (Maison de Balzac, unpublished, 2008).

Dousteyssier-Khoze, Catherine, *Zola et la littérature naturaliste en parodies* (Paris: Eurédit, 2004).

Drakakis, John (ed.), *British Radio Drama* (Cambridge: Cambridge University Press, 1981).

Drew, William M., *D. W. Griffith's 'Intolerance': Its Genesis and Vision* (Jefferson, NC and London: McFarland, 1986).

Duffy, Larry, '*Madame Bovary* and the institutional transformation of pharmacy', *Dix-Neuf*, 15, 1 (2011), 70–82.

Dugelet-Chignac, Jacotte, 'La deuxième mort d'Emma', *www.lexpress.fr/culture/livre/fiches-de-lecture-sur-italique-contre-enquete-sur-la-mort-d-emma-bovary-italique_822218.html*, accessed 1 April 2011.

Duhamel, Bruno, 'Balzac en bande dessinée: l'image en mémoire', *L'Année balzacienne* (2011), 365–81.

Dumas, Olivier, *Voyage à travers Jules Verne* (Quebec: Stanké, 2000).

Eisenstein, S. M., 'Literature and cinema: reply to a questionnaire', in S. M. Eistenstein, *Selected Works*, vol. 1: *Writings, 1922–1934*, ed. and trans. R. Taylor (London: British Film Institute, 1988), pp. 95–9.

Ellis, John, *Visible Fictions: Cinema, Television, Video* (London: Routledge, 1992).

Enright, D. J., *Fields of Vision: Essays on Literature, Language and Television* (Oxford: Oxford University Press, 1988).

Epstein, Jean, *Ecrits sur le cinéma*, 2 vols (Paris: Seghers, 1974–5).

——, 'Notes de lecture: résumés, citations, notes personnelles', notes held at the Paris Cinémathèque, EPSTEIN9 B 1 (packet 1 of 10, no date, no pagination).

Everson, William K., *American Silent Film* (New York: De Capo, 1998).

Eyre, Jean, 'Comment on tourne un orage la nuit', *Mon Ciné*, 70 (21 June 1923), 7–8.

——, '*L'Auberge rouge*', *Mon Ciné*, 85 (4 October 1923), 18–19.

Faber, Claude, *Jules Verne: le roman de la terre* (Milan: Éditions Milan, 2005).

Falconer, Graham, 'Le travail de "débalzaciénisation" dans la rédaction de *Madame Bovary*', *Revue des Lettres Modernes*, 865–72 (1988), 123–56.

Farnoux, Lucile, '*Gemma Bovery*: une adaptation de Flaubert en bande dessinée?', *Actas do Congresso Internacional da Associação de Literatura Comparada*, 3 (May 2001), *www.eventos.uevora.pt/comparada/VolumeIII/GEMMA%20BOVERY.pdf*, accessed 1 September 2010.

Felton, Felix, *The Radio Play* (London: Sylvan Press, 1949).

Finch, Alison, 'The stylistic achievements of Flaubert's fiction', in Timothy Unwin (ed.), *The Cambridge Companion to Flaubert* (Cambridge: Cambridge University Press, 2004).

Fiske, John, *Television Culture* (London: Routledge, 1989).

Flaubert, Gustave, *Madame Bovary*, ed. Claudine Gothot-Mersch (Paris: Garnier, 1971).

——, *Correspondance*, ed. Jean Bruneau, 4 vols (Paris: Gallimard, Bibliothèque de la Pléiade, 1973–98).

——, *Madame Bovary*, adapted and illus. Daniel Bardet and Michel Janvier (Creteil: Adonis, 2008).

——, Brouillons de *Madame Bovary*, vol. 1, folio 243v, *http://lettres.ac-rouen.fr/francais/BOVARY_6/accueil-0.html*, accessed 3 October 2010.

—— and Du Camp, Maxime, *Par les champs et par les grèves*, in Flaubert, *Œuvres complètes*, ed. Jean Bruneau and Bernard Masson, 2 vols (Paris: Seuil, L'Intégrale, 1964).

Fox, Soledad, *Flaubert and 'Don Quijote': The Influence of Cervantes on 'Madame Bovary'* (Brighton and Portland: Sussex Academic Press, 2010).

Frandon, Ida Marie, *Autour de 'Germinal': la mine et les mineurs* (Geneva: Droz, 1955).

French, Philip, '*Bel-Ami* – review', *www.guardian.co.uk/film/2012/mar/11/bel-ami-review-donnellan-ormerod*, accessed 22 March 2012.

Freud, Sigmund, *The Interpretation of Dreams*, ed. Ritchie Robertson and trans. Joyce Crick (Oxford: Oxford University Press, 2008).

Frølich, Juliette, 'Charles Bovary et *La Belle au bois dormant*', *Revue Romane*, 12, 2 (1977), 202–9.

Furse, John, 'David Hopkins: obituary. Filmmaker with a passion for all things independent', *www.guardian.co.uk/news/2004/jun/16/guardianobituaries.film*, accessed 19 November 2010.

Gallot, Didier, *Simenon ou la comédie humaine* (Paris: France-Empire, 1999).

Gänzl, Kurt, *The Musical: A Concise History* (Boston: Northeastern University Press, 1997).

Gaudon, Jean, 'Hugophobie et modernité', *Elseneur*, 10 (July 1995), 9–34.

Genette, Gérard, *Palimpsestes: la littérature au second degré* (Paris: Seuil, 1982).

Giddings, Robert, Keith Selby and Chris Wensley, *Screening the Novel: The Theory and Practice of Literary Dramatization* (London: Palgrave, 1990).

Gielgud, Val, *British Radio Drama: 1922–1956* (London: Harrap, 1957).

Gleizes, Delphine, *L'Œuvre de Victor Hugo à l'écran: des rayons et des ombres* (Paris and Saint-Nicolas, Canada: L'Harmattan and Presses de l'Université Laval, 2005).

Grant, Elliott M., *Zola's 'Germinal': A Critical and Historical Study* (Leicester: Leicester University Press, 1970).

Gravett, Paul, 'The Posy Simmonds interview', *The Comics Journal*, 286 (November 2007), 26–67.

Gray, F. 'The nature of radio drama', in P. Lewis (ed.), *Radio Drama* (London: Longman, 1981), p. 51.

Green, Anne, 'Flaubert and the Sleeping Beauty: an obsessive image', in Tony Williams and Mary Orr (eds), *New Approaches in Flaubert Studies* (Lewiston, Queenston, Lampeter: Edwin Mellen, 1999), pp. 65–80.

Griffiths, Kate, *Emile Zola and the Artistry of Adaptation* (Oxford: Legenda, 2009).

——, 'Mythical returns: televising *Thérèse Raquin*', *Nineteenth-Century French Studies*, 39 (2011), 285–95.

Grojnowski, Daniel, 'L'amateur de nouvelles', in J. Lecarme and B. Vercier (eds), *Maupassant miroir de la nouvelle* (Saint-Denis: Presses Universitaires de Vincennes, 1988), pp. 10–20.

Grossman, Kathryn M., *Figuring Transcendance in 'Les Misérables': Hugo's Romantic Sublime* (Carbondale and Edwardsville: Southern Illinois University Press, 1994).

——, *'Les Misérables': Conversion, Revolution, Redemption* (New York: Twayne, 1996).

Gunning, Tom, 'An aesthetic of astonishment: early film and the (in)credulous spectator', *Art and Text*, 34 (1989), 31–45.

Gural-Migdal, Anna and Robert Singer (eds), *Zola and Film: Essays in the Art of Adaptation* (Jefferson: McFarland, 2005).

Gurkin, Janet, 'Romance elements in *Eugénie Grandet*', *L'Esprit créateur*, 7, 1 (1967), 17–24.

Hansen, Miriam, *Babel and Babylon: Spectatorship in American Silent Film* (London and Cambridge, MA: Harvard University Press, 1991).

Harris, Trevor, *Maupassant: Quinze Contes* (London: Grant and Cutler, 2005).

Haynes, Christine, *Lost Illusions: The Politics of Publishing in Nineteenth-Century France* (Cambridge: Harvard University Press, 2010).

Heath, Stephen, *Flaubert: 'Madame Bovary'* (Cambridge University Press, 1992).

Hollander, Anne, *Moving Pictures* (London and Cambridge, MA: Harvard University Press, 1991).

Howe, I., 'Zola: the poetry of naturalism', in D. Baguley (ed.), *Critical Essays on Emile Zola* (Boston: G. K. Hall, 1986), pp. 111–24.

Hugo, Victor, *Œuvres complètes*, ed. Jean Massin, 18 vols (Paris: Le Club français du Livre, 1967–70).

——, *Les Misérables*, trans. Norman Denny (London: Penguin, 1982).

——, *Les Misérables*, ed. Guy Rosa and Nicole Savy, 2 vols (Paris: Poche, 1998).

——, *Les Misérables*, adapted and illus. Daniel Bardet, Bernard Capo and Arnaud Boutle, 2 vols (Luçon: Glénat, 2010).

Huss, Roger, 'Some anomalous uses of the imperfect and the status of action in Flaubert', *French Studies*, 31 (1977), 139–48.

Hutcheon, Linda, *A Theory of Adaptation* (New York and London: Routledge, 2006).

Huyssen, Andreas, *Twilight Memories: Marking Time in a Culture of Amnesia* (New York and London: Routledge, 1995).

Ippolito, Christophe, *Narrative Memory in Flaubert's Works* (New York: Peter Lang, 2001).

Ithurria, Etienne, 'Claude Santelli et Maupassant', in Y. Reboul (ed.), *Maupassant multiple* (Toulouse: Presses Universitaires du Mirail, 1995), pp. 107–19.

Jeanne, René, 'Balzac au cinéma', *Cinémagazine*, 46 (2 December 1921), 5–8.

Joly, Bernard, 'Maupassant et Zola', *Cahiers naturalistes*, 46 (1973), 205–26.

Kelly, Dorothy, 'Balzac's *L'Auberge rouge*: on reading an ambiguous text', *Symposium*, 36 (1982), 30–44.

Kirkham, Pat and Sarah Warren, 'Four *Little Women*', in D. Cartmell and I. Whelehan (eds), *Adaptations: From Text to Screen, Screen to Text* (London: Routledge, 1999), pp. 81–97.

Knight, Diana, *Flaubert's Characters: The Language of Illusion* (Cambridge: Cambridge University Press, 1985).

Kristeva, Julia, *Semeiotiké: recherches pour une sémanalyse* (Paris: Seuil, 1969).

Laforgue, Pierre, *Gavroche: Etudes sur 'Les Misérables'* (Paris: SEDES, 1994).

Lamy, Thierry, Philippe Thirault and Bruno Duhamel, *'Le Père Goriot' d'Honoré de Balzac*, 2 vols (Paris: Delcourt, 2009).

Lapierre, Marcel, *Les Cent Visages du cinéma* (Paris: Grasset, 1948).

Larminat, Astrid de, 'Rebondissement dans l'affaire Bovary', *www.lefigaro.fr/livres/2007/05/24/03005-20070524ARTFIG90242-rebondissement_dans_1 _affaire_bovary.php*, accessed 6 January 2010.

Laster, Arnaud, *Pleins feux sur Victor Hugo* (Paris: Comédie-Française, 1981).

——,'Hugo et l'opéra', *L'Avant Scène Opéra*, 208 (May–June 2002), 6–15.

Le Blanc, Michelle and Colin Odell, *Jackie Chan: The Pocket Essential* (Harpenden: Pocket Essentials, 2000).

Leider, Emily W., *Dark Lover: The Life and Death of Rudolph Valentino* (London: Faber and Faber, 2003).

Le Rocambole: Bulletin des amis du roman populaire, 30 (2005).

Lethbridge, Robert, 'Etienne Lantier "romancier": genèse et mise en abyme', *Cahiers naturalistes*, 59 (1985), 43–54.

Lloyd, Rosemary, *Flaubert: 'Madame Bovary'* (London: Unwin Hyman, 1990).

M. P., 'Avant *La Cousine Bette*: quelques minutes avec Max de Rieux', *Cinémagazine*, 27 (6 July 1928), 13.

McCloud, Scott, *Understanding Comics: The Invisible Art* (New York: HarperPerennial, 1994).

McFarlane, Brian, *Novel to Film: An Introduction to the Theory of Adaptation* (Oxford: Clarendon Press, 1996).

'*Madame Bovary*: réécritures et expansions', *http://flaubert.univ-rouen.fr/derives/mb_reecri.php*, accessed 4 March 2010.

Marcoin, Francis, 'Mutisme de Maupassant', in J. Lecarme and B. Vercier (eds), *Maupassant miroir de la nouvelle* (Saint-Denis: Presses Universitaires de Vincennes, 1988), pp. 61–9.

Marcus, Millicent, *Filmmaking by the Book: Italian Cinema and Literary Adaptation* (Baltimore: Johns Hopkins University Press, 1993).

Marder, Elissa, *Dead Time: Temporal Disorders in the Wake of Modernity (Baudelaire and Flaubert)* (Stanford, CA: Stanford University Press, 2001).

Marel, Henri, 'Etienne Lantier et les chefs syndicalistes', *Cahiers naturalistes*, 50 (1976), 26–39.

Matthews, J. H., 'Maupassant écrivain naturaliste', *Cahiers naturalistes*, 16 (1960), 655–61.

Maturin, Charles, *Melmoth the Wanderer*, ed. Douglas Grant and Chris Baldick (Oxford and New York: Oxford University Press, 1989).

Maupassant, Guy de, *Bel-Ami* (Paris: Gallimard, 1973).

——, *Contes et nouvelles*, ed. L. Forestier, 2 vols (Paris: Gallimard, 1974–9).

Mayle, Peter, *A Year in Provence*, illus. Leslie Forbes (London and New York: BCA, 1991; first published 1989).

Mazade, Charles de, 'Chronique de la quinzaine', *Revue des Deux Mondes*, 9 (1857), 211–23.

Mellerski, Nancy C. and Richard B. Kline, 'Liberating Maupassant: Christian-Jaque's *Boule de suif*, *French Review*, 72 (1999), 867–76.

Mitterand, H., 'Ideology and myth: *Germinal* and the fantasies of revolt', in D. Baguley (ed.), *Critical Essays on Emile Zola* (Boston: G. K. Hall, 1986).

Montchanin, 'Balzac à l'écran', *Mon Ciné*, 67 (31 May 1923), 10–11.

Morley, Sheridan, *Spread a Little Happiness: The First Hundred Years of the British Musical* (London: Thames and Hudson, 1987).

Moyal, Gabriel Louis, 'Retranslation and ideological unravelling: Balzac's *conte philosophique* takes a return trip', *www.umass.edu/french/people/profiles/documents/Moyal.pdf*, accessed 20 August 2011.

Mura-Brunel, Aline, *Silences du roman: Balzac et le romanesque contemporain* (Amsterdam and New York: Rodopi, 2004).

Murphet, Julian and Lydia Rainford (eds), *Literature and Visual Technologies. Writing After Cinema* (London: Palgrave 2003).

Murray, Alison, 'Film as national icon: Claude Berri's *Germinal*', *The French Review*, 76 (2003), 906–16.

Muscarnera, Pascal, 'Les dessous de Maupassant, révélés par Gérard Jourd'hui', *www.allocine.fr/article/fichearticle_gen_carticle=18483535.html*, accessed 21 October 2011.

Naremore, James, *Film Adaptation* (London: Athlone, 2000).

Niven, David, *The Moon's a Balloon* (London: Penguin, 1994).

O'Leary, Liam, *Rex Ingram: Master of the Silent Cinema* (Dublin: Academy Press, 1980).

Ong, W., *Orality and Literacy* (London: Methuen, 1982).

Pagès, Alain, 'La lysogenèse du texte romanesque', *Cahiers naturalistes*, 59 (1985), 127–34.

Pasco, Allan H., *Allusion: A Literary Graft* (Charlottesville: Rockwood, 1994).

Penketh, Adrian, 'Adapting Balzac for the Friday play', *www.bbc.co.uk/blogs/radio4/2011/01/adapting_balzac_for_the_friday_play.html*, accessed 10 March 2012.

Perrault, Charles, *Contes*, ed. Gilbert Rouger (Paris: Garnier, 1967).

Pilcher, Jeffrey M., *Cantinflas and the Chaos of Mexican Modernity* (Wilmington: Scholarly Resources, 2001).

Place-Verghnes, Floriane, 'Il fallait brûler Maupassant. Du danger d'adapter *Bel-Ami*', *Bulletin Flaubert-Maupassant*, 12 (2003), 61–84.

Pliya, José, *Le Complexe de Thénardier* (Paris: Quatre-vents, 2001).

——, *Le Complexe de Thénardier*, dir. Jean-Michel Ribes, Arte, 2004 [on DVD].

Poe, Edgar Allan, 'The Pit and the Pendulum', in *The Collected Tales and Poems of Edgar Allan Poe* (London: Wordsworth, 2009).

Poteau-Tralie, Mary L., *Voices of Authority: The Criminal Obsession in Guy de Maupassant's Short Works* (Oxford: Peter Lang, 1994).

Poulosky, Laura J., *Severed Heads and Martyred Souls: Crime and Capital Punishment in French Romantic Literature* (New York: Peter Lang, 2003).

Prece, Paul and William A. Everett, 'The megamusical: the creation, internationalisation and impact of a genre', in William A. Everett and Paul R. Laird (eds), *The Cambridge Companion to the Musical* (2nd edn, Cambridge University Press, 2008), pp. 250–69.

Prendergast, Christopher, *Balzac: Fiction and Melodrama* (London: Edward Arnold, 1978).

Raitt, Alan, 'Le Balzac de Flaubert', *L'Année balzacienne* (1991), 335–61.

Ripoll, Roger 'L'avenir dans *Germinal*: destruction et renaissance', *Cahiers naturalistes*, 50 (1976), 115–33.

Robb, Brian J., *Silent Cinema* (Harpenden: Kamera, 2007).

Robb, Graham, *Victor Hugo* (London: Picador, 1997).

Robert, Guy, *'La Terre' d'Emile Zola: étude historique et critique* (Paris: Les Belles Lettres, 1952).

Rodger, Ian, *Radio Drama* (London: MacMillan, 1982).

Roman, Myriam and Marie-Christine Bellosta, *'Les Misérables': roman pensif* (Paris: Belin, 1995).

Rubin, Leon, *The Nicholas Nickleby Story: The Making of the Historic Royal Shakespeare Company Production* (London: Heinemann, 1981).

Rzepka, Charles J., *Detective Fiction* (Cambridge: Polity, 2005).

Sabin, Roger, *Comics, Comix and Graphic Novels: A History of Comic Art* (London and New York: Phaidon, 1996).

Saint-Gelais, Richard, 'Spectres de *Madame Bovary*: la transfictionnalité comme remémoration', in Susan Harrow and Andrew Watts (eds), *Mapping Memory in Nineteenth-Century France* (Amsterdam: Rodopi, 2012), pp. 97–111.

Sanders, Julie, *Adaptation and Appropriation* (London and New York: Routledge, 2006).

Scaggs, John, *Crime Fiction* (Abingdon: Routledge, 2005).

Scepi, Henri, *'Les Misérables' de Victor Hugo* (Paris: Gallimard, 2009).

Schmeling, Manfred, 'Labyinthus subterraneus: *Germinal*', *Cahiers naturalistes*, 84 (2010), 255–88.

Seebacher, Jacques, *Victor Hugo ou le calcul des profondeurs* (Paris: Presses Universitaires de France, 1993).

Seylaz, Jean-Luc, 'Une scène de Balzac: le transport de l'or dans *Eugénie Grandet*', *L'Année balzacienne* (1980), 61–7.

Shakespeare, William, *King Lear*, ed. Elspeth Bain, Jonathan Morris and Rob Smith (Cambridge: Cambridge University Press, 1996).

Sherrington, R. J., *Three Novels by Flaubert: A Study of Techniques* (Oxford: Clarendon Press, 1970).

Silverman, Kaja, *The Acoustic Mirror* (Bloomington: Indiana University Press, 1988).

Simmonds, Posy, *Gemma Bovery* (London: Jonathan Cape, 2001).

Singer, Ben, *Melodrama and Modernity: Early Sensational Cinema and Its Contexts* (New York: Columbia University Press, 2001).

Smirnoff, Renée de, 'Sur une Cosette balzacienne: Pierrette', in Pierre Brunel (ed.), *Hugo: 'Les Misérables'* (Mont-de-Marsan: Éditions InterUniversitaires, 1994).

Smith, Diane and Robert Singer, 'A drunkard's representation: the appropriation of naturalism in D. W. Griffith's biograph films', *Griffithiana*, 65 (1999), 96–125.

Stam, Robert and Alessandra Raengo, *Literature and Film: A Guide to the Theory and Practice of Film Adaptation* (Oxford: Blackwell, 2005).

Steiner, George, *After Babel: Aspects of Language and Translation* (Oxford: Oxford University Press, 1992).

Sternfeld, Jessica, *The Megamusical* (Bloomington and Indianapolis: Indiana University Press, 2006).

Sullivan, Edward D., *Maupassant: The Short Stories* (London: Edward Arnold, 1962).

Sultanik, Aaron, *Film: A Modern Art* (New York, London, Toronto: Cornwall, 1986).

Surville, Laure, *Balzac: sa vie et ses œuvres d'après sa correspondance* (Paris: Jaccottet, Bourdilliat, 1858).

Suwala, Halina, 'Zola et Maupassant, lecteurs de Flaubert', *Cahiers naturalistes*, 65 (1991), 57–77.

Tanner, Tony, 'The "morselization" of Emma Bovary', in Harold Bloom (ed.), *Gustave Flaubert's 'Madame Bovary'* (New York and Philadelphia: Chelsea House, 1994).

'*The Conquering Power* starring Rudolph Valentino and Alice Terry', *New York Times*, 10 July 1921, *www.silentsaregolden.com/conqueringpowerreview.html*, accessed 9 April 2011.

Thorpe, Adam, '*Madame Bovary:* the Everest of translation', *www.guardian.co.uk/books/2011/oct/21/translating-madame-bovary-adam-thorpe,* accessed 10 March 2012.

Todd, Jr, Michael and Susan McCarthy Todd, *A Valuable Property: The Life Story of Michael Todd* (New York: Arbor House, 1983).

Ubersfeld, Anne, '*Les Misérables,* théâtre – roman', in Anne Ubersfeld and Guy Rosa (eds), *Lire 'Les Misérables'* (Paris: Corti, 1985), pp. 119–34.

Unwin, Timothy, *Le Tour du monde en quatre-vingts jours* (Glasgow: Glasgow Introductory Guides to French, 1992).

——, 'Gustave Flaubert, the hermit of Croisset', in Timothy Unwin (ed.), *The Cambridge Companion to Flaubert* (Cambridge: Cambridge University Press, 2004), pp. 1–13.

——, *Jules Verne: Journeys in Writing* (Liverpool: Liverpool University Press, 2005).

Vanderwolk, William, 'Memory and the transformative act in *Madame Bovary*', in Harold Bloom (ed.), *Emma Bovary* (New York and Philadelphia: Chelsea House, 1994).

Vargas Llosa, Mario, 'Flaubert, our contemporary', in Timothy Unwin (ed.), *The Cambridge Companion to Flaubert* (Cambridge: Cambridge University Press, 2004).

Venuti, Lawrence, *The Translator's Invisibility: A History of Translation* (London: Routledge, 2005).

Vermette, Margaret, *The Musical World of Boublil and Schönberg* (New York: Applause Theatre and Cinema Books, 2006).

Verne, Jules, *Le Tour du monde en 80 jours* (Paris: Gallimard, 2004).

——, *Robur-le-Conquérant* (Paris: Librairie générale française, 2004).

Vierne, Simone, *Jules Verne: mythe et modernité* (Paris: Presses Universitaires de France, 1989).

Vincendeau, Ginette, *Stars and Stardom in French Cinema* (London and New York: Continuum, 2000).

Wainwright, Martin, 'Newcastle, not Paris, may set TV scene for Zola classic', *www.guardian.co.uk/media/2008/apr/05/television.bbc,* accessed 21 November 2011.

Wargny, Danielle, 'Emma, version BD, version GB', in Nicole Terrien and Yvan Leclerc (eds), *Le Bovarysme et la littérature de langue anglaise* (Rouen: Université de Rouen, 2004), pp. 209–18.

Warren, Paul, *Zola et le cinéma* (Sainte-Foy: Presses de l'Université Laval, 1995).

Watts, Andrew, *Preserving the Provinces: Small Town and Countryside in the Work of Honoré de Balzac* (Oxford: Peter Lang, 2007).

——, 'Cracks in a cartoon landscape: fragmenting memory in Posy Simmonds's *Gemma Bovery*', *Essays in French Literature and Culture,* 48 (2011), 45–65.

——, 'Footsteps in the snow: piecing together time in *Madame Bovary* and *Contre-enquête sur la mort d'Emma Bovary*', *South Carolina Modern Language* Review, 10, 1 (2011), 13–34.

Wehle, Philippa, interviewed by Stéphanie Bérard, 'D'une langue à l'autre: le vrai défi, c'est trouver la voix de l'auteur, son rythme, sa musique', *www.afribd.com/article.php?no=9354,* accessed 24 March 2012.

Weldon, Fay, 'Dying? I don't want to do that again', *Daily Telegraph*, 12 March 2009, *www.telegraph.co.uk/culture/4980926/Fay-Weldon-Dying-I-dont-want-to-do-that-again.html* accessed 4 January 2010.

Wilsher, Peter, Donald Macintyre and Michael Jones, *Strike: Thatcher, Scargill and the Miners* (London: André Deutsch, 1985).

Wolk, Douglas, *Reading Comics: How Graphic Novels Work and What They Mean* (Philadelphia: Da Capo, 2007).

Wrigley, Amanda, *Greece on Air: Engagements with Ancient Greek Culture on BBC Radio, 1920s–1960s* (forthcoming, Oxford: Oxford University Press, 2013).

Yon, Jean-Claude, *Eugène Scribe: la liberté et la fortune* (Paris: Broché, 2000).

Zakarian, Richard, *Zola's 'Germinal': A Critical Study of its Primary Sources* (Geneva: Droz, 1972).

Zola, Emile, *Nana* (Philadelphia: T. B. Peterson and Brothers, 1880).

——, *Les Rougon-Macquart: histoire naturelle et sociale d'une famille sous le Second Empire*, ed. Henri Mitterand, 5 vols (Paris: Gallimard, Bibliothèque de la Pléiade, 1960–7).

——, *Œuvres complètes*, ed. Henri Mitterand, 15 vols (Paris: Cercle du Livre Précieux, 1966–9).

Radio, television, film and stage adaptations

Around the World in Eighty Days (Jules Verne), dir. Michael Anderson, produced by Michael Todd, 1956.

Around the World in Eighty Days (Jules Verne), dir. Frank Coraci, 2004.

L'Auberge rouge (Honoré de Balzac), dir. Jean Epstein, 1923.

Chez Maupassant (Guy de Maupassant), 3-part series created by Gérard Jourd'hui and Gaëlle Girre. Series one (director of each episode in parentheses): Histoire d'une fille de ferme (Denis Malleval), La Parure (Claude Chabrol), L'Héritage (Laurent Heynemann), Deux amis (Gérard Jourd'hui), Le Père Amable (Olivier Schatzky), Hautot Père et fils (Marc Rivière), Miss Harriet (Jacques Rouffio), Toine (Jacques Santamaria); series two: Le Rosier de Madame Husson (Denis Malleval), L'Ami Joseph (Gérard Jourd'hui), Aux champs (Olivier Schatzky), Le Petit Fût (Claude Chabrol), Ce Cochon de Morin (Laurent Heynemann), Une soirée (Philippe Monnier), La Chambre 11 (Jacques Santamaria), Au Bord du lit (Jean-Daniel Verhaeghe); France 2, 2007, 2008 and 2011.

Le Complexe de Thénardier (José Pliya), dir. by Jean-Michel Ribes (Arte, 2004 [on DVD]).

The Conquering Power [Eugénie Grandet] (Honoré de Balzac), dir. Rex Ingram, 1921.

Germinal (Emile Zola), adapted by David Hopkins, BBC Radio, 1982.

Germinal (Emile Zola), adapted by Diana Griffiths, BBC Radio, 2007.

Les Misérables (Victor Hugo), musical, Alain Boublil (lyrics) and Claude-Michel Schönberg (music), West End, Barbican Centre, 1985.

Index